D0898111

THE
KING'S MINION
Richelieu,
Louis XIII,
and the Affair of
Cinq-Mars

The KING'S MINION

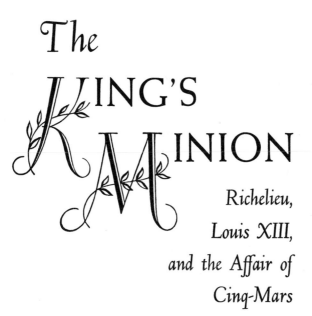

Richelieu,
Louis XIII,
and the Affair of
Cinq-Mars

et by
Philippe Erlanger

PRENTICE-HALL, INC.
ENGLEWOOD CLIFFS, NEW JERSEY

The King's Minion: Richelieu, Louis XIII, and the Affair of Cinq-Mars
By Philippe Erlanger
Translated from the French by Gilles and Heather Cremonesi
English translation copyright © 1971, 1972 by Elek Books
Published in England © 1971 by Elek Books (*Richelieu and the Affair of Cinq-Mars*)
Published in France © 1962 by Librairie Académique Perrin (*Cinq-Mars*)
Illustrations of *demi-écu* and of letter from Louis XIII to Richelieu reproduced in
the illustrated section, courtesy of Tam Mossman. All rights reserved.
First American Edition published by Prentice-Hall, Inc., 1972
Printed in the United States of America • 3

Library of Congress Cataloging in Publication Data
Erlanger, Philippe, 1903–
   The King's minion.
   Translation of Cinq-Mars; ou, La passion et la fatalité.
   1. Cinq-Mars, Henri Coiffier, Ruzé d'Effiat,
marquis de, 1620–1642. I. Title.
DC123.9.C5E713   1972   944'.032   75-37256
ISBN 0-13-516310-2

Contents

THE
KING'S MINION

Richelieu,
Louis XIII,
and the Affair of
Cinq-Mars

One

The First Strands of Destiny

AT A TIME when it was fashionable to behave as outrageously as Henri IV, the Vert Gallant, Madame d'Effiat was a model of marital virtue. She was a devoted wife and personally supervised her children's upbringing—behavior which her contemporaries regarded as almost unseemly. Her virtues were counterbalanced, however, for she was also a proud, mean, ambitious, and extremely domineering woman.

Marie de Fourcy had married a captain of the light cavalry, Antoine Coiffier-Ruzé, Marquis d'Effiat, in 1610, the same year that Henri IV's death plunged France into one of the grimmest episodes of her history. Nevertheless, it was an excellent marriage. Marie's dowry consisted of 90,000 *livres tournois,* and the Marquis himself was handsome, strong, agile, and possessed every possible quality for a brilliant career. Effiat, already the owner of considerable estates in the Auvergne and Touraine, was given the domains of Chilly and Longjumeau by his mother's brother, Beaulieu-Ruzé, then Secretary of State. This uncle, who had managed to flourish at court for sixty years, was an inspiring example for Effiat to follow.

His success was rapid. He managed to increase his personal fortune, and his wife's parsimony did not deter him from living on a grand scale. He commissioned the celebrated Métézeau, who was later to build the La Rochelle dike, to tear down the old chateau at Chilly and replace it with a sumptuous house in the best architec-

tural style of the day. Simon Vouet, Perrier, and Sarrazin decorated it, and soon it excited the admiration, if not the envy, of
everyone. Festivities of unrivaled splendor took place in the great
galerie where Vouet had painted "The Loves of the Gods."

From his uncle, Antoine d'Effiat learned that it was best to remain loyal to the King regardless of the vicissitudes of politics.
Beaulieu-Ruzé had been loyal throughout the Civil Wars, which the
grands seigneurs had so relished and which Henri IV had suppressed, only to have them flare up again after his death. Effiat also
lived by this principle. His devotion to his King during the troubled
years of Louis XIII's minority was rewarded when Louis came of
age in 1619 and sent d'Effiat as ambassador to Flanders.

It was five years later that Cardinal Richelieu was appointed
Head of the Council (he did not become Prime Minister until
1629). France was then like a ship adrift. As Richelieu himself recalled, royal authority "was so unlike what it should have been
that it was nearly unrecognizable. Every man measured his merit
by his audacity." Internally the country was subject to a thinly disguised anarchy, while abroad the House of Austria, having taken its
revenge on Henri IV, prepared to crush France in a vise between
Madrid and Vienna.

Louis XIII loathed Richelieu. The Cardinal had been the favorite
of his mother, Marie de Médicis, and it was only the fear of rousing
her titanic wrath that forced the young King to submit to Richelieu's arrogant tutelage. But after several weeks, however, Louis had
to admire Richelieu's mastery of intrigue. Once he realized that the
ambitious priest could bring "glory and grandeur" to his Crown, he
stifled his personal feelings and gave the Cardinal whatever support
and authority he required.

In fact, it was only by the King's support that Richelieu maintained his position. The Cardinal found no allies among the Catholic and Protestant factions, none in the nobility and Parlement,
none in the *bourgeoisie* and still less among the rank and file of the
population. Had his political position been based on popular feeling, he could not have held it for six months. But he had formu-

lated his policies and drafted a truly Cartesian plan of action, and he depended on the young King to remove all possible opposition. It was Louis who said, "It's enough that I want him."

Of course, there were many at court who did not feel that the King's will was reason enough, but Antoine d'Effiat wisely chose not to believe them. He resolutely offered the Cardinal his services. In 1624 he was entrusted with the delicate mission of negotiating the marriage between the King's sister, Madame Henriette, and England's Prince of Wales, who later became Charles I. His success was rewarded with the *Cordon Bleu.* Thereafter his talents were more fully exploited. He was very successful both as diplomat and soldier—he was made *Grand Maître* of the Artillery—and later was appointed Superintendent of Finances. During a particularly critical period, Richelieu asked him to "re-establish the accounts of the Kingdom." This artillery officer managed the assignment so skillfully that he virtually provided the resources the Cardinal needed to pursue his enterprises.

This assignment hardly completed, he was recalled to the field of battle. His conduct at Veillane, where the Duc de Savoie's forces were totally defeated, won him a maréchal's baton and the governorship of the Auvergne. When he died suddenly of "scarlet fever" at Lutzelstein in 1632, the French army in Germany had just been placed under his command. Monsieur de Pradines conveyed his heart and last will and testament to the inconsolable Madame d'Effiat.

She was left with three sons and three daughters. The youngest daughter died in infancy, while the eldest, Charlotte, was forced to mourn her passing youth in a convent, a fate she shared with so many of her rank. The fate of the second daughter, Marie, was equally cruel. At the tender age of nine she was married to the widower Gaspard d'Alègre. The little girl grew to adore him, even though the marriage could not be consummated. Regrettably, the Cardinal had the habit of expressing concern for his friends' welfare by intervening in their family affairs, and he soon realized that little Marie would be an excellent match for his cousin, the Duc de La

Meilleraye. Her parents were cooperative and ambitious enough to consent. The heartbroken little girl was removed from her beloved Alègre and remarried to the Duc. As she was already rather unstable, this shock completely deranged her. When she was eighteen, she left her harsh world during a miscarriage. Her surviving son, the future Duc de Mazarin, inherited her mental instability.

Martin, the eldest son and heir to the Effiat title and domains, was already a soldier when his father died. His mental faculties were also rather weak. He used to cut up the tapestries at Chilly to resole his worn shoes; he died completely mad in 1645. Jean, the youngest son, went into the Church, for which he had no calling, and his exuberant nature inevitably involved him in scandals which marred his career as a court abbé.

The perpetuation of the house of Effiat thus fell to the second son, Henri, who had been born on March 27, 1620. He was spared the religious career that usually awaited the younger members of noble families, for his father had given him a large estate in Touraine which Beaulieu-Ruzé had originally acquired from Jacques de Broc. The Castle of Cinq-Mars, an old fortress with magnificent terraces, dominated the estate. Its outer walls were 135 feet long and 45 feet wide; the tower had three surrounding walls and could easily withstand a siege. Twenty-five towns and villages were the feudal property of whoever bore the feudal title of Marquis de Cinq-Mars. When he was ten, Henri was appointed chief bailiff and Lieutenant General of Touraine.

The Cardinal Richelieu could be a ruthless enemy, but he was loyal and generous to those who served him well. His sense of duty to his family was particularly strong. The sacrifice of poor little Marie to the Duc de La Meilleraye made the Effiats the Duc's relatives; and after the death of the Maréchal, Meilleraye easily persuaded his mother-in-law to submit to the Prime Minister's despotic will and make him the protector of her fatherless children.

Richelieu often visited Chilly, which the Maréchal d'Effiat himself had had so little time to enjoy. The Cardinal soon came to regard the house as his own. It was here that he carried on many of the government's secret activities. Political prisoners were spirited away to the mysterious chateau to be questioned and perhaps even silently disappear at the bottom of an oubliette. There was said to be a terrible tipping chair which could dispose of unsuspecting victims during the interrogations. Richelieu, encircled as he was by conspirators eager to assassinate him, felt no compunction in resorting to the methods of Louis XI.

The little Marquis de Cinq-Mars saw the more convivial side of the Cardinal's nature. If Richelieu saw the hapless Martin's lack of capabilities, he was enchanted by the lively, intelligent, and handsome Henri. In his heart of stone he may have felt some fleeting affection for the son of his dead friend. But Henri must certainly have been terrified before the awesome Cardinal clad in his grandiose scarlet robes. The boy was equally in awe of his fierce mother, whose widowhood now made her absolute head of the family. He grew up under the yoke of this twofold tyranny, at a time when convention prevented his being shown the kind of affection he obviously needed.

Henri had "a marvelous grace in everything he did." He inherited Maréchal d'Effiat's handsome features, but in place of his father's virile self-confidence, he had a charmingly languid air slightly touched with sadness; his dreaming, seductive, and disquieting expression betrayed the weakness and the instability of someone easily hurt. He concealed this weakness in frequent and capricious outbursts of violence. Had he been brought up in the twentieth century, he would have been studied, cared for, and possibly given stability and confidence; but this was quite inconceivable in the seventeenth century. The educational theorists of the time rigorously avoided "softening" a childhood which from infancy was bent to strict discipline and complete submissiveness. A child ate at the far end of the table, bareheaded in contrast to his elders and without breathing a word. He sat only when given permission, and before the last courses were served, he rose, took his plate, bowed low to his parents, and quietly withdrew to his room. "Well brought-up children with wise mothers never speak in their presence except in whispers and are always found in their mothers' rooms," Angelique Arnauld used to say. Henri IV, regarded as an excellent father, used to tell his son the Dauphin, "I am the master, and you are my servant."

By temperament, Madame la Maréchale d'Effiat was inclined to tighten rather than relax this rigorous control; her ambitions, in fact, intensified her authoritarian needs. It was to be Henri's duty to maintain and increase the House of Effiat's recently acquired fortunes—which could easily have been jeopardized by the Maréchal's untimely death. Madame d'Effiat felt, therefore, that she should retain absolute control over her son and guide him with an iron hand, to which she devoted all her formidable energies. But she went too far. Even if he never got over a slight atrophy of his willpower, Henri bitterly resented his own weakness and spent much of his life in fruitless and awkward revolt against those who tried to control him. Only once was he to succeed, and that once was his undoing.

When Henri was fifteen, he was sent, on Richelieu's advice, to attend Monsieur de Benjamin's academy in the rue Vieille-du-Temple. The Cardinal himself had drafted the military academy's founding statutes. Monsieur de Benjamin was to concern himself with "modeling [young men's] manners. No man was better fit to instruct the young in the rules of virtue." Besides virtue, Cinq-Mars was taught "all that concerns the profession of arms": geography, mathematics, surveying, the art of fortification, fencing, horsemanship, dancing, and many other skills. The Cardinal actually "insisted on receiving minutely detailed accounts of his conduct." Cinq-Mars' letters show that he also received the usual thorough grounding in the classics. As an adolescent he was deeply fond of fashionable novels. He and the rest of his generation grew up under the spell of *Astrée* and its code of love. Thus at sixteen, when the ailing Monsieur de Benjamin decided to close down his academy, Cinq-Mars too was longing to follow the "Map of Tenderness," get out into the world, and accomplish great deeds.

Richelieu appraised his protégé with his notoriously perceptive eagle eye and saw a vigorous young man, handsome as a Greek hero, bursting with laughter, impetuous, eager to taste the joys of life. The Cardinal decided to terminate Henri's studies and send the young Lieutenant General of Touraine (now also lieutenant in the government of Bourbonnais) to the Court. During the previous year of 1635, France had begun a war against Spain and the Emperor, a war which was to last a quarter of a century. New companies had been added to the King's Guard, and Cinq-Mars was given the command of one of them. He was presented to His Majesty, who paid him no attention.

Cardinal Richelieu was directing a colossal enterprise, which was about to reach a decisive phase. His plans had gone smoothly so far, but the scale of the whole undertaking now threatened to overwhelm him. At the same time, his popularity was at a low ebb. He was the object of even greater disgust, misunderstanding, and hatred than in 1624. He was still admired, but his only support continued to be the general belief in royal authority—in other words, the will of the King.

Indeed, the King had written to his Minister saying, "Be assured that I shall love you to my last breath." But the King never lifted the protective sphinxlike mask which he donned before the Cardinal as an instrument of revenge and as a safeguard. For Louis was not the "illustrious slave" that Madame de Motteville was to describe, although he was quite willing to appear so at court. He may have disdained to share his minister's glory, but every single decision that went toward establishing that glory was first referred to the King, who studied, weighed, and finally approved it.

Yet his family, his entourage, and his confessor all insisted that the Cardinal was leading the kingdom to ruin. There were many who eagerly awaited the King's slightest nod to rid him of this scourge. Richelieu was constantly faced with the examples of the assassinated Concini who had preceded Richelieu in the service of Marie de Médicis; the assassinated Duke of Buckingham who had been too successful in his suit for the Queen's affections; the murdered Wallenstein. He knew that a mere word or even a silence from the Monarch could dispense with him just as easily. (Louis XIII had chosen, for instance, to keep just such a silence at Vitry when the Duc de Luynes' second, Déageant, speaking of Concini in the King's presence, said, "The King hears he's being killed.")

This explains why "this great genius who performed nothing but miracles," as Corneille put it, was condemned to wait upon his master's every change of mood, to watch for the very slightest intimation of a frown that could herald his downfall. Richelieu's sudden bouts of feverishness were simply reactions to his master's frequently equivocal, if not mysterious, silences. It explains why he was constrained to be a subtle, vigilant, and artful courtier, as well as a consummately versatile actor, a master of tearful scenes and sudden improvisations.

Once the King said to him in anger, "You go first, for it's said you are the real king."

"Yes, Sire," the Cardinal riposted, seizing a blazing torch, "I go first so that I can light your way."

In the end, Louis and Richelieu were united by the political confusion of the times and by the dangers that faced them both; each knew he was indispensable to the other. The minister's existence hung upon the King's fate, and the kingdom's fate depended upon Richelieu's existence. The King wished to be kept informed of every detail of the affairs of state; and Richelieu gave far more time and energy to the four square feet of the King's desk than to the rest of the world. He threw a tight network of spies over the entire court, enrolling priests, doctors, court favorites, and servants. After twelve years of practically ruling alone, his apprehension, far from diminishing, had become an obsession. As we have seen, he had some justification, for the year 1636 saw a terrifyingly successful invasion finally turned back at Corbie, only to be followed by an almost fatal attempt on Richelieu's life.

The cold and steely outer casing of the Scarlet Courtier concealed an anxious, intensely emotional man worn down by illness and almost superhuman labor. It was only natural that he should come to regard the affairs of state as inextricable from his personal survival. He could not afford to allow any moral scruple to take precedence over this concern; nor could he afford ever to forget it. Even Cinq-Mars' astonishing good looks entered this concern. It suddenly occurred to the Cardinal that this boy might win the King's affection as Baradas and Saint-Simon had already done.

Saint-Simon, now a duc and peer, had started life as a humble stable page. Until he was nineteen he was nothing but a rough and ready rustic of no great subtlety or wit, although lively and nice enough. His Eminence himself had introduced Louis XIII to the lad, who had then become the royal favorite. On the Day of Dupes in 1630, when Richelieu thought that his ex-patron Marie de Médicis had contrived his downfall, it was this same "smelly little chap" who had led the Cardinal back to his master and without doubt saved France.

Richelieu felt that he had the right to expect even greater loyalty from the son of his old friend Effiat, whom he had protected and helped bring up. At that moment Louis' heart was divided between two women: the proud Marie de Hautefort and the gentle Louise de La Fayette. Both women loathed the Cardinal, and both worked to be rid of him. If Henri managed to supplant these two, Richelieu could relax and be able to devote himself wholly to the greater glory of France.

The King had not yet even noticed Cinq-Mars; the young man himself regarded the King as a distant divinity whom he wished to serve but whose personal characteristics repelled him. The Cardinal was ready to spin the web which would fatally ensnare them both.

Two

The Vain Struggle

WHEN THE YOUNG Cinq-Mars joined the Court eager for pleasure and renown, he discovered a baffling universe.

Left to his own penchants, the King would have led an almost monastic existence. Only duty, the demands of government, and the traditional pomp that inevitably surrounded his position forced him to participate in the dazzling spectacles given at the Louvre and at Saint-Germain. Even so, he did all he could to dim the brilliance of these official displays. He tried to abolish dueling and banish extravagant fashions by passing the sumptuary laws, but nothing could induce the French to stop converting their fortunes into lavish attire or to forgo the pleasure of slitting each others' throats.

Henri IV's son was a sickly and neurasthenic King, masochistic and his own worst enemy. He did not share the Spanish princes' morose habit of dreaming over their ancestors' tombs, however; he was an active, athletic man. Louis devoted as much energy to war, travel, and hunting as he did to politics. Once when it was raining, he expressed the frustration of a huntsman denied his favorite pastime by banging on the streaming windowpane and muttering to one of his servants, "Let's bore each other!" Hunting was an escape from his obsessions and made him feel more at ease, especially when he took refuge in his beloved Versailles. "This little castle of playing cards, which even the humblest gentleman would not boast of owning," was set in a subdued and melancholy countryside with a few scattered farms and vineyards surrounded by marshes and an infinity of forests well supplied with game. It was here that His Most Christian Majesty realized that there was much misery beneath so much splendor and resigned himself to living between these two extremes.

His Majesty had other pastimes which revealed the childish streak in his habitually grim nature. He liked weaving nets, gardening, making preserves and armaments as well as coins. Then suddenly the royal craftsman decided to reveal his aptitudes for composing, decorating, and dancing! The magnificence of the last Valois was revived at the Louvre and the Hôtel de Ville. The royal family and the nobility intermingled with hundreds of artists. Multitudes, whose social status was defined by their brilliant attire, gasped in admiration at weird and wonderful spectacles whose splendor our gray age cannot imagine. There were extraordinary mechanisms, disguises where gold and precious stones were employed like ordinary cloth. Giants and dwarfs, tightrope walkers, fabulous animals, mythological deities, knights, and enchantresses peopled the solemn pageants and comic fantasies. Even the "hypochondriac king" himself was known to dance as a clown or a devil or a farcical Mahomet!

None of this, however, could persuade the court to excuse his tense, reserved nature, his halting speech and awkward movements, or his inability to express his feelings, which he seemed to be ashamed of. His ascetic ideals were out of step with the gallant, adventurous, theatrical gestures inspired by the fashionable *Précieuses* of the day. His virtues, worthy of being called stoic,[1] were not understood or appreciated by a court which had been weaned on *Astrée* and seduced by *Le Cid* and which nevertheless remained

---

[1] The *Manual of Epictetus* (Epictetus was a stoic philosopher of the first century A.D.) was one of the most popular books of the day and gave rise to a philosophy whose enduring success was assured by the works of Guillaume Du Vair.

Rabelaisian to the core. The King did not have the grace of a Caladon or the heroic dimensions of a Rodrique or the robustness of a Gargantua. His restive nobility regarded him as a martinet determined to forbid anything that represented the joy of living: festivities, duels, intrigues, lechery, independence. "That idiot," Madame de Chevreuse called him, when her seductive ploys were spurned. Her words were not forgotten. To while away the time until they were rid of this nuisance, courtiers composed possible epitaphs for their sovereign:

> *Here lies a king who, under a priest,*
> *Played his despicable little role*
> *He had all the virtues of a servant*
> *But not one of a master.*

Only when the King was dead would these same proud and savage gentlemen appreciate his true worth. Finding themselves subjected to Mazarin, they would pay him belated homage.

Queen Anne of Austria could have animated a cheerful and brilliant court, as indeed she would during her regency, but her morose husband would not permit her. He even went as far as forbidding her her own circle of friends. At thirty-five, Anne was slightly heavy, but she still retained much of the beauty and attraction that had fascinated Buckingham and had even turned the Cardinal's head. One day, His Eminence had even been known to grant her whim and dance a saraband for her dressed in a green habit trimmed with little silver bells. But the request had been a joke, and his compliance made him a laughingstock. She never finished paying for it.

The greatest Queen in the world led a harassed, miserable life. The declared enemy of the Prime Minister, she was distrusted by her husband and was constantly watched and spied upon. Her sterility exposed her to still worse indignities. She was everything that Louis XIII was not: sensual, lazy, gluttonous, muddleheaded, flirtatious. The King loathed her elaborate toilette, her chatter, her

Spanish cosmetics. He accused her of appearing more like an Infanta than a French Queen. He was convinced that she had played a part in the Chalais plot to kill him so as to marry Monsieur, his brother, and he resented this to his dying day. He performed his conjugal duty only to perpetuate his line, and even though he had dedicated France to the Virgin in the hope of begetting a son, his visits to his intimate enemy had become few and far between. (Louis XIII's impotence is a myth, as his doctor's journal proves. Anne of Austria suffered three miscarriages before Louis XIV was born.)

His court was thus a very different one from that of François I or Henri IV. Still, it had never been peopled so brilliantly. The Queen was attended by splendidly witty and lively ladies-in-waiting: the Princesse de Condé and her daughter, the future Duchesse de Longueville; the Princesses Marie and Anne Gonzaga, Madame de Montbazon, Madame de Hautefort, Mesdemoiselles de La Fayette, de Chémerault, de Ponchâteau, de Vigean, d'Escars, de Saint-Louis, and twenty others who made up her peerless retinue.

Cinq-Mars was very much at ease among the spirited, bellicose, debauched, and gloriously vain young men for whom extravagance was a title of respect. He shared their taste for astonishing, dazzling pursuits—natural to the young of any century, but ones which this age pushed too far. Seeking a chance to be noticed was his dominant preoccupation.

Life was sweet; springs and summers were spent on the battlefield, and winters were for Paris and pleasure. His prowess on the battlefield and in the bedchamber excited the admiration of his peers. In his handsome features there was something anxious, innocent, and even mysterious that inspired friendship as well as love. But this sort of reputation was not to be won at the court of Louis the Chaste. It had to be consecrated at the Hôtel de Rambouillet and the other *salons* by the society that gathered at the Place Royale. Cinq-Mars made himself count beneath the painted ceilings of noble houses of the glittering *Précieuses* and in the chambers of the ravishing hostesses of the notorious Marais district.

There he came to know the notorious Libertines, whose leader was the famous Des Barreaux, nicknamed the Illustrious Débauché or Théophile's widow (after the poet Théophile de Viau, who died in 1626), even though he was then madly in love with a provincial girl called Marie Delon de Lorme. These Libertines were free-thinkers in a world wholly given over to religion. With a swaggering audacity, they ridiculed anything sacred and any conformity, preached an aggressive materialism, published scandalous poems, and "reveled in orgy." Still the captive of a strong maternal authority, Henri greatly admired these reprobates who feared neither Heaven nor Hell and braved the fulminations of both Church and Parlement. He met them at their favorite cabarets, at the Pomme de Pin in rue de la Juiverie near Notre Dame, at Coffier's in rue du Pas-de-la-Mule, at Cormier's in rue des Fossés-Saint-Germain-l'Auxerrois, where they drank heavily and recited wickedly salacious verse.

The young Marquis also enjoyed the more delicate intellectual pleasures of the Marais *salons,* entering eagerly into literary jousts. This won him the reputation of a wit; but most importantly he still had to prove himself a mettlesome swordsman. He fought Louis Foucault, Comte du Daugnon, in a duel, and defeated him. He had doubly risked his life, since dueling had recently been made a capital crime. But this time, the Cardinal looked the other way, apparently delighted to see that his protégé had proved himself.

Handsome, witty, courageous, Cinq-Mars would not fail to captivate both the Court and the capital. He conquered the right mistresses and won devoted friends. The closest of them was Henri de Massue, Marquis de Ruvigny, whom Cinq-Mars loved like a brother and who was respected and very popular despite his Protestant faith.

These satisfactions so quickly followed his emotionally deprived childhood that they were bound to give him an exaggerated opinion of himself. He began to feel that nothing was beyond his reach. A charming young rooster who preened himself with disarming presumption, he was sure of a dazzling future. The son of the Maréchal d'Effiat would surpass his father. Until his dreams came true, he would live the life of his companions—a life of battles, duels, romances, adventures, and madcap escapades; of chases, sword-fights, silken ladders, and drunken street brawls, a life that brought him the intoxicating illusion of total freedom.

Cinq-Mars had not given any thought to the complaints of the Marquis de la Force, Grand Master of the Wardrobe, who wanted to sell his office to Monsieur d'Aumont. The King had practically given his consent, but Richelieu asked him to delay. Cinq-Mars did not consider the transaction could affect him and so ignored it, but finally His Eminence asked him whether a dandy so concerned with his own appearance might not be pleased to concern himself with the King's as well.

The young man grew pale at the suggestion. The Grand Master of the Wardrobe was forced to share the King's most intimate life, receive his confidences, and bear the brunt of all his moods. The office may have been an important and highly coveted one, but Cinq-Mars knew it to be a euphemism for slavery. He had just begun to feel free for the first time in his life and had no intention of becoming the slave of a gloomy, cantankerous, maniacal prince.

Overcoming his timidity before the Cardinal, he firmly refused. Richelieu did not press the point. He gave the young man a condescending, knowing smile and dismissed him.

Then in March of 1637, when Father Gordon relinquished his post as confessor to the King, the Marquis de Cinq-Mars had the honor of escorting to the Louvre his successor, the Jesuit Father Caussin. Henri could not foresee how the crisis opened by this implacable enemy of Richelieu's would affect his own future.

The King was then tragically in love with Louise de La Fayette. He had started courting the sweet young girl in order to make Marie de Hautefort jealous, with the unexpected result that they both fell into a chaste, sad, and timid love. Louis and Louise were to be seen whispering together in alcoves, meeting at the hunt and at court ceremonies, exchanging messages. That was all—and that would have been enough, if only the world had left them in peace.

But politics intervened. Richelieu, delighted with Hautefort's fall from favor, promptly offered his alliance to La Fayette, only to find that his enemies had already hit on the same idea and had succeeded in winning her sympathies. The pious Louise was shocked by the Cardinal's approaches. She was convinced that it was her personal mission to reconcile the King with his Queen and to liberate the French people from the Cardinal's tyranny, and she gave herself zealously to these tasks. Richelieu outmaneuvered her by playing on her piety and giving Louis a rival for her affections who was none other than God. On his instructions, Father Carré, the young lady's confessor, lured her toward a convent, while Richelieu played on Louis' religious inclinations to prevent his standing in the way of her calling.

Father Caussin did his best to thwart Richelieu's maneuver. He bolstered La Fayette and by fanning her horror of Richelieu, persuaded her to stay at Court for the sake of France. The unfortunate monarch's private life thus became the political instrument of the Cardinal on the one hand and of the rival Spanish faction on the other. Richelieu's ends were finally served by the frailties inherent in the relationship itself. One day the exasperated ascetic dared to ask Louise, "Would you like me to keep you at Versailles and live under my orders and be entirely mine?" The virgin recoiled in terror, and the shamefaced suitor regained his self-control. As Madame de Motteville put it, "the mutual fear they had of each other induced them to part."

Louis XIII now realized that he could not afford to become attached to any one person, for it might lead him to neglect his Christian duty to God, the true Sovereign of the State. He could be harsh toward others only if he were harsh toward himself. He informed the Cardinal of his sacrifice with a tear-stained note, and on the 19th of May Mademoiselle de La Fayette entered the Convent of St. Mary of the Visitation. Louis lapsed into despair. He might even have abdicated had there been anyone less despicable than his brother to succeed him.

Father Caussin was not so easily deterred. He assailed the King with the peril he was putting his soul in by waging a sinful war and refusing to live with his Queen. Louis would hear an echo of these arguments again during his interminable visits to the Convent of the Visitation where he went to see Louise, now in her novitiate habit.

Richelieu was thus constrained to fight off internal enemies while conducting a gigantic conflict. At this point he again took up the matter of the Marquis de la Force's position with Cinq-Mars, and this time he exhorted and admonished. Henri fought back tooth and nail. His affair with Mademoiselle de Chémerault, Madame de Hautefort's best friend, reinforced his determination not to yield to the Cardinal. This beautiful creature excited in him all the exalted, sublime sentiments of the characters of *Astrée:* "The soul should love the soul which is its equal, rather than the body which is its inferior." These shepherds of Lignon, however, did not sacrifice all carnal pleasures to metaphysical joy. Wits of the day observed that when they set out to attain the summit of chaste love, they were wont to rest halfway up.

In any case, Cinq-Mars refused, and the Cardinal was forced to look elsewhere. He did not look very far: Mademoiselle de Chémerault was ambitious and had a natural gift for intrigue and far fewer scruples than her suitor. She did not refuse the Cardinal's offer. When Richelieu spoke to the King about her, however, he was silenced. "I have resolved," Louis said, "not to become involved with anyone ever again." The King was deluding himself, for already his interest was returning to his Aurora, the proud and brilliant Marie de Hautefort.

Summer came. In July, Richelieu obtained conclusive evidence that with France in the state of war, the Queen was committing treason. She had been maintaining an extensive and highly compromising correspondence with her brother, the King of Spain, with the Duc de Lorraine, and with England. Anne did not hesitate to give false testimony, but she knew she had been discovered. She was in danger of being publicly denounced and dismissed to a convent. Louis would probably have been glad to untie the odious marital bond. In a mystical way, her undoing would have brought him closer to Louise.

Having considered the alternatives, however, the Cardinal decided that the conspirators' desire for a united royal household was equally necessary to his own ends. Ironically, the Queen—who never tired of plotting Richelieu's downfall—was the only person who could fulfill his greatest hope by giving birth to a Dauphin, a wish his adversaries naïvely shared. He therefore decided to treat himself to the pleasure of being merciful to a dangerous enemy. The daughter of the Habsburgs had to eat her pride and even humbled herself to say, "Your Eminence must be so full of goodness." She even tried to press his hand in gratitude. Louis forced himself to bestow a kiss of peace, which he gave with his lips and not with his heart.

Meanwhile Louise de La Fayette and Father Caussin were still under the illusion that a reconciliation between the King and his wife would bring about the Cardinal's undoing; and they continued their efforts. On December 5, a series of romantic coincidences served their cause by leading the reluctant Louis XIII into the conjugal bed at the Louvre.[2] On December 8, Father Caussin, certain of victory, enlarged his usual indictments against Richelieu. He described the ravages of the war, the resulting distress of the population, and the impious alliance with the Protestants. He reminded the King that he was responsible for the welfare of his own kin and ended the tirade by dramatically presenting a letter from the Queen Mother, Marie de Médicis, who had been in exile for six years.

Louis was deeply moved by this portrayal of his distressed kingdom. It exacerbated his insomnia, anxiety, doubts, and guilt. The following morning he instructed Father Caussin to go before the

---

[2] See Philippe Erlanger, *Louis XIV* (New York: Praeger, 1970).

Cardinal at Rueil and restate his case. Louis would follow Caussin and "uphold all he had said." But the tables were turned on the Jesuit. A *lettre de cachet* exiled him to Rennes as of the following day. Richelieu had scored another victory, but it was one of those situations which constantly arose to remind him of the danger he was compelled to risk.

Abruptly he turned on Cinq-Mars and subjected the youth to another round of intensive persuasion. Henri continued to oppose him with the negative obstinacy which is often the weapon of the weak. Henri put up a desperate fight against the minister's violent temper and refused to accept the dubious honor which was being thrust upon him. Richelieu was disappointed and angry. Having dealt with the chaste virgin and the King's confessor, he now had to face a former royal favorite. That old ditty cropped up again:

> *Hautefort the marvel*
> *Awakens all Louis' senses*
> *When her vermilion lips*
> *Show him a smile*

But Louis' senses, in fact, were as unaffected as they had been when this odd lover had used a pair of tweezers to remove a suspicious message from Madame de Hautefort's bodice.

"Banish the word desire," the King told Boisrobert, after reading a poem dedicated to his beautiful mistress, "for I desire nothing." And then he quoted one of his favorite expressions: "May God please that adultery never enters my house."

He nonetheless allowed himself to be dominated by Marie de Hautefort who was known as "Hermione" among the *Précieuses*. She was not capable of the epic furies of Racine's princess, nor did she have Hermione's eagerness to be married—she waited until she was thirty before choosing a husband—but she did have her pride, haughtiness, courage, and cruelty, none of which she spared her sighing suitor. When her beauty eventually faded, it was described as giving her "more strength and nobility than lightness and grace." She had an essentially pitiless, overbearing nature and could not abide anyone who preferred hunting to the subtler pursuits of the "Carte du Tendre." Whenever conversation strayed from the King's outdoor pleasures, it invariably deteriorated into bickering. It was a strange relationship which created two martyrs through mutual irritation and vexation. Marie never hid her preference for the Queen and delighted in avenging Anne of Austria. Anne, in turn, heaped all her bitterness and boredom not on the "mistress," as might have been expected, but on the "lover" instead. Madame de Motteville was to write of Louis, "This soul, accustomed to bitterness, had compassion only so that it could feel its pains all the more." These sorrows were what bound him to his beloved tyrant.

In January of 1638 the incredible, prodigious news broke: After twenty-two years of marriage, Anne of Austria was pregnant. The King renewed his vow to the Virgin in the hope of obtaining a Dauphin who would decide the fate of France, but he did not change his hostile, icy attitude toward his wife. Marie de Hautefort, ever devoted to her Queen, was determined not to let the Cardinal rob the Queen of her glory in her motherhood. The haughty creature decided to win over her royal lover by treating him kindly. Louis XIII was transported, but Richelieu quaked. He could not afford to let this little schemer play with the King, to let her poison his mind without the Minister ever knowing the substance of what passed between them. Their trifling exchanges terrified the scourge of Europe.

The Cardinal went to Madame d'Effiat, pointing out that her son's indiscretions threatened to nip his fortunes in the bud. Richelieu arranged an advancement worthy of a royal favorite, and he had refused out of pure caprice! If Henri persisted, he and his family could expect nothing further from the Cardinal.

Richelieu need not have gone so far to incite the ambitious woman to action. She swooped down on her son, who had never had the courage to disobey her. But he made a last stand, and once more dared to remain insensible to Richelieu's blandishments.

Richelieu set about the problem in another way: He saw to it that the King began to hear talk of Cinq-Mars. Louis had scarcely noticed the charming officer, although he had been in the King's Guard for eighteen months. But now the courtiers in the Minister's service voiced their delight with Cinq-Mars and maneuvered conversations round to praise "this young man in the first flower of his youth, who distinguished himself by his striking appearance, his elegant manners, and lively wit." One evening as His Majesty was retiring, his retinue talked of nothing else.

The King finally took note of the object of all this praise and was struck by Cinq-Mars' beauty. He spoke to him and was pleased by his manner. Richelieu then reminded him of the late Maréchal d'Effiat, eulogized the son, and suggested that the office of Grand Master of the Wardrobe might suit him perfectly. This enthusiasm roused the King's suspicion. Nonetheless he chose to forget his previous half-promise to Monsieur d'Aumont and raised no objections.

Now only the boy's intransigence still had to be broken. Madame d'Effiat used all the resources of her authority to threaten and frighten Henri. The Cardinal reserved for himself the more advantageous role of peacemaker.

Henri would have needed a will of iron to withstand such pressure. He capitulated, fully aware of the consequences of his defeat. On his eighteenth birthday, March 27, 1638, he became Grand Master of the Wardrobe.

Three

ADONIS AND THE STOIC

MATHIEU LE NAIN has left for posterity a portrait of the most handsome and gallant of all Masters of the Wardrobe. The finely modeled face is surrounded by an exquisitely curled wig. The gentle eyes have a slightly malicious glint which emphasizes the sensual mouth. The young Marquis is dressed in a white satin doublet trimmed with aglets and a pair of gold-embroidered breeches finished with a cascade of lace that overlaps his top boots. His cuffs and collar are of fine Venetian lace. A magnificent gold baldric lies across his chest.

Madame d'Effiat's parsimony had never yet permitted Henri to offset his good looks with fine clothing. But now that all the tailors of the land were at his feet, he could begin to amass at no great expense a fantastic collection of clothes. The inventory of his estate confirms that at his death he possessed fifty-two outfits valued at fifty to a hundred livres each, not to mention all the cloaks, hats, and accessories. One such outfit comprised "a surcoat, doublet, and breeches in nut-brown cambric, the surcoat lined in the same cambric, the breeches lined in white satin and the doublet in *gris de lin* satin; each garment edged in silver and gold lace, the buttons being embroidered with gold and silver; the breeches trimmed in Scottish satin aglets and gold and silver lace." Then there were the plumes and jewels and those strong and costly scents with which dandies were supposed to anoint themselves.

As Cinq-Mars was responsible for choosing the King's apparel, the clothing industry assumed that this paragon of elegance would persuade the monarch to dress less austerely. Cinq-Mars did, in fact, try to make his own taste prevail, but he did not know Louis XIII. His Majesty would not dress more lavishly and reproached the young man for his indiscretion. Their relations thus started off on the wrong foot. The King often scolded the rascal, who controlled himself and kept a cheerful face. A short while later, Henri suffered no further rebukes; instinctively, he had understood that they were harbingers of royal favor. Louis liked playing the pedagogue and preaching virtue. Instructing and reprimanding a charming novice afforded his tormented soul a deep satisfaction.

Was Henri IV's son simply an unhappy man or was he a great king? He was assuredly both, and certainly he was also a very unhealthy man and a conscience-stricken Christian. His ill health is extensively documented. He had contracted tuberculosis when he was twenty-one. However, as his excellent physician Héroard observed, he had "a body of iron." It was this constitution which enabled him to survive to the age of forty-two despite the barbarous remedies inflicted on him by the Faculty of Medicine after Héroard's death. If his royal status had not commanded the indefatigable attentions of all the Diafoiruses of the time, his malady might have been held in check still longer. In fact, his physicians were often naïvely astonished by his miraculous recoveries when they stopped treatment, having given him up for lost. They never noticed the logical relations between recovery and the cessation of treatment. The laws of medicine were as inflexible as those which governed tragedy, and even a crown prince dared not disobey them. In one year alone, the fearsome Bouvard, whom Louis was publicly to blame for his death, prescribed 47 bleedings, 212 medications, and 215 enemas!

The court never ceased to marvel at the King's physical endurance. He was not deterred by wind, mud, snow, or Dog Days. He would lay his hands on the heads of eleven hundred ailing subjects at a time, stay in the saddle for seventeen hours at a stretch, walk eight leagues without stopping to rest, and share his soldier's fatigue till the battle was over. He was always up by six o'clock and never retired before midnight.

Nature rebelled, and Louis paid the toll for maintaining this pace. At thirty-seven, this "thin Jupiter was a pointed moustache" with an ageless, pale, feverish, consumptive face. His personality also suffered. His dwindling strength made him more restless, more eccentric, more obsessed by lugubrious thoughts.

The physical imbalance aggravated his spiritual torments. Louis had not inherited his father's skepticism. He feared a God whom he loved to serve and enjoyed hearing his choir sing His praises. He was devout to the point of superstition; his beliefs were absolute; his religious observances, like all his formal behavior, were impeccable. He built chapels and was truly devoted to the Virgin. He never was guilty of the religious hypocrisy of contemporary monarchs, but his belief in kingship constituted a second faith to which he was no less passionately devoted. It was unfortunate for him that his duty to the Church and his duty to his kingdom so rarely coincided. His Most Christian Majesty could dedicate France to Notre Dame with one hand and stave off the Pope with the other. He made alliances with Protestant kings and waged a fierce war against His Catholic Majesty of Spain. He persecuted his wife and his brother, and he forced his mother to suffer and die in exile, sacrifices that always weighed heavily on him. These perpetual conflicts wore him down.

A lad of eighteen could scarcely be expected to grasp the complexities and grandeur of such a sovereign. Living at such close quarters with him, Cinq-Mars was bound to notice all his pettiness, his foolishness, his blunders, his ill humors, his contradictions. In fact, the King was not an easy man to understand. He was timid but given to terrible fits of violence. He was an oversensitive, suspicious, jealous despot who practically abdicated to his

Minister and could be intimidated by his mistress' slightest frown. He was indecisive but stubborn, a rigid moralist with a taste for puerile pleasures, a wounded soul given to passing stringent judgment on others, a compound of anguish and conviction, pride and self-effacement, dynamism and submissiveness. Seeing his King's avarice deny the Court ladies an ordinary bowl of soup, it probably never struck Henri that this singularly awkward person might personify the very ideal qualities Corneille celebrated in *Le Cid*, a play which had enjoyed a great success the previous winter. In fact, the second Bourbon King's reign displayed "the triumph of the will applied to some extraordinary duty" [1] in the best Corneillian manner.

Had Louis not been born a King, he would never have attained much distinction. But as it was, he created an ideal of what the King of France should be, which was too oppressive for such a mediocre personality to follow. He did not doubt that he was superhumanly endowed with miraculous powers which enabled him to heal subjects ill with scrofula. His word was sacrosanct and any resistance to his commands an unpardonable crime. In his eyes, sovereign, state, and country were confused; they became a single supernatural entity to which all other considerations were sacrificed. It was natural that lesser men kiss the feet of the man who embodied these ideals, as it was that his subjects should say, "Rule well, Sire, and all that we have is yours."

Corneille was to exalt this suppression of the individual and magnify the importance of the autocrat whose personal fortune was bound up with that of the whole world. Long before Louis saw *Cinna*, he had decided to emulate the Prince who was master of himself and of the universe. This concept of kingship was diametrically opposed to the superb egolatry of Louis XIV. Louis XIII's King was the semidivinity who demanded total submission from his subjects, while sacrificing his own personal existence to the ideal of

---

[1] Jules Lemaitre.

kingship. If he was the absolute monarch, he remained the servant of his people, for his omnipotence was divinely granted for their protection. From the very beginning of his reign he had recognized the terrible discrepancy between the weak man he was and the King he wanted to be, and he made constant and enormous efforts to lift the one to the level of the other. These efforts were all the more poignant because he could not allow himself any assistant or even a witness.

"I should not be King had I the sentiments of ordinary men." With these words he refused Montmorency's blessing; they define his ambition exactly. They would have been less pathetic and less Corneillian had they been strictly true, for Henri IV's son was only too subject to ordinary feelings, most often when he needed most to eschew them. His conscience dictated that he overcome them; he tried to obey, and eventually the regal functions absorbed the individual.

Despite his disastrous marriage, Louis applied equally rigid principles to his love affairs. Anne of Austria's complicity did not throw him into Marie de Hautefort's arms; she was never his mistress. When Saint-Simon offered to be their go-between, he received a celebrated scolding: "It is true that I am in love. I could not help this because I am a man and subject to my senses. But I am also King and can thus be certain of obtaining whatever I desire. But the more I am King and the more I am obeyed, the more I must remember that God forbids me this. He made me King that I might obey His Command and make all those obey me whom He has subject to my command."

Louis's scrupulous continence occasionally relaxed when he took a fancy to a young girl or a youthful courtier. He treated both sexes identically, was susceptible to both, and all his infatuations followed the same pattern: He poured out his soul, wrote childish, long-winded letters, flew into rages, and made amends. This masochistic despot's idea of amorous bliss was to feel completely dominated by his beloved, to whom he could unbosom himself endlessly and confide all "the movements of his heart." Marie de Hautefort's imperious tyranny over him satisfied his secret desire for this type of relationship. Henri must have laughed at this strange pair or perhaps even felt sorry for them.

Throughout the Queen's pregnancy, Louis and "the Creature" quarreled incessantly. He tried to appease her by promoting her to the Queen's lady-in-waiting, with little effect. When he wrote to Richelieu about affairs of state, he often broke off to bemoan his miseries: "The Creature is always angry with me. . . ." "The first day of our reconciliation passed with coldness on her part and submission on mine. . . ." "This evening I thought I should award Madame de Hautefort a pension of 1,200 écus . . . to show her how I shall always return her ill humor with kindness. . . ." "Each day I discern that ill will which she bears me and, loving her as I do, I can only despair. . . ." "One never knows how to conduct oneself with a person who finds fault with all that one does to please. . . ."

The King's patience eventually came to an end. On August 25 he decided to leave her. The next morning they were reconciled. "Their affection won through," Chavigny wrote to Richelieu, "the reconciliation was easily effected, and the King, who had approached the encounter drawn and very nervous, emerged from it in good spirit, and his stomach went down without recourse to the usual remedies."

Ten days later Anne of Austria was in labor. Her condition aroused some concern. Madame de Hautefort was upset and on the verge of tears; Louis reprimanded her coldly: "Keep your thoughts on the child. There will be ample opportunity for you to mourn the mother." When the future Louis XIV was born and Château de Saint-Germain resounded with jubilation, Marie had to "urge him to go to the Queen's side and kiss her."

France was overjoyed at the news. So was Richelieu. The fruition of the Spanish faction's plot gave him solid ground on which to operate and guaranteed his ultimate success. His mortal enemy,

Gaston d'Orléans, the King's brother, was now no longer heir. The Cardinal's future no longer depended upon the waning strength of a sickly monarch, and the birth of a son satisfied in Louis that universal need for posterity. He gave ardent prayers of thanksgiving, but he was incapable of unadulterated joy and soon began to feel strangely jealous of the little child who was already worshipped as a rising sun.

The God of War had begun to favor France. At such a time Richelieu was concerned to find the King under the spell of a dangerous woman. She strove to undermine policies she did not understand and could only upset her happy "lover's" moral judgments. Cinq-Mars was not making the progress Richelieu had expected, even though the King's ears rang with the young man's praises. But at least the King was growing used to him, and the Cardinal had reason to hope for the future. For the time being Richelieu had to turn his attention to more immediate problems.

He asked Mademoiselle de Chémerault to inform him of everything she saw and heard between her close friend Marie de Hautefort and the King. She did not refuse the distasteful task. Cinq-Mars' behavior would also fall "within her province." And if this were not enough, she was instructed to provoke quarrels between the King and his beloved. Most cunning of all, she was to attract the King's attention to the young man who was in love with her.

Henri did not realize that he was walking into a snake pit. His cheerful spirit often performed the miracle of soothing His Majesty's temper when Marie's biting tongue provoked it. In the autumn of 1638, the courtiers in waiting noticed signs of an important change: The "hypochondriac" had begun to smile openly at his Master of the Wardrobe's lively jokes.

A devout and upright man, Monsieur Delon de Lorme had tried unsuccessfully to preserve his daughter from the entanglements of love. After many romantic wanderings, the adventurous girl finally settled down in Paris with Des Barreaux in a delightful house in the *faubourg* Saint-Victor. The Libertine poet had named his retreat "The Isle of Cyprus" and indiscreetly advertised his joys and pleasures:

I die and rise again. O great master of gods,
Love, how much pleasure and glory I have through
you!

His decision to introduce his conquest to Parisian society was his greatest indiscretion. He took her with him everywhere and presented her to the celebrated Ninon de Lenclos, who then plied this new discovery with all manner of advice. Under her influence, the provincial girl became an irresistible, beautiful coquette who thirsted for pleasure and radiated joy. Marie Delon became Marion de Lorme; she was twenty-five when she embarked upon the career which was to make her immortal. Despite the influence of the Church, people were not puritanical in the nineteenth-century sense. No door was ever closed to her because she was the mistress of a notorious man. Her incredible beauty graced the noblest houses as well as those of the opulent bourgeois.

Cinq-Mars met her and was dazzled. He courted her ardently, and she did not discourage his attentions. She was attracted by his dandy good looks, and his prestigious position as Master of the Wardrobe flattered her growing aspirations. She loved Des Barreaux, however, and would not betray him. Henri was forced to play the role of pining lover as dictated by the Hôtel de Rambouillet's code of love.

Cardinal Richelieu kept careful track of what happened throughout the kingdom, but he made a special point of knowing everything that went on in the Place Royale. He knew Des Barreaux well. He had saved the famous debauchee when he committed "some outrage against a young Jesuit." And he also kept a very close watch on Cinq-Mars' conduct. He was especially interested in anyone who could enslave both a Libertine and a prince charming.

Abbé Boisrobert, who was his closest confidant, kept Richelieu abreast of every intricacy in this double intrigue. He was so lyrical in describing the young lady's charms that he excited something more than the Cardinal's curiosity. There was a popular jingle sung in Paris at the time:

> *Those who flatter His Eminence*
> *For the virtue of continence,*
> *Take their authority*
> *From the saying that in Rome,*
> *A saint is merely a priest*
> *Who makes love in secret.*

The Minister's amorous life was, in fact, common knowledge. The saraband incident had made the Court roar with laughter and joke endlessly about his weakness for the Queen. His affair with his niece, Madame de Combalet, who had become the Duchesse d'Aiguillon, also added spice to the chronicles. Indeed, Marie de Médicis' jealousy of the young woman alienated her from her ex-protégé. Madame de Chaulnes and Madame de Fruges were among the few women of real social standing who bestowed their favors on the Scarlet Courtier; he recruited the majority of his conquests from the lower ranks of society.

Monsieur le Cardinal now wished to become acquainted with the most celebrated beauty of the day. Boisrobert brought Marion and her friend Ninon de Lenclos to lunch in the Château de Rueil's magnificent park. While fountains plashed and violins played serenades, Richelieu studied Des Barreaux's mistress carefully from the secrecy of his window. The next morning Boisrobert began making arrangements for a tryst between the two. Contemporary reports disagree on the conditions stipulated by the two parties, but it is known that Marion did not resist the lure of the Cardinal's purple. She arrived at the Palais Cardinal disguised as a page. Richelieu also wore an unusual outfit—a *gris de lin* satin habit trimmed with silver and gold lace, lace-trimmed boots, and a plumed hat. How their encounter proceeded remains a mystery. Marion later boasted of carrying away a "trophy"—a ring worth sixty gold pistoles belonging to Madame d'Aiguillon.

The politician never lurked very far behind the Cardinal's diverse façades, even when fortune smiled on him. It seems that no sooner was he satisfied than he tried to recruit her as an agent and proposed that she spy on Cinq-Mars. But when Des Bournais, His Eminence's *valet de chambre,* went to deliver a hundred gold pistoles to her and to ask her to return to the Palais Cardinal, the young woman scornfully refused and threw the money into the messenger's face.

The story ran round town, much to the Cardinal's discomfort. Marion became famous. Des Barreaux forgot his short-lived humiliation and gloated over his victory. He immediately sat down to write a poem on "His Mistress's Preference for the Author Over His Sometime Rival, the Cardinal," which ended triumphantly:

> *I had it from her own faithful mouth*
> *That she would rather die than be unfaithful to*
> *me.*

But Des Barreaux was tempting fate. The adventure had only made the lady the more desirable to Cinq-Mars. And no young woman who yearned to conquer Paris and revel in its pleasures could hold out indefinitely against an Adonis who occupied one of the most important posts at Court. She yielded, and Cinq-Mars returned her passion. The two blissful lovers soon became the talk of the Marais. Defeated, Des Barreaux sank into despair, vainly casting curses upon the traitress:

> *No, you are no longer my angel,*
> *No longer an object so worthy of praise,*
> *For whom I always disclosed*
> *My heart by my sighs, my soul through my verses.*

And Marion merely laughed, unmoved by the great cynic's down-fall. The Prince of Libertines was so deranged that he was actually converted. "He made an utter fool of himself and kissed a lot of relics," the heartless Tallemant remarks.

For a time, Cinq-Mars and Marion were the happiest and most fêted lovers in Paris. Richelieu was annoyed, and Madame d'Effiat violently indignant. Henri was no longer so afraid of his mother, and her reprimands only threw him back into his lover's delightful arms. He did not, however, relinquish Madame de Chémerault! They continued to be lovers, and the treacherous lady continued to give her reports to the Cardinal, some of which are mentioned in his *Memoires.*

Henri was not aware of the slightest threat to his future. He was no longer troubled by the King, whose benevolence had not yet begun to curtail his pleasures. These triumphs naturally went to the eighteen-year-old's head. His family background and his own inclinations did not temper his success with the necessary circum-spection. The young Marquis was convinced that his good fortune was entirely due to his own merit. Adonis became Narcissus. But as youth and grace add luster to all things, his reckless vanity only added to his charm.

Four

The "Workings of Nature"

𝒆𝕩 THE ENSUING WINTER proved both bitter and glorious for Louis. The capture of Brisach had been crucial. The Emperor was cut off from the Netherlands; a wedge had been driven between the talons of the Habsburg eagle. Victory now seemed possible, though still far off.

The hero of the Pas de Suze, whom Bassompierre had credited with an "assurance and valor in battle which even the late King, his father, never displayed," had originally thrown himself into the war with much less anxiety than Richelieu. Three years of war had made them change places. The minister advocated war with ferocious tenacity while the King yearned for peace. His Most Christian Majesty's health was declining. He was increasingly tormented by the ailments which Callot described in such detail. He trembled at the prospect of having to meet his Sovereign Judge before he had ended this sinful war.

His people's sufferings also worried him. He had always been well loved, but now he was becoming painfully aware of the diminishing number and volume of the cries of "Long live the King!" that accompanied his travels throughout the country. Then, no sooner had the troubles in Périgord died down than the Norman "Bare-feet" began slitting tax collectors' throats and committing other atrocities. Another cycle of violence, counterviolence, sentences, and executions ensued. Overwhelmed by his public responsibilities, Louis continued to endure his private martyrdom.

He was surrounded by intrigue, espionage, and duplicity. La Chesnaye, one of his valets, was a secret agent of the Cardinal's. Mademoiselle de Chémerault spied on both Cinq-Mars and Madame de Hautefort. Madame de Hautefort, in turn, reported her sad lover's every word to the Queen. Louis often wished to sever this bond. "The King wanted to break loose," wrote Chavigny to Cardinal de La Valette, "but he could not find the pretext." Later he wrote, "The Hautefort matter has not yet been decided, but I think it is over and done with." But it always seemed to mend. Louis was fascinated by Hermione, and would have accepted his bondage if the Cardinal's legion of agents had not undertaken to liberate him, telling him of how she ridiculed him and provoked unpleasant incidents and misunderstandings.

One day an incredible rumor was broadcast: The Marquis de Gesvres had dared talk of marriage with the King's favorite, and she had not been outraged by it. The King was, however. His anger swept through the Court. The Duc de Gesvres, the rogue's father, was made to endure a Homeric diatribe, whereupon he rushed back to his son to make him sign an oath that he would never again presume to the hand of the Queen's lady-in-waiting. The Marquis was disgraced. Louis regained his equanimity slowly.

Such minor dramas became melodramas to the "hypochondriac." His daily letters to his minister betrayed a curiously distorted sense of proportion. Madame de Hautefort's cruelties were given as much weight as the affairs of state.

In this sinister world where even the simplest pleasures were suspect, Cinq-Mars was a breath of fresh air. He radiated youth and liveliness. He was a happy and fulfilled lover—Louis realized it with some envy, but it also added to Cinq-Mars' charm. Henri even had the fortunate knack of loving both Marion and Mademoiselle de Chémerault without rousing their jealousies, although each obviously knew of the other, since his affairs were on everyone's tongue.

Marion's beauty made her immortal, but her rival's beauty was just as dazzling. "She was remarkable," La Rochefoucauld wrote of her, "and her delightful intellect was no less pleasurable than her beauty." She was not financially independent—she was called the "Pretty Pauper"—and she was therefore forced to be a resourceful schemer. But Cinq-Mars ignored such considerations. He sometimes spoke of marrying the schemer, and sometimes the hussy.

When Marion was made to go home with her parents to their chateau at Baye, he galloped after her. Travel was hazardous in those days. The Master of the Wardrobe's haste attracted suspicion. "A band of men concerned with catching thieves overtook him and bound him to a tree. Had no one come forward to verify who he was, they would have carried him off to prison."

Madame d'Effiat took a dim view of her son's libertinage. Marion de Lorme had not yet become an experienced courtesan, but she did her best to play the part in style and was incredibly extravagant. One can easily imagine how she must have worried the parsimonious Madame d'Effiat. Ruvigny, whose gallantry and military prowess Cinq-Mars greatly admired, advised him to break away from his mother's intolerable control. Cinq-Mars mustered up his courage and left his mother's home after a particularly violent scene to take up residence at Ruvigny's "by the Couture Sainte-Catherine." He spent his nights with Marion and punctuated his days with no fewer than four visits to her, each in a different suit of clothes. Madame d'Effiat choked with rage, but the few months which the young man spent with his lively companion, a time entirely taken up with the pursuit of love, were probably the happiest in his life.

Cinq-Mars suspected that Ruvigny was the lover of a very noble and worthy lady because he pursued his love with such secrecy. Henri would see him leave impeccably dressed every morning at seven for the Hôtel de Rohan. At first he thought the object of his pursuit was the Duchesse herself. On further reflection, however, he realized that Ruvigny was too proud to share his mistress with another man, for it was well known that Madame de Rohan [1] had

---

[1] The Duchesse de Rohan was Sully's daughter. Her daughter, Ruvigny's mistress, eventually married Chabot and founded the family of Rohan-Chabot.

a number of lovers, one of whom was Monsieur de Jerzay. Henri decided to trick Ruvigny into telling him who his mistress was. "I nearly boxed a fellow's ears on your behalf," he told him. "He said some foolish things about you and Mademoiselle de Rohan."

"Then you very nearly did me a grave disservice," Ruvigny replied.

Cinq-Mars swore to keep the secret. He would have been very happy if all his friends had been like Ruvigny and if all his secrets had always been amorous ones.

Louis d'Astarac, Marquis de Fontrailles, harbored other secrets. This "gentleman of Languedoc, hunchbacked before and aft, and of a wondrous ugly face" was a born conspirator, dedicated to a life of intrigue. He was remarkably intelligent, but obsessed with the need to avenge the humiliations of his physique. He would have liked to impart some of his strength and courage to the Duc d'Orléans, always ready to form plots and equally ready to betray his collaborators. Richelieu knew of Fontrailles' shady dealings, but was unable to interfere with them. He disliked the man intensely.

One day, when Richelieu was on his way to an ambassador's offices, he found the hunchback in the antechamber. "Out of my way," he said. "You should not present yourself. The Ambassador has no love of monsters."

Fontrailles gnashed his teeth and swore under his breath. "You devil, you may stab me today, but I shall do the same to you one day if it is the last thing I do." Later the Cardinal beckoned him in and tried to laugh the incident off; but the hunchback never forgave him.[2]

Fontrailles had perceived Richelieu's intentions and guessed that the King would fall prey to Cinq-Mars' charms. He thus set out to win the young man's confidence. Henri, who could never resist intelligent, strong-willed people, did not reject Fontrailles' friendship. Fontrailles "became his intimate friend, entering his rooms at any hour he pleased, receiving the young man's confidences," and

---

[2] Tallemant des Réaux.

whispering all manner of dangerous counsels in his ears. The role of evil genius suited him to perfection.

François-Auguste de Thou, on the other hand, had the appearances of a guardian angel. He was the son of an illustrious parlementary family who had known Henri since early childhood. His father owned the property of Villebon, near Chilly. His extensive travels took him to England, Flanders, Italy, the Levant, and gave him a precocious experience of the world. At nineteen he was made Parlementary Counselor. He was then made magistrate and an officer of the quartermaster's staff. It was through the latter appointment that he received a wound and was enabled to reveal his military gifts.

His career promised to be brilliant, but it was abruptly curtailed by a chivalrous if rather ill-conceived gesture. At the Queen's behest, the young counselor advanced the necessary funds to stop the sale of Madame de Chevreuse's jewels, which had been pawned just before the treacherous lady had been forced to flee after the exposure of the same conspiracy that very nearly brought about Anne of Austria's downfall. De Thou's chivalry was reported to Richelieu, who gave the impetuous gallant a thorough dressing down. Without punishing him, he nevertheless placed him in the category of the untrustworthy. Thus disgraced and reduced to the ignominious post of "Master of the King's Library," he became a subscriber to the widespread opinion that the Cardinal was a despotic subordinate and a plague on the kingdom. De Thou was convinced of this, or rather he believed he was, for he was essentially loyal and scrupulous and yearned to attain Christian perfection. He had studied theology from his earliest years and had spent much time in meditation and in search of absolute truths—meditations which only tormented him, however, and made him the more indecisive. His normal state of anxiety was taxed to breaking point when he fell in love with the glowing and very devout Princesse Guéméné. His love for her was bound to be guilty and even sinful, for despite her piety, she offered him temptations which he struggled to resist. His old wound was painful and also taxed his nerves. He felt a need to work for noble causes and for the good of others.

He began to regard the terrible Minister as the embodiment of all evil. It was his duty to destroy him. As Le Vassor says, "He took it into his head to contrive his downfall, convinced that in worldly terms it was the greatest possible achievement and that it would be the best way of serving his God." This obsession soothed his fevers and exorcised his demon.

Despite his austere demeanor, he was very fond of young Cinq-Mars, whom he intended to rescue from his youthful flush of riotous living and lead back to God. Henri recognized and admired his friend's "exceptional merit," his "lofty soul," his courage, and his "noble penchants." He may have made light of his stuffiness, ridiculed his scruples, and called him "His Disquietude," but he respected him.

One day de Thou had the same premonition that Fontrailles had had and understood what role the Cardinal wished the Master of the Wardrobe to play. He was thrilled. His earthly mission was now revealed. Heaven had predestined him to prepare the scatterbrained youth to be the King's guardian angel and savior of the state.

Cinq-Mars was so involved in his various love affairs that he failed to notice the nets that were being woven about him. Richelieu, Fontrailles, and de Thou filled his ears with advice as to how to conquer Louis XIII, each for completely different reasons. Cinq-Mars listened. His successes multiplied and fortified his self-confidence and ambition, and his former timidity disappeared. It might be fun to play the pretty wench and seduce a devout, neurotic king. A young man's giddy head could easily be turned by the fabulous tales of Epernon or Luynes or Buckingham.

For some time, Louis XIII had evaded the trap he knew the Cardinal had laid for him. Nonetheless he finally yielded. The Cardinal's direct pressures had not increased his interest in the Master of the Wardrobe. On the contrary, it was Cinq-Mars' youthful spontaneity which eventually broke down his defenses. When Marie upset him, he sought comfort in Cinq-Mars' pretty face and his almost childish laughter. Then one day, he suddenly discovered the personality behind these attributes and saw Cinq-Mars in a completely different light.

On March 27, 1639, the King wrote to the Cardinal of Madame de Hautefort: "The attachment continues." At the beginning of May, Madame de Hautefort could still upset him, as La Chesnaye, the Cardinal's spy and *valet de chambre,* reports: "His only malady is a form of self-torment. Having sufficiently tormented himself and all those about him, [the King] was restored to reason. He even took it into his head to get down on his knees and beg our forgiveness. . . ." Louis solemnly proclaimed, "I love her more than all the rest of the world together." But by May 25, when His Majesty left Saint-Germain to take command of his army, Richelieu already knew that his plan had succeeded.

Louis XIII arrived at Abbeville on May 30. He was to leave on June 4. It was during these four days, according to Montglat, that "he began addressing Cinq-Mars more than was his wont." The Court noticed this new familiarity immediately. Substantial evidence indicates that it was at this time that he yielded to the new emotions which had been tempting him.

It seems probable that this was a new experience for the King. The young Louis was not even eleven years old when Luynes, who was then thirty-three, comforted him in his unhappiness and helped the boy to overcome his infatuation for him. Baradas was a coarse blockhead, and that ex-stableboy Saint-Simon, "The Manurist" as he was called, was hardly less boorish. Louis loved Luynes as a hero, Baradas as a faithful animal, and Saint-Simon as a confidant.

A good deal of malicious speculation surrounds the nature of these relationships. When Luynes took power (the King was then fifteen), the Tuscan ambassador wrote, "*La buggara he passato i monti* [Buggery has crossed the Alps]." It seems difficult to believe Louis Vaunois' opinion, that "the only reason for these spiteful insinuations was the universal envy that attended Luynes." The

King's "Italian" inclinations were as obvious as those of his illegitimate brother, César de Vendôme. However, Louis was devoutly religious and always regarded the sexual act as shameful. This would indicate that he did not follow his inclinations. Furthermore, he had remarkable powers of self-control. His childhood miseries may have thrown him into Luynes' arms—he used to have his mattress placed alongside his friend's bed to ward off his nightmares, or so he claimed—but it was very unlikely that he should have participated in "a hundred obscenities" with Baradas; and his famous reprimand to Saint-Simon would become meaningless had any such relations existed between the two. In any case, none of his past loves resembled his lightning attachment to Cinq-Mars. In fact, "It was a total infatuation, an obsession, a madness. Now no one sees in Louis the least resistance, the slightest hesitation. There will be no turning back."

Thus at Abbeville Cinq-Mars learned that he had become a favorite. He may not have been surprised at being the object of such passion, but he was probably astounded at its vehemence. He had heard of nothing else for two whole years, and then all at once the game was on. He may not have calculated the outcome of these two years' efforts. It would have been impossible to predict Louis XIII's passions.

Cinq-Mars did not have the virtues of a saint, but his own inclinations did not lead him to any such "deviations," of which the company of the Libertines had already offered him several glimpses. Louis' attachment presented him with a dilemma. How could he possibly refuse a man whom he had effectively seduced, especially when this man was a King, the Lord's Anointed, the absolute lord and master of all souls and properties? Even a thoroughgoing womanizer like Cinq-Mars might find some excitement in the conquest of the sacred person to whom God had entrusted France.

The affair has provoked bitter controversies. Many modern historians have shrunk in horror before this scandalous hypothesis and rejected it out of hand, while others have elected to give Louis XIII the benefit of the doubt. But his contemporaries had no doubt whatever. Perrault wrote to the Prince de Condé, "Your Highness will be able to recall what he knew of King Henri III's affection for Monsieur d'Epernon and remember how he behaved and how he could give him presents." Vittorio Siri tacitly shared this opinion. So did the dignified Henri Arnauld, the future bishop of Angers and a brother of the famous Jansenists, who frequented the Hôtel de Rambouillet, "and who always had firsthand knowledge of what went on at court and in the city." He kept President Barillon, then in exile, informed as to every development in the Cinq-Mars affair. Tallemant des Réaux draws his facts from eyewitness informants whom he never fails to name. His *Historiettes* were long regarded as the work of a petty scandalmonger and were dismissed as extremely suspect. Today his nonconformism is felt to warrant considerably more attention. His realistic depictions of the seventeenth century should often be preferred to other more decorative portraits.[3]

We cannot therefore ignore the probability of a most singular liason; the vanity and curiosity of the one man gave free reign to the passion of the other.

---

[3] Cf. Antoine Adam, *Introduction à la nouvelle édition des Historiettes de Tallemant.*

Five

MONSIEUR LE GRAND

⚛ HAVING TAKEN HESDIN and several other towns, the King proceeded on to Stenay to inspect Maréchal de Châtillon's troops, then entered Mézières, where he stayed for four days. It was there, on July 26, that some of France's foremost officers gathered and dined together. The Duc de Nemours was among them: "He was as spirited and handsome a prince [of the House of Savoie] as anyone in the kingdom, but he was very young and impulsive." That evening, no doubt irritated by Cinq-Mars' sudden rise to royal favor and at all the rumors that surrounded it, he set about needling the Master of the Wardrobe.

Social rank then demanded that a mere gentleman respect his superiors. He was not expected to respond to any insult a prince might choose to hurl at him. Henri ignored such considerations. He allowed himself to be impetuous and answered for himself. Taken aback, the Duc proceeded to redouble his attack; Cinq-Mars redoubled his counterattack. Nemours was furious and flung a cherrystone at the insolent upstart's face, only to have a similar projectile shot back at him, which caught him in the eye. He sprang at Cinq-Mars, and they started struggling with each other. The other guests finally succeeded in dragging them apart.

This puerile incident shocked and divided the Court. Henri could count on those who recognized his potential and not on those who wished his downfall. The King, naturally, was informed.

It was expected that Louis, who always demanded strict conformity to formal etiquette, would decide in the Prince's favor. In this case, however, he reproved Monsieur de Nemours for his conduct, defended the Master of the Wardrobe, and bestowed favors on the young Marquis' apologists.

The King's surprising reaction caused a scandal, and the incident served to convince everyone that Cinq-Mars had indeed become His Majesty's favorite. Louis provided further proof of his favor by starting to call Henri "dear friend" before a speechless court. Even the older courtiers had never heard of such a flagrant indiscretion; Henri III himself would never have dared flaunt his affections so publicly.

Only twenty-five years before, the celebrated Francis Bacon had described for Buckingham a favorite's superb and yet precarious position: "You are the King's shadow. If he commit some error, it is you who have committed it, or have permitted it, and you will have to pay the consequence. You may even be sacrificed to please the multitude. You must be his constant watchdog." But Henri was not acquainted with these shrewd words. He did not yet realize that since the beginning of the century, in Spain, in England, and in France, the exercise of absolute power seemed naturally linked to the establishment of a royal favorite (Richelieu had been Marie de Médicis'). He was content to savor the reflected glory of an absolute monarch. Only nineteen, he had the world at his feet.

Henri's strange victory was followed by three unique, unproblematical, joyful months. When Louis rode across his kingdom directing sieges, inspecting his fortresses, breathing the odor of gunpowder, he kept his persecuting demons, his ailments, and manias at bay. The habitually tormented King even managed to feel happy. During the numerous trips that occupied that active summer and early autumn, he and his favorite enjoyed the best months of their tragic friendship.

Louis made no effort to conceal their relationship. When Cinq-Mars joined the Court again at Langres after spending a few days in Paris, Louis actually sent the royal coach to meet him at Châtillon. Nonetheless, His Majesty had just sent Madame de Hautefort a "casket" which had raised many a speculating eyebrow.

The King traveled throughout the Ardennes and Champagne until the end of August, then went down toward Savoie to rescue his sister Christine, Madame Royale. She was the Duc de Savoie's widow and the Regent of his duchy until her young son came of age. She had been forced to flee Turin when her brother-in-law, an ally of Spain, had marched on her.

The King and the Cardinal met at Dijon and proceeded together to Grenoble, where Madame Royale threw herself at her brother's feet. Louis comforted her and sent a rescuing army to Piedmont. He continued to Lyon, went to Roanne on the waterway, participated in the festivities of All Saints' Day at Montargis, and finally returned to Fontainebleau on November 3.

The Cardinal's presence on these journeys afforded him the opportunity of observing Louis and Cinq-Mars at close quarters over an extended period. He had reason to hope that this relationship might afford him a personal triumph, the disgrace of Marie de Hautefort. "The Cardinal's instructions to Cinq-Mars to insinuate himself into the King's heart marvelously reveal the vitality of this minister's genius," wrote Vittorio Siri. Henri was so delighted with his newfound glory that for once he was quite prepared to listen to his protector's advice. He was easily convinced that Hautefort could ruin his good fortune and that he had to vanquish this rival. With this in mind, Henri began to sulk more and more noticeably on their way back to Paris. Worried, Louis finally asked Henri why.

"Alas, Sire," the boy answered, "When Your Majesty sees Madame de Hautefort again, he will no longer love me, and the whole Court will wonder what I could have done to lose my master's good graces."

He would not be reassured or cheered. Madame de Hautefort inadvertently helped his scheme by treating the King to her cruel mocking tongue when they met. The Cardinal's spies immediately reported these dissonances back to him. The King turned to his favorite and did his best to make his handsome face smile. He gave him a gift of 1,500 écus and hinted that he would make him First Equerry, a post which Baradas and Saint-Simon had held before him. But Henri swore he would never enjoy anything unless Louis promised never to look at Madame de Hautefort again. Louis finally gave in, probably without regret, for as Montglat says in his *Memoires,* "although it may not be impossible to have both a friend and a mistress, *he* found it difficult to reconcile the two."

Louis went to great lengths to appease this young man whose sensibilities he believed to be as delicate as his own. He even swore a veritable oath of allegiance: "I have given you my heart, and I swear you shall never share it with another." When this declaration was broadcast to the royal retinue, it assumed the importance of an affair of state. Chavigny, the Cardinal's right-hand man, wrote to Mazarin, a fellow collaborator: "We have a new favorite at Court, M. de Cinq-Mars, who depends wholly on Monseigneur le Cardinal. Never has the King shown such violent passion for anyone." But did Henri "wholly depend on Monseigneur le Cardinal"? The impetuous adolescent was conscious of his new power and had begun to wonder how to liberate himself from his old protector and from his imperious, meddlesome mother and be master of his own destiny.

François de Thou may have helped him reach this ambitious decision, or Henri may have made up his own mind. What is certain, however, is that Henri set about trying his strength against those who thought they had him fenced in. He decided he would not be made First Equerry, a post the King and the Cardinal had chosen for him, but rather Master of the Horse, one of the most important offices in the kingdom.

It was a dangerous move, but Henri played it daringly and with unexpected Machiavellian skill. He spread conflicting rumors that he would secretly marry Marion de Lorme and alternatively that he had already done so. This propelled a horrified Madame d'Effiat to Parlement to obtain "injunctions" against the marriage. She

even filed charges against Marion, accusing her of "rape and seduction." Louis was distraught and Richelieu furious. Henri sulked,
took exception to it all, and never revealed his true motives. The
King tried to humor him by nominating him First Equerry. Cinq-
Mars acted indignant.

"Since I am already Master of the Wardrobe, this post could not
possibly elevate me. It was awarded to other favorites with whom
I do not wish to be compared. Is the son of a Maréchal de France
to be put on the same footing with mere pages who were only too
delighted to shed their livery?"

Crestfallen, Louis asked "what would make him happy?" Henri
continued playing his game and finally announced that "he would
either remain what he was, or would accept the post of Master of
the Horse."

Richelieu was astonished by Henri's gall. His own nephew, Maréchal de Brézé, had sought the post for years, but it was tenaciously
held by the old Duc de Bellegarde. The King would not listen to
the Cardinal. The situation was threatening his health, for "the
least of his passions disrupted the economy of his entire person."
Henri had to be placated and pleased at all costs.

Louis dispatched Monsieur de Saint-Aoust to prostrate himself
before Bellegarde to ask him in His Majesty's name to relinguish
his post in exchange for a considerable sum—five thousand livres.
The old man hesitated, sighed, and recalled his own youth; for he,
too, had been a favorite, Henri III's last *mignon* and Gabrielle
d'Estrée's first lover. He was a legendary seducer whose charms
had conquered many a princesse and many a fashionable young
person. Now the poor old man was left with his memories to
console him in his disgrace. Detested as he was by the Cardinal,
childless and with one foot in the grave, he was scarcely in a position to gainsay his master's request. The sometime *mignon* may even
have been amused by the idea of serving the same set of circumstances he had enjoyed half a century before. But none of these
considerations weakened his bargaining powers. He demanded

that the office of the Master of the Wardrobe be awarded to his eldest nephew, the Marquis de Montespan (the future father-in-law of Louis XIV's mistress).

The terms for Bellegarde's resignation were still being negotiated when the Queen joined Louis at Fontainebleau—the Queen and her retinue, including her lady-in-waiting, Marie de Hautefort. Louis was uncertain as to the outcome of both the Marion de Lorme situation and the Bellegarde case. He was at the mercy of Cinq-Mars, who played on his anxieties like an accomplished coquette. One thing was certain, however: Madame de Hautefort had lost her hold over Louis. She would not believe it, as she was convinced that her mere presence was enough to make Louis her slave. In fact, all she did merely hastened her own downfall. Louis' affections were solidly engaged, and as Richelieu once put it, one did not fall from Louis' favor by degrees, but all at once.

The court was astonished that Louis should introduce Cinq-Mars to the Queen "in words that fully revealed his passion." When Marie de Hautefort appeared, he gave her an icy look and did not speak to her. At Fontainebleau Louis took every opportunity of displaying his exceptional attachment to Henri. He even went off to the hunt on horseback in order to leave his carriage behind for the young man, who was not an early riser.

Louis finally approached Madame de Hautefort in the company of Cinq-Mars on the evening of November 7.

"Madame," he said, "my affections are now entirely for Monsieur de Cinq-Mars. I have learned that you take pleasure in speaking ill of him. I am very unhappy about that. If you continue, you will have cause to regret it. I wish you to know that I shall punish all those who have the effrontery to conspire against me."

He turned his back on the speechless and furious woman. The Court hurried to pay their respects to His Eminence and to the Master of the Wardrobe. But Henri was still not satisfied.

The following day, November 8, the nomadic King decided to

leave Fontainebleau. At a very early hour an officer called upon Madame de Hautefort to deliver a *lettre de cachet* bearing the King's private seal which banished her from the Court. The proud young woman blushed with shame, tore up the letter, and chased the officer out, shouting that the order had not come from the King and that she would believe its contents only if he communicated them to her directly.

An hour later, as Louis was stepping into his carriage, a veiled woman appeared before him. Marie brusquely disclosed the face of an angered goddess, bowed and begged His Majesty to explain a commandment contrary to all his promises. The King did not appear in the least concerned; on the contrary, he donned that near-inhuman expression that he wore when refusing Montmorency's and others' blessings. Nonetheless, he politely held his hat in his hand throughout their long and painful farewell.

"Get married," he said. "I shall provide for you."

Marie refused to listen and demanded further explanation. Finally when she had lost all hope, she asked, "What do you want to happen to me?"

"What would have happened had you left the Court every time you threatened to do so."

These were the last words they exchanged, according to Henri Arnauld, who witnessed the scene. "She has been provided," he adds, "with assets worth a hundred thousand écus [the King had given her the port of Neuilly for thirty years]. She will marry very well, being highly esteemed for her virtue and courage."

Madame de Hautefort left the Court and would not return until the death of her former adorer. But she was not the only one to go. Louis may have felt frantic, but he did not yield to Cinq-Mars without exacting his own pound of flesh. Bellegarde's capitulation would prevent Cinq-Mars' dreaded marriage to Marion, but she was not his only rival. Mademoiselle de Chémerault would have to be sacrificed to the ambitious young man's career. Louis may also have learned of her excellent services to the Cardinal. The Pretty

Pauper was to share the lady-in-waiting's exile and bowed out of the chronicles of the time.[1]

On November 8 the King slept at Villeroy. The next day he called on Madame d'Effiat at Chilly Castle, not to negotiate a reconciliation between mother and son, but to impose one at the grasping lady's expense. Madame d'Effiat was forced to surrender "whatever personal effects Henri might require."

On November 10 the King reached his beloved Versailles accompanied only by servants and personal staff. Amid the forests, marshes, and the autumn mists, the melancholy huntsman was in his element. He could spend his days with Cinq-Mars in this temptation-free haven and savor a kind of happiness that fate rarely allowed him.

Meanwhile, the lawyers of the kingdom were working overtime. For sixty years the Church and Parlement had argued over clandestine marriages. Many young people married precipitously and secretly to avoid parental, and even royal, disapproval. This practice had greatly increased during the wars of religion. Many a rich heiress was forcibly carried off in the midst of the general commotion and then made to marry her abductor. Parlement sometimes annulled such unions and sometimes upheld them, depending on the province. The Church violently objected to these decrees that dealt with marriages, regarding them a civil infringement on their domain.

Under Henri IV, lawyers had started to draft legislation which would reconcile all factors, but they did not manage to make much headway in the bog of legal minutiae. Then, suddenly, when the King and the Prime Minister learned of young Cinq-Mars' marital impulses, they ordered their lawyers to work something out im-

---

[1] There are several contradictory accounts that deal with Madame de Hautefort's disgrace and with the so-called clandestine marriage. Having examined all the texts, we have adopted the ones which we consider to be the most acceptable. Dreux de Radier and Tallemant differ greatly in their versions of the marriage. No historian who has since treated the subject has thought fit to follow the incidents of Louis' and Cinq-Mars' life in chronological order. This method makes the truth accessible.

mediately. The lawyers and clerks worked day and night drawing up a statute, just as Bellegarde's last defences were falling.

On November 13, Saint-Aoust returned with the old favorite's resignation. Two days later the new Master of the Horse was sworn in. Henri thus became Monsieur le Grand. On November 19, His Majesty signed a law on civil marriages which conceded a nominal victory to the Church, even if it did leave some scope for flexibility. The law, in fact, stipulated that, on pain of annulment of the marriage and confiscation of all estates—which would be donated to the hospitals—"the marriage banns shall be proclaimed by the curate of each of the contracting parties with the consent of fathers, mothers, tutors, or trustees, if they be children of families or in the keeping of others, and that the marriage shall be celebrated before four trustworthy witnesses other than the priest who shall receive the consent of the parties and join them in matrimony, following the form practiced by the Church."

Louis breathed freely again. His "dear friend" would no longer be prey to fallen women and petty intriguers. "He could not allow them whom he honored with his friendship to marry, and yet he was a chaste man and wished his subjects to be chaste." Lavisse and Mariéjol, who wrote these lines, may have allowed discretion to blunt their perspicacity.

Cinq-Mars rejoiced. The loss of the dangerous Chémerault was a small price to pay for this triple victory: a double victory over the King, who had made him Monsieur le Grand in his twentieth year and yet could not prevent him from being Marion's lover; and a further victory over the Cardinal before whom he had finally proved his independence and power. He did not realize that in sounding this advantage so loudly he might be taking his first step toward destruction.

Seeing the boy he had always regarded as his own creation prove capable of achieving his own personal ends, Richelieu flew into one of those rages that could make Europe tremble. He made holes in his bedroom tapestry with his cane and beat his servants, as he always did when in one of these tempers. Then he became reflective and uneasy. He realized it had been a serious, if not fatal, mistake to create such an ambitious, headstrong favorite. Henri might well prove to be his downfall. Marie de Hautefort had been a less redoubtable antagonist; the King knew of her bribed allegiance to the Spanish party and distrusted women. Richelieu even imagined bringing her back from exile and breaking Henri before it was too late.

But it was already too late. Louis XIII would never countenance the removal of his favorite after going to such extremes to secure his good graces. Rather than launch into a doubtful battle, Richelieu thought it wiser to conceal his fury and make the best of the situation. A dispute between the King and his adolescent friend soon rewarded his prudence: He was asked to play the role of arbiter.

Cinq-Mars was convinced his battle was won, and his admirable caution and restraint left him overnight. He had controlled himself during their long travels through France. He had conducted himself irreproachably throughout his daring game of setting up a loose woman as rival to His Most Christian Majesty, and he had emerged victorious. But youth rebelled. No sooner had he been made Monsieur le Grand than he rushed off to make love to Marion with all that pent-up ardor that had accumulated during those frustrating months. The lovely young woman hastened to broadcast the news of their reunion, delighted at the chance of snubbing those who had thought this unlikely after their clandestine marriage had failed to materialize. The Queen of the Marais was now nicknamed "Madame la Grande."

The King was deeply hurt. Very possessive, very pious and misogynistic, he thought Cinq-Mars was monstrously ungrateful. He took a masochistic delight in needling his lovers into hurting him—as Marie de Hautefort knew only too well. He was afraid, however, to discuss the real cause of his despair with Henri. He picked quarrels on the pretext of taking exception to the young madcap's extravagance. Henri had just bought a golden coach. Their first quarrel, then, burst less than a week after Cinq-Mars' triumph, and it acquired epic proportions. Louis upbraided the young man harshly, denounced his careless extravagance, his debauched tastes, his dissipation, his laziness. He predicted dire consequences if he did not renounce his dissolute ways.

Henri did not give an inch. He no longer looked upon Louis as his King, but as an infatuated, jealous, feeble, bickering man who was also something of a hypocrite. He answered bitingly that he would neither waste his youth nor let himself be cloistered. He then returned to Marion to sulk, knowing this would produce the best results.

Louis, sick with sorrow, turned to his Minister, told him of his favorite's depravity and wickedness. Richelieu was pleased to have the opportunity of reaping his revenge: He summoned Monsieur le Grand and scolded him thoroughly. His Eminence's reprimands had a different ring from those of the King. The mere sight of the scarlet robes could revive Henri's old terror of the Cardinal. He promised to apologize and make amends. The incident was the sole topic of conversation at Court for some time. The great Cardinal, wrapped in the pride and pomp of his Roman purple, had become a paternal arbiter between the King and his "dear friend"!

Louis was so overjoyed that he wished to give gossips written proof of the restored harmony. This is how the following extraordinary document was written:

> We, the undersigned, certify to whomsoever it may concern that we are most satisfied and contented the one with the other and that we have never been in such perfect mutual understanding as we are at present. In witness whereof we have signed this present certificate:
>
> *Louis*
> By my command: *Effiat de Cinq-Mars*
> Written at Saint-Germain the twenty-sixth of November 1639.

The King wrote to the Cardinal on the same day, "I appreciate your concern for my welfare. I felt a little unwell last night, which constrained me to take a small remedy this morning. I may take medicine this evening. The certificate I enclose will indicate how well your reconciliation of yesterday has succeeded. When you intercede to lend your assistance, nothing can go wrong."

And the rainbow shone radiantly. Louis had the portrait of his favorite painted. Monsieur de Nyert, His Majesty's head valet, was to recount to Tallemant des Réaux (who is our source), certain intimate scenes which provide ample food for thought. "Fontrailles once entered Monsieur le Grand's bedchamber at Saint-Germain rather abruptly and discovered him being rubbed from head to foot with oil of jasmine. He got into bed and said rather unconvincingly, 'Ah, that's much better.' A second later there was a knock at the door. It was the King. It would seem he was oiling himself for combat. . . .

"On one of his trips the King retired at seven o'clock. He was in a state of disarray. Two huge dogs leaped onto the bed, upsetting the bedclothes and licking him. He sent word that Monsieur le Grand should undress and come to him. When he came he was dressed like a young bride. 'Come to bed, come to bed!' said the King impatiently. He had the dogs taken away, but did not have his bed freshly remade. The *mignon* had scarce climbed into bed when the King started kissing his hands. When he noticed that Monsieur le Grand, whose affections were otherwise engaged, was not responding to his ardor, he said, 'Dear friend, what is the matter, what do you want? You seem so sad.'"

*"I would not be King if I had the sentiments of
ordinary men."* Louis XIII crowned by Fame,
by Philippe de Champaigne.

A letter in Louis' hand-writing to Richelieu, from Chantilly the 16th of July, 1633: "My Cousin, I am extremely happy that you are writing me again. I alert you that the state of the garrisons in Champagne isn't that which I asked for: what I want is companies of infantry in the towns, and not private garrisons. Bassan's relatives and brothers fear that their brother will be condemned; I beg you to take care of this matter. Assure yourself of my affection and that I am very impatient to see you, awaiting which I shall pray the Good Lord with all my heart to hold you in His holy protection."

"*The greatest servant France has ever had.*"
Armand-Jean Du Plessis, Cardinal de Richelieu, by Philippe de Champaigne.

Louis XIII and Mademoiselle de Hautefort. The King holds the pair of tongs which he used to remove "a suspicious note" from her bodice.

"The greatest Queen on earth led an anxious and humiliating life." Anne of Austria, by Van Dyck.

"The Château de Chilly belonging to Madame la Mareschalle d'Effiat, four leagues from Paris on the chemin d'Orléans," where Cinq-Mars was born.

Henri, Marquis de Cinq-Mars.
(MUSÉE DE RICHELIEU: STUDIO TREMBLIER)

"*A radiant creature, thirsty for pleasure, whom no one could resist.*" *Marion de Lorme, the most celebrated courtesan of the day. The inscription of this eighteenth-century print credits her with having lived for 135 years (1606-1741). In reality, she died before she was fifty.*

A ball at the Court of Louis XIII.

*"The most illustrious
Princesse Marie de
Gonzaga de Cleves, Prin-
cess of Mantua, Duchesse
de Nevers and Rethel,
Sovereign of Mézières,"
was Gaston's ex-fiancée,
and spurred Cinq-Mars on
so that he could become
worthy of her.*

*Gaston de France, Duc d'Orléans, was the hub of
constant intrigue against his brother the King
and ever ready to sacrifice his co-conspirators in
order to save himself. Painting by Van Dyck.*

*François-Auguste de Thou,
"His Disquietude," whose
pious hope of reforming
Cinq-Mars only drew him
into an ill-fated conspiracy
against Richelieu.*

*The Palais de Justice at Lyon, where Cinq-Mars'
trial was held.*

The Execution of Cinq-Mars. Actually this contemporary print depicts de Thou's beheading: note Cinq-Mars' body being carried to the carriage at left. It was de Thou who asked for a blindfold, as shown here.

The ruins of the Château de Cinq-Mars as they are today.

COLLECTION VIOLLET)

A gold demi-écu minted in 1643, the year of Louis' death.

(PRIVATE COLLECTION: PHOTO JOHN PITKIN)

Six

Rows and Wrangles

꧁ IN THE WINTER of 1639–1640, events began to take shape that were to change the course of European history. The King wanted peace more than ever. He called a convention of diplomats to Cologne to seek a peace settlement, but their search was to last eight years! Father Joseph, the "Gray Eminence" of foreign affairs, died, and Richelieu recalled from Italy the only man capable of succeeding him.

Giulio Mazarin had once been Papal Nuncio in Paris. He now resigned from the service of the Holy See and openly entered that of His Most Christian Majesty. He had been involved in French politics for some time. He returned to the Louvre on January 5, 1640 (this date alone refutes those who insist that Mazarin was Louis XIV's father), as a naturalized Frenchman after four years' absence.

While Richelieu and Louis XIII tried to put an end to the conflict, they continued to plan the spring campaigns. They would have to fight on four fronts: Artois, Piedmont, the Basque country, and Roussillon. News from Roussillon was promising, despite the Spanish victory at Salse. Catalonia was preparing to shake off her Spanish yoke, and separatist delegates were coming to Paris to ask Louis XIII to be their King. These vast and costly campaigns would require new taxes and further sacrifices. Richelieu was confident that victory would soon reward his efforts, but other worries claimed his attention. He confessed to his close friends, "I am only a zero, signifying nothing unless a number stands before me."

The number was the old, fragile sovereign. Richelieu had to protect him from illness, worry, doubt, nervous attacks, and bouts of mysticism, or the unfinished edifice of France's grandeur would come tumbling down and bury its architect beneath the debris. Louis XIII's peace of mind was as important to Richelieu as the strength of his armies. This is why he thought Cinq-Mars important and why, despite the recent humiliation, he continued to hope he could make use of him. He swallowed his pride in the hope that the young fool would soon stop sowing his wild oats and help him manage His Majesty's moods. In any case, the King was so completely devoted to him that the Cardinal was to appoint himself their protector and arbiter. He would have to devote as much attention to keeping them on good terms as to the conduct of wars, intrigues, and the business of government.

From the start, however, all his good intentions met with poor results. When Cardinal de La Valette died, he left a number of ecclesiastical benefices vacant which the Minister then redistributed, reserving a somewhat meager abbey for Jean d'Effiat, Cinq-Mars' reluctantly ecclesiastic brother. Louis, however, had become fond of this foolish youngster whom he jokingly called "the little Cardinal," and he was infuriated by Richelieu's slighting appointment. He tore the order to pieces and insisted "that the Abbé d'Effiat be awarded the best abbey available." Richelieu had to obey.

Again the Cardinal's fury terrified his retinue. For days, Rueil and the Cardinal's palace buzzed with possible ways of getting rid of the favorite. The rage abated, and Richelieu took hold of himself. He would stick to his plans, but he began to hate his former pupil.

Henri tried to reconcile his "duty" with the pursuit of pleasure. He loathed life at Saint-Germain. As Montglat put it, "The Court was always there, and the principal entertainment consisted of looking for foxes in their holes and blackbirds hawking in the snow in the poor company of a dozen hunters." Cinq-Mars felt so self-confident that he was certain he could lure even the most Spartan of Capetians into "debauchery."

Indeed this was the only time that the son of the Vert Galant was known to stay up drinking, dancing, and feasting. Monsieur le Grand did foster splendor, as his position demanded, or at least he manifested it in his own person. He invited the lords of the land to magnificent feasts and balls. He dressed sumptuously. The Court began to regain some of its past Valois brilliance, though not for long. The King was haunted by the image of his people's misery and felt guilty. He had not only inherited his Protestant grandmother Jeanne d'Albret's tuberculosis but also her toughness, her sense of duty and puritanism. He soon resumed his morose habits and issued a new sumptuary edict. Boredom again fell over Saint-Germain.

Cinq-Mars could not bear the gloom. Again, Montglat points out that "Since he was very young, he did not have the prudence to dissimulate his sentiments. He too openly expressed his regrets at not being able to taste the pleasures of Paris, even in the presence of the King. . . . Rather than revel in the exalted favors he enjoyed, he spent his days complaining of misfortune to his friends, claiming that they enjoyed far greater liberty than he, and that he was attached to a man whose company bored him."

He no longer had the excitement of charging across France and plotting and conducting skillful intrigues. Louis was his old self: He preached, moralized, talked of God, burdened Cinq-Mars with all his worries and endless accounts of his dogs and birds of prey. He also insisted that Henri never leave his side, a tyranny that Marie de Hautefort had been able to escape. Henri could not endure it. "Ambition, the passion of maturity, was of little interest to a young man seduced by passions of a more youthful nature," and certainly could not relieve his intolerable burdens.

The King was now in the habit of retiring early, which freed Cinq-Mars to gallop off to Paris and make love to his Marion. The young lovers would then join the gleeful band of Marais Libertines at the Hôtel de Rohan, where they actively participated in the nightly festivities. When the sky began to pale, Cinq-Mars would leap back in the saddle and race back to Saint-Germain in time to be present at the King's rising.

This routine of sleepless nights, lovemaking, and nocturnal jaunts followed by the daily exasperations soon took its toll on his appearance and conduct. Louis reacted by becoming worried and irritable. He started to fear that he had become an object of aversion to his friend and suffered a thousand deaths. His jealousy caused him to have his favorite watched, and so he got to know of his escapades. New quarreling arose. As soon as the King awoke he would scrutinize his beloved's face, and if he discerned the slightest look of fatigue, he would pounce on Cinq-Mars and reproach him bitterly. Henri would either deny his imputations or answer back impertinently.

The Cardinal's agents carried back all these developments. The ambitious La Chesnaye was one of his agents; he had helped bring about Madame de Hautefort's fall from favor, and now had hopes of "changing his role from that of confidant to that of favorite." He hated Cinq-Mars but disguised it so well that the young man was convinced of his devotion and talked freely. This enabled Richelieu to be a well-informed peacemaker. After each quarrel, he paternally scolded Cinq-Mars and soothed the King.

> I am always concerned to think that His Majesty is discontent, [wrote the Cardinal to Louis] which is why I am writing this morning to inquire after His Majesty's disposition, knowing that he left here [Rueil] yesterday feeling dejected. I beg His Majesty's leave to proffer the following counsel: Should he not voice his discontent as soon as it is roused; should he not inform His Master of the Horse of his wishes, these avoidable pains will continue to plague him. It is impossible to be young and also wholly wise. His Majesty can make good his subjects' frailties by guiding them with his wisdom. I would beg His Highness to decide to act upon this advice for the sake of his well-being, as I am convinced that they will produce the best

results. I entreat him to give the matter thought and assure him that until my very last breath, I will be a hundred times more devoted to him than to myself.

The Cardinal was responsible for another truce. The treaty stipulated that the favorite should no longer frequent the "gentlemen of the Marais." Louis felt something akin to revulsion for these men, chiefly for their impiety but also for the open homosexuality practiced by their patron, Théophile. He feared that Cinq-Mars might be wooed away from him. As it was, women seemed to be enough for Henri. Mademoiselle de Chémerault, "who had entered religion in Paris" (that is, she lived in a convent), had taken up with him again. Not that this prevented him from visiting Marion's lovely bedchamber, decorated with crimson damask and silver fringe. These irresponsible escapades upset the King's equanimity and interrupted the Prime Minister's work.

As Tallemant recalls, "One evening he [Cinq-Mars] met Ruvigny at Saint-Germain and said, 'Follow me. I must go out to speak to La Chémerault. Two horses are waiting for me in a ditch nearby.' When they got to the ditch, they found that the groom had fallen asleep on the ground, and both horses had been taken. Monsieur le Grand was in despair. They went into the town in search of other horses and then noticed a man following them at a distance. It was a guardsman of the Light Cavalry, one of the spies the King had put onto his Master of the Horse. Cinq-Mars recognized him, called him over, and spoke with him. The man pretended he had thought the two friends were about to fight one another; Cinq-Mars told him that that was not the case, and the guardsman rode off. Ruvigny advised the Master of the Horse to return and spare the King irritation. He should go to bed and then two hours later call his gentlemen in attendance to help him dispel his sleeplessness. In this way he could shake the King's faith in his spies' information, for the King was bound to hear of his escapade the next day. The Master of the Horse did as his friend counseled. The next morning the King said to him, 'You went to Paris, I hear,' Cinq-Mars brought forward his witnesses, the spy was confounded, and he was able to go into Paris the next three nights."

The Queen liked the Master of the Horse. She never demonstrated any of the jealousy she had toward her friend Madame de Chevreuse (when the latter had tried to seduce the King) and toward Mademoiselle de La Fayette, to whom she was so indebted. Her situation had changed since the near-miraculous birth of the Dauphin a year before, and she was forced to operate with greater discretion and deviousness. Before the Dauphin's birth, when she had been the sterile, ignored wife, the suspected and treacherous accomplice of the enemy, she had lived in constant fear of being subjected to a humiliating divorce, if not a trial. Her best hopes had then been a dishonorable widowhood or seclusion in some convent. But as the mother of the next King of France, Anne of Austria had to be careful, prudent, and cunning. She could not count on faithful supporters, who were, in any case, rather scarce. Her political ally, her dangerous and seductive brother-in-law Gaston d'Orléans, would immediately become her rival and contest her position as Regent if the King died.

The King and the Cardinal had the means to prevent her from becoming Regent before they left the scene. Fortunately for her, however, they both suspected and feared Gaston more than they did the King of Spain's sister. When Louis died, it was certain that the Cardinal would assume the tutelage of the future Louis XIV himself, but then the Cardinal was unlikely to survive the King. It was nonetheless essential that she play for time, avoid making mistakes, and above all not incur the King's anger.

This is why the Queen was so charming to the King's favorite. Cinq-Mars was easily won over by his sweet and lovely Queen, but he too had an ulterior motive: He hoped that a reconciliation between the royal couple might give him more freedom. He set about bringing them together as Marie de Hautefort and Louise de La Fayette had done before him. On Christmas Eve at Saint-Germain, the King took everyone by surprise by ordering that his "pillow be placed" in his wife's bed. Thus was conceived Philippe, the founder of the House of Orléans, ancestor of all the Catholic princes alive today. One wonders whether the strange atmosphere which surrounded this even might have influenced the temperament of the future Monsieur, Louis XIV's brother. Many and mysterious are the ways of nature.

But Henri's servitude was not relaxed by these marital intimacies. The King's tyrannical passion for him continued, and the young man defended himself with the same mockery and ill temper as before. They resumed their rows on the very first day of the new year, and continued over a period of several weeks, interrupted by an occasional, short-lived reconciliation. "The Cardinal and the Master of the Horse were aloof and cold toward each other," observed Henri Arnauld. "His Eminence is displeased that the Master of the Horse quarrels so often with the King." The man who was becoming the "greatest king in the world" was reduced to despair by the slightest sign of ill temper, by the merest note of harshness he detected in his beloved.

On January 23, 1640, Louis wrote to his Minister, "I shall go hunting. My sorrow is such that nothing pleases me. The Queen is well, and we have more reason to believe she may be pregnant. I was reconciled with my Master of the Horse last evening. I hope he will be more prudent in future."

But Henri refused to be prudent. On January 29, Henri Arnauld related the following to Président de Barillon: "His Eminence spent two days in Paris. He was not at ease and returned on Friday to make peace between the King and the Master of the Horse, who had just had a new dispute, besides the two big ones they have had in the past two weeks. Nothing good will come of this."

At first Henri took a secret feminine delight in these rows. Despite his apparent submissiveness, he always emerged victorious. But the game began to pall when his jealous master's recriminations became really bitter and the Cardinal's scoldings grew more threatening. Tallemant indicates that the King's "caresses" were beginning to become odious. Cinq-Mars was regretting and cursing his fortune which a few months before had seemed so blessed and joyous. Where were the gay, boisterous days of his eighteenth year? He never stopped bemoaning their loss to the King, who was invariably hurt by his complaints. He would lash out at Louis remorselessly, and the King was cruelly wounded despite the childish nature of the assaults.

"Monsieur le Grand," wrote Henri Arnauld, "has taken it into his head to refuse to go hunting with the King. No one dares broach the subject with him." This was a way of spoiling the unhappy Sovereign's greatest pleasure and depriving him of whatever mental solace he usually gained from hunting. But Henri suffered the backlash of the King's resulting nervous tension. If Henri had the coquetry of a woman, now he showed feminine weaknesses. He had nervous attacks and hysterical crying fits of unexpected violence. His worried friends did not know how to soothe him. If he had been a twentieth-century screen idol and not a seventeenth-century favorite, he would have been declared the victim of a nervous breakdown.

At the beginning of February Louis had gout, and Richelieu was disturbed to see him so downcast. He set his skillful mind to devise some sort of diplomatic solution, and he succeeded. February 11 saw a complete reconciliation. "Monsieur le Grand is now more in favor than ever," remarked Arnauld the following day. But the Cardinal's pleasure at his success was soon soured. The insufferable boy had snubbed him once again. A deliriously happy Louis had promised his friend the Comté of Dammartin, whose revenues were worth 23,000 livres. Then the King expressed his desire to enjoy the pleasures of the reconciliation in peace, but dutiful as ever, he did not leave before checking with Richelieu that the interests of the state would not suffer from his absence.

Richelieu kept him waiting anxiously for two weeks and then wrote to Chavigny in an acidly ironical vein:

The King may go to Chantilly without prejudice to his affairs. I think he could do no better than to amuse himself. . . . I am pleased to hear of Monsieur le Grand's reinstatement. As you may well imagine, I should prefer to see him before the King's departure, but I would not ask him to come here [to Rueil]. I shall judge his intentions by his actions.

Cinq-Mars was not wise enough to be wary of the Minister's growing irritation. Dammartin had been given to him on the condition that His Majesty retain the usufruct (this clause, imposed by Richelieu, was revoked in June) and that the title revert to the Crown in the event that he died without leaving an heir. This had prompted the young man to announce jocularly. "I am the King's heir, and he is mine."

Louis XIII was not always jealous, nor did he always talk of hunting and religion. His serener moments were spent in confiding to his friends the more serious aspects of his life and trying to explain some of the Corneillian dilemma posed by his kingship. Nor did Cinq-Mars lend an unsympathetic or heartless ear on such occasions. He would stop playing the spoiled child and feel a mixture of pity and admiration for the stoic capable of such sacrifices for his country. But like nine tenths of his fellow Frenchmen, he was quite incapable of appreciating Richelieu's work. He would accuse the Cardinal of barbarous cruelty when the King spoke sadly of his exiled mother whom he would never see again, of his brother whom he was forced to persecute, or those friends whom he had had to decapitate, of the war against other Catholics whom he was forced to fight with the aid of Protestant princes.

Louis said that Richelieu was "France's greatest servant," but this inquisitorial despot's personality and methods did cause Louis much suffering. "I should not be King had I the sentiments of ordinary men," Louis insisted, although he did have such sentiments, of which he was not always master. When he confided in Cinq-Mars, it was an indulgence, a way of finding some ephemeral solace by sharing what he usually hid beneath his sinister mask. He always regretted his revelations and would make the young man swear never to repeat his words.

This exposed Cinq-Mars to very grave dangers, for Richelieu wanted to know precisely these sentiments and revelations. Richelieu had pressed him repeatedly that winter, with disastrous results. Henri would not answer the Cardinal's questions to his satisfaction. However, His Eminence did not wish to lose what little hold he had over the young man. He decided it would be unwise to put too much pressure on Henri for the time being; he could still rely on La Chesnaye for such information.

Apparently it was at Chantilly that Monsieur le Grand learned of the valet's duplicity. His suspicions had been aroused when he surprised Richelieu whispering heatedly with his supposed friend in the garden—a conversation "which ended with His Eminence dismissing him like a schoolboy." Henri set about obtaining sufficient proof to expose and destroy the spy. The King had to be humored and prepared before he launched his attack. Then, on March 21, Louis XIII wrote to Richelieu, "I slept very well last night. It is my hope that Monsieur le Grand and I shall have no more misunderstandings. As soon as I see you, I shall tell you a great deal about La Chesnaye's wicked ways." The favorite had worked so well that one day, Vittorio Siri reports, "the King entered the Gentleman's Chambers in the company of Cinq-Mars and brusquely ordered La Chesnaye to quit the Court at once for being seditious and a sower of discord." Louis fumed at the thought of all the painful wrangles the traitor had engineered. "In mistreating La Chesnaye," Tallemant wrote, "Louis turned to his retinue and said, 'At least he was not a gentleman.' He called him a knave and threatened him with his cane."

The valet naturally sought refuge with the Cardinal, but His Eminence refused to receive him and ordered him to disappear. Richelieu never supported his agents once they committed the folly of being caught. He was furious nonetheless.

Henri, rather uneasy at this too complete victory, also ran to His

Eminence to "explain the reason which had made the King get rid of La Chesnaye." He was greeted with fire and brimstone. Father Griffet says that the Cardinal "reprimanded him severely for his shortcomings which he foresaw would finally have dire results unless he took pains to correct them." Cinq-Mars thought he could stem the Cardinal's ire by "saying that the rogue had caused trouble with the King, which had hindered him from fulfilling his duty to His Eminence."

He could not have said anything worse. Richelieu took him at his word. As Monsieur le Grand seemed so well disposed, the Cardinal would be pleased to pardon him on the condition that he stepped into La Chesnaye's shoes and reported back every single word the King said.

Cinq-Mars saw the trap and refused point-blank. Richelieu lost control and gave vent to all he had withheld. He told him how and why a dandy who had no greater claims to fame than a pretty face had been made to rise to the summit of favor, why he had been chosen and practically forced on the King. Henri d'Effiat was a total nonentity, an insignificant nothing, and Monsieur le Grand even less than nothing. The only existence he had was that of a servile instrument created in the interests of the Cardinal.

It was a shock, a rude awakening. Cinq-Mars was barely twenty, and despite his precocious experience of the world, he knew little of the wiles of politics, of the base dealings of politicians acting in the interests of the state. He did not like Richelieu, but he feared him and would never have dreamed that a friend of his father's would sanction serving him up to Louis XIII as a spy. Henri expressed his humiliation, his disgust, his rage, and then fled, weeping convulsively.

The following day his brother-in-law La Meilleraye, now Maréchal de France, visited him. La Meilleraye was startled by the chaotic situation. He reasoned paternally with Henri, impressing upon him the dangers that might ensue as a result of his behavior, and persuaded him to return to Rueil. Once again the trembling boy stood before the scarlet robes. La Meilleraye took up Henri's defense and with a great flurry of words "declaimed his apology." His Eminence condescended to show some indulgence. The victorious Maréchal begged his brother-in-law to return the Cardinal's great kindness by immediately signing "a written pledge that he agreed to tell the Cardinal all that the King might say." Henri almost consented, but he had his pride, courage, and a good deal of obstinacy. He declared that to do so "would be signing his own condemnation," whereupon he bowed and walked out. La Meilleraye gave him up dramatically and went to pay his compliments to La Chesnaye.

This was a declaration of war. Richelieu did not forgive offenses, much less humiliations he was made to suffer. This child had once been the object of his hopes, of his generosity, and had then proceeded to wound his pride by letting himself be loved by Marion; then he betrayed his confidence, then foiled his maneuvers, and finally presented him with an adversary in place of the submissive creature he had counted on.

As for Cinq-Mars, he had received a blow which his friends did their best to aggravate. Fontrailles fanned his rage, de Thou his indignation. Both convinced him that he should fear the tyrant's vengeance. Henri saw the wisdom of their arguments. The admirable Minister had a truly vile soul. He was too young to understand that such a man would regard as tantamount to treason the refusal to commit an evil act for the good of the state.

Seven

THE ARRAS AFFAIR

𝒞𝔥𝔵 IT WAS THE early spring of 1640. That year France was to recover her ground, and Louis the Just would live through his finest hours. It was to be a year of victories, the year when *Horace* and *Cinna* were first performed. A few lucid minds began to see the emergence of a new France eager for pre-eminence; a powerful, impetuous, magnificent France of brilliant men, of Condé and Turenne, of Descartes and Pascal, of Corneille and Poussin.

The King and his Minister felt the resurgence of this new life, but the Parlement, the nobles, and the people ignored it. Revolts, dissent, and plots continued to proliferate. Three Spanish spies disguised as hermits were discovered and confessed that they had been hired by French princes—by the Duc de Vendôme in particular—to assassinate the Cardinal. But this dampening discovery did not delay preparations for the campaign which Louis hoped would finally bring his desired "blessed peace." He applied himself to the task with something akin to passion. And as Richelieu put it, the God of War did work miracles for them in Piedmont. The Comte d'Harcourt defeated the Marquis de Leganez and recovered Casal. They had to push northward and complete the campaign by taking Arras and thus Artois.

The conquest of Arras was a risky undertaking. The town was an important Spanish stronghold. The Catholic King's subjects as well as Richelieu's enemies sang the jingle:

When the French take Arras,
Mice will eat cats.

The army was enlarged to 200,000 men, and the campaign was entrusted to three maréchaux, Châtillon, Chaulnes, and La Meilleraye, to whom Richelieu announced, "You will answer with your heads if you fail to take the town." Louis XIII had planned the siege during a relatively peaceful sojourn at Chantilly.

The King and his favorite continued to squabble. Louis had given up trying to conceal his jealousy of Marion. He dared not exile the impudent young woman, but he ordered her to leave Paris whenever he was there. Richelieu also disapproved of Monsieur le Grand's liaison with the woman who had snubbed him.

Marion defied them both. She encouraged her lover to be as debauched, insolent, and extravagant as possible. Louis did not have the courage to deal with her himself or the strength of will to ignore their relationship. He was being made to look as ridiculous as Molière's Arnolphe and Bartolo; the situation was becoming dangerous.

To ensure a difficult military victory, Richelieu had felt it essential to terrorize his maréchaux, and now he turned to the equally essential task of pacifying his master. He would have preferred to remain the arbiter-general of their extravagant quarrels, but his recent encounters with Cinq-Mars had been particularly explosive and required a sort of mediation he could no longer provide. He turned to the Secretary of State, Sublet de Noyers, and asked him to shoulder this responsibility with the same solemnity he would use toward a matter affecting the security of the kingdom. The King and Cinq-Mars both admired this great steward who had been responsible for the singlehanded resurrection of the army. It seemed ironical, if not ridiculous, that a war minister should have to referee an intimate lovers' quarrel on the eve of a major offensive. The situation would have been truly farcical had the individuals involved not had the power to influence the outcome of the war itself. De Noyers proved himself to be as excellent a

peacemaker between these incompatibles as he was a military orga-
nizer. The Cardinal knew he had won when the King left Chantilly for the north on May 7.

On May 9 at Soissons, a new "reconciliation" was concluded in the
form of a treaty. Louis XIII dictated a solemn document to de
Noyers:

> Today, the ninth of May, the King being at Soissons, His
> Majesty has agreed to promise Monsieur le Grand that through-
> out the duration of this campaign, he will have no quarrel
> with him, and should it occur that the said Sieur le Grand offer
> him any cause for complaint, it shall be brought, without
> malice, by His Majesty to the attention of Monsieur le Cardinal,
> without bitterness, in order that on His Eminence's advice, the
> said Sieur le Grand can correct whatever might displease His
> Majesty and so that all His subjects may continue to find their
> peace of mind in that of His Majesty. These terms have been
> agreed by the King and my said Sieur le Grand in the presence
> of His Eminence.
>
> Signed: *Louis*
> *Effiat de Cinq-Mars*

His Eminence appears to have forgotten his grudges, for he gave
his blessing to this truce, which favored Henri. Henri also affected
to be in good spirits and did not flaunt his advantage. Paris was a
long way off, and Marion was at her family chateau at Baye. Then
on May 20, a joyous King wrote to the Cardinal, "I can assure you
that Monsieur le Grand and I have attained a perfect understanding." Henri, however, decided that his good behavior should not
go unrewarded.

The only authentic glory the seventeenth-century gentleman could
win was to be found on the battlefield. The social functions, the
purpose and the authority of the nobility, its pre-eminence, its
privileges, and its abuses were all justified on the battlefield. When
Henri IV restored a long-forgotten state of peace to France, the
gentry were forced into unemployment, which reduced them to

subsisting on royal generosity. When Louis XIII came to power and war broke out, young nobles were again afforded a thousand opportunities of excelling themselves in the service of the King or in opposing him.

The favorite had already proved that he was a man of stout heart, but he had not yet distinguished himself in battle. A year before, it would have satisfied him to achieve this recognition by the mere demonstration of valor, but now his growing ambition and still childish pride spurred him to attain more lasting recognition. He decided that the laurels of a victorious general would forever safeguard him from being treated "like a schoolboy." Monsieur le Grand complained "of the vile inaction which prevented him from acquiring the reputation of a man of arms which he had always longed to win." Louis was distressed to see his beloved dejected, but he was also a soldier and was even proud of the young man's ardor.

Arras was under attack by mid-June. A Spanish army commanded by the Infante-Cardinal, the Queen's beloved brother, marched to rescue the town and to besiege the besiegers. The French were cut off from their supplies and soon found themselves in a critical situation. An immense convoy of six or seven thousand heavily escorted carts was requisitioned to save them from starvation.

The siege held the general public in suspense. "News is awaited with a marvelous impatience," wrote Henri Arnauld. The outcome of the war was in the balance. Every young Frenchman wanted to take part in the decisive battle. Cinq-Mars was pretentious enough to want to win it himself. He asked the King to give him the command of the troops that were to force the blockade. Louis hesitated for a moment. He was reluctant to be separated from his beloved, but he was touched by the bellicose impatience of a boy whom he had so often accused of frivolity. The seductive ploys and persuasions Henri adopted to win command of the army could have won him the crown jewels. Louis finally consented. A general of twenty was, perhaps, about to make history.

Richelieu was astounded and horrified by the news. He rushed to the King and launched into one of his long Cartesian discourses to prove the danger of entrusting the outcome of the war to the inexperience of a young dandy better suited to debauchery than military strategy. But a mere look from the King silenced him. It was one of those times when the Cardinal could hear the whistle of gunshot as he confronted his "illustrious slave." He feigned submission, bowed, and left. But that same evening Monsieur le Grand was summoned before His Eminence.

Richelieu, like most great statesmen, was a gifted actor. He played this scene brilliantly. He started by adopting the right paternal pitch in which to warn the young stalwart against being overimpetuous; then in a touching voice he evoked the sorrows that would befall the kingdom if the Arras operation failed; he finally donned his terrifying mask and swore he would never countenance a folly which might prove so disastrous for the whole country. No match for Richelieu, Cinq-Mars was overwhelmed and hypnotized. By the time Richelieu adopted a dulcet tone in which to suggest he make the gesture of spontaneously renouncing the disproportionate honor which had been bestowed on him, Henri had already given ground. But this great sacrifice merited compensation. The flower of the nobility were to form a corps of 1,400 volunteers who would not fail to acquit themselves gloriously in battle. Despite the presence of three princes, Monsieur le Grand would be given the command of these "Immortals." This would enable him to exhibit his abnegation as well as his valor.

Henri capitulated. He told the King of his decision in the most touching terms, and Louis was filled with tender admiration for his consideration and courage. Meanwhile, Richelieu hastened to make amends with his old enemy du Hallier, one of the army's best strategists. Du Hallier (later the Maréchal de l'Hôpital) was given general command of the operation, and Monsieur le Grand was put at the head of the volunteers.

Then at the last minute the King showed signs of weakening. Cinq-Mars feared the King would make him remain with him at the army headquarters in Amiens. Before letting him go, Louis made him promise to write to him twice a day.

Henri was wild with joy at the prospect of leading such a brilliant detachment, prancing behind drum and standard toward glory, François de Thou riding at his side. But his vainglorious dream was to be tempered by reality. The Duc d'Enghien, the Prince de Condé's son, and the Ducs de Mercoeur and de Beaufort, His Majesty's nephews (they were grandsons of Henri IV and Gabrielle d'Estrées), refused to take orders from a mere gentleman. Bitter quarreling erupted among the young men. But the King was looking out for his favorite, even at a distance, and the princes were made to accept Cinq-Mars.

The great day arrived—August 2, 1640. The Spaniards had attacked the half-starved besiegers and Maréchal de Châtillon had had two horses killed beneath him before the relief army arrived. The battle seemed lost. The enemy held the fort of Rantzau. "Someone came to tell the Maréchal that all was lost and that the entrenchments were falling." Châtillon reined back the young soldiers from rushing into the fray. He was reluctant to throw Monsieur le Grand into the melee. "Wait," he said, "wait until they have done their worst." He finally gave the order to charge and was promptly struck in the shoulder by a musket shot.

The volunteers "charged so fiercely that the Spaniards were pushed back from the entrenchments to the far end of the battlefield."

Cinq-Mars acquitted himself remarkably. His horse was shot from beneath him, but he leaped up immediately and fought on while spiteful onlookers were eager to discern a certain all-too-natural pallor. The princes and their friends were heard to whisper that "Monsieur le Grand looked better in the ballroom than on the battlefield."

But such remarks were quite unjustified, as Henri was soon to prove. When he saw the infantry assembling to lay siege to the fort of Rantzau, he hurried to join them. But Châtillon, who had remained at his post despite his wound, was reluctant to let him expose himself to such danger. If the favorite died or was disfigured, Louis XIII's eternal wrath might well descend on the Maréchal's head. He decided not to allow the volunteers to lead the assault.

"By the force of my own entreaties and orders, I had Monsieur le Grand removed from the lines," he wrote to Comte de Charost. "Everything turned out well."

The favorite was safe and sound, and the battle was won. Châtillon felt he would ingratiate himself by exalting Cinq-Mars. His report stated, "Monsieur le Grand arrived with many notable volunteers. Had Monsieur le Châtillon not restrained him by entreaty and by order, which he was obliged to obey, he would have charged . . . the fort that the enemy had just regained. His arrival was welcomed by the officers and troops who had withstood the enemy's onslaught for two continuous hours." The *Gazette de France* sounded its trumpets on Cinq-Mars' behalf. The August 8 issue read:

> Our volunteers were commanded by the Master of the Horse, who acquitted himself with such excellence that those who witnessed his charge at the enemy's squadrons deemed him a worthy heir of the titles and virtues of his father, the great Maréchal who, even though he was on his deathbed, accomplished the feat of leading His Majesty's armies to victory in Germany.

Châtillon's zeal and the *Gazette's* eulogy were ill placed, according to the Cardinal. He had never expected to see his one-time protégé win such a dangerous halo. Théophraste Renaudot, the editor of the *Gazette,* was severely reprimanded. He then published an official account of the Arras engagement, indicating that the first report had not been the official one. Richelieu himself dictated the text. Cinq-Mars was not even mentioned, nor was François de Thou. The *Mercure* went even further and coolly attributed the command of the volunteers to the Duc d'Enghien.

Since his departure from Amiens, Henri had not thought of his promise to write to Louis. His continued silence turned Louis' initial fury into sheer misery, which Tallemant claims actually made him weep. As the King's resentment did not diminish, the

Cardinal took the opportunity of minimizing his favorite's accomplishments by reporting that the brazen boy had behaved like a coward, an inexcusable crime in the eyes of a warrior king. He told His Majesty in mocking tones that "he had been very happy that the generals had appeared so zealous in guarding his [Cinq-Mars'] person; that the accident that had befallen his horse had so frightened him that he had not recovered in time to join the army in the retaking of Rantzau; and that it was a pity that he had not chosen to demonstrate some of the valor which he had flaunted when he was far from actual danger."

Arras fell on August 9. On the fifteenth the King dealt with all the amnesties and the necessary procedures for the occupation of Artois, which was now restored to France for good. Two weeks later, Cinq-Mars joined him at Chantilly. Louis had rehearsed a terrible reception for him, but his anger dissolved at the sight of the boy tanned by the winds of battle. Henri proffered a host of good reasons to explain his negligence, and he was very charming. Their reconciliation was complete. "The understanding between Monsieur le Grand and myself is very great," wrote His Majesty to the Prime Minister. "There were a few clouds, but they have now passed."

Louis, who had always been reluctant to befriend any of the Cardinal's creatures, was now secretly pleased to find that the Cardinal and Monsieur le Grand had fallen out. It was his turn to seize the opportunity of separating and ensuring that they would never be reconciled. He told Henri of what Richelieu had said about his performance at Arras.

Cinq-Mars was thunderstruck. To question a gentleman's courage was the worst of insults, and the injustice of this particular one only exacerbated the outrage. The naïve boy was convinced that Richelieu had wanted to dishonor his old friend's son because he was annoyed that Cinq-Mars had refused to become his spy. Monsieur le Grand had hated the Cardinal since that day at Rueil, and now he swore to reap his own vengeance.

On September 7, the King returned to Saint-Germain where the Queen, eight months pregnant, awaited him. He went to see the two-year-old Dauphin, who he thought looked "very much prettier than before." Cinq-Mars wanted to fondle the infant, but the future Louis XIV would have none of it and shrieked. His father's intervention merely doubled his cries. The King was violently angry. "With a face full of rage," he said to the Queen, "My son cannot bear the sight of me. His upbringing seems most strange, but I shall put it in good order." That evening he wrote to Richelieu about the incident, concluding, "My son is . . . very willful. [Henri IV had once said the same of him]. I am not prepared to suffer his ill humors." Then, two days later, "I am ill pleased with my son. No sooner does he set eyes on me [Cinq-Mars was always with him] than he cries as though I were the devil incarnate, and always calls for his mother. His evil temper must be made to disappear, and he must be removed from the Queen's side as soon as possible."

A distracted Anne of Austria sent a messenger to ask for the protection of her enemy, the Cardinal. The court was excited by the incident for a full week. The King threatened to take the Dauphin away from his mother and entrust him to the care of guardians if his conduct did not radically improve. Everyone knew that these guardians would be the King and his favorite. On September 13, however, Louis obtained satisfaction: "My son begged my pardon on his knees," he wrote to His Eminence, "and then played with me [and Cinq-Mars] for more than an hour. I gave him some toys, and we are now the best friends in the world." Once again, the Master of the Horse's intimate participation in family matters indicates the extent of his power.

On September 21, Anne of Austria gave birth to a second son, to the great joy of the somber monarch. A few days later the King went to Monceaux. He informed Richelieu that amid this gentle countryside, which autumn had made the lovelier, his soul was at peace—an almost unique experience for him. He was hunting wolves, and he and Cinq-Mars were "happy together."

Eight

THE *Femme Fatale*

Marie Gonzaga, Duchesse de Nevers et Rethel, Princess of Mantua, was descended from Nordic adventurers and sophisticated Italian despots. Her ancestors were Albrets, Lorraines, and Paléologues. She was the daughter of the Rhine through the Clèveses and the daughter of the Renaissance through the Dukes of Mantua. Her coat of arms thus both bore the arrogant Gonzaga eagle and the mystical Clèves swan. She was a tough, hard-headed princess (Albret), courageous and ambitious (Lorraine), and a somewhat illusionistic Greek besides (Paléologue), whose father had hoped to become emperor of Byzantium.

Without going back further than two generations, her family history resounded with her ancestors' exploits. Her grandfather Luigi Gonzaga, the third son of the Duke of Mantua, married Henriette de Clèves and became Duc de Nevers. He was one of Catherine de Médicis' principal counselors, and mentor of the young Henri III, whom he accompanied on his trip to Poland. He was remembered and respected for his singular wisdom and moderation, even though he had helped organize the St. Bartholomew's Day Massacre.

Henriette de Clèves became the mistress of the magnificent Annibal de Coconnas, the idol of the young. In the Bartholomew Massacre he was said to have slain some thirty heretics with his own dagger. Henriette wept for him publicly when, condemned to death for attempting to kidnap the Duc d'Alençon and the future Henri IV, his head rolled off the executioner's block after that of Queen Margot's beloved La Mole. At the same time, in Italy, Luigi Gonzaga's namesake and cousin was in the process of becoming Saint Aloysius Gonzaga.

Henriette de Clèves' and Luigi Gonzaga's son Charles was an extravagant gadfly. He astonished Rome with his fabulous ambassadorship, then undertook to wage war against Louis XIII. He occupied Champagne, in fact, before he had come of age. Then he went on to organize a campaign to recapture his rightful inheritance of Constantinople. His fleet, and with it his hopes, went up in flames, but in 1627 the fortuitous death of his cousin Vincenzo II gave him the duchy of Mantua.

Mantua was then a key principality in Italy. Neither the Emperor nor the King of Spain wanted to let it fall into the hands of an ally of the King of France. They tried to give it to the Duc de Savoie, but Richelieu intervened, and war broke out. Charles was finally recognized Duke of Mantua and Marquis de Montferrat in 1631. His sons had disappeared at a very early age, and he was left with three daughters, Marie, Anne, and Bénédicte.

Louise-Marie Gonzaga, born in September, 1611, lost her mother when she was seven and was brought up by her aunt Catherine Gonzaga, Duchesse de Longueville, who took pains to educate her as an Italian princess. She also gave her an ardently religious education and elaborate instruction in all the superstitions then prevalent in the land of her paternal ancestors. Marie divided her time between churches and shrines on the one hand, and astrologers, magicians, and alchemists on the other. When she died, she left a considerable work on "the great profession."

Marie Gonzaga possessed that intractable pride and that passion for grandeur and "la gloire" which Corneille personified in his heroines. She followed her father's exploits with avid interest and was intoxicated when he became Duke of Mantua. Unfortunately the Duchy could never be hers, but no matter. Mademoiselle de Nevers, as she was then called, had greater designs in mind. When she was at an age when most girls pine for their first love, Princess Marie was dreaming of crowns; for no throne was beyond the young lady's reach. This is what she would request of the Virgin of the Dove, also called the Virgin of Beautiful Love, when she went to prostrate herself before her image in the Church of Saint-Etienne de Nevers. A portrait painted of Marie when she was fifteen shows her young face encircled with enormous pearls, full of grace but also marked with malice and resolution. The child's smile recalls that of a Reims angel, but her eyes are not the kind that would lower readily.

When she was seventeen, Mademoiselle de Nevers shone amid the beauties who surrounded the Queen. She was not one of the fragile, heart-wrenching, simpering creatures subject to the "vapors," who wrung so many fashionable hearts in the eighteenth century. The gentlemen of her day were once described as "wild beasts held on a leash of Christianity," and their female companions held their haughty heads high above their vigorous bodies. They loved good food, the smell of battles and, despite the "Carte du Tendre," they enjoyed their warriors' lusty embraces. These headstrong women managed to make of their favors such an honor that their suitors were convinced that no effort was too great for such a recompense. This enabled the women to smooth down their men's rough edges, not without exciting their natural mettle and taste for danger and rebellion. Marie was the equal of all these Amazonian *Précieuses* but was unfortunate in her choice of a suitor whom no other woman in France would have dared aim for.

In 1628, Monsieur—as Gaston d'Orléans, the King's sole brother, was called—was heir apparent to the throne, already a widower at the age of twenty, and the favorite son of the Queen Mother, Marie de Médicis, still the ruling deity of the court. He was also the hope of Richelieu's adversaries. What a contrast between the lugubrious Louis XIII and this jasmine-scented prince who sauntered about, hands in his pockets, whistling like an oriole! He was as handsome and scatterbrained as a page, and his grace and charm reminded everyone of his father, Henri IV. There were those who wanted to see Monsieur become the defender of the Cardinal's victims and the feudal and Catholic (in the domain of foreign policy) order which this scarlet tyrant sought to destroy. When the plot that was to seize power in his name was discovered, however, Gaston showed little integrity and none of the courage of his convictions. He promptly denied friendships, betrayed colleagues, and sacrificed Chalais' life in order to save himself.

Marie de Médicis was intending to remarry him to one of her relatives, the sister of the Grand Duke of Tuscany, when Marie Gonzaga captured his hitherto fickle heart. Richelieu, who was still managing the mother's raging tempers, promised to thwart any plans the young couple might have of marriage. But Monsieur seemed genuinely in love. Despite his earlier sarcastic sallies against the *Précieuses* and their simpering suitors, he started writing love poems to his beloved:

> *Youthful goddess whose new graces*
> *Augment today my secret cares . . .*
> *By your beautiful eyes, I pledge you my faith.*

A sonnet bearing his signature arrived almost daily at the Hôtel de Nevers, where he was to be seen sighing like a shepherd out of *Astrée*. Marie could realistically dream of becoming Queen of France.

The War of the Mantuan Succession interrupted the idyll abruptly. At the Cardinal's instigation, Gaston was appointed general in command of the French army, for which he received the sum of 50,000 écus. Gaston was to restore the Duke of Mantua to his estates, but the restoration was not to win him the Duke's daughter. On the contrary, the Cardinal had made a deal with him: For the glory he would win, he was to renounce all plans he might have of marrying Marie Gonzaga. Monsieur actually subscribed to the unchivalrous bargain, but he was not given the chance to reveal his intentions. Louis XIII, who had suffered Marie de Médicis' preference for his younger brother throughout their childhood, drew the line at conferring so great a military honor on him. He decided to command his armies himself. Freed and furious, Gaston proclaimed his firm intention of marrying the Princesse. He abandoned the army and the King near Grenoble and turned back for Paris.

In the meanwhile, Mademoiselle de Nevers and her aunt had set out for the Alps. The Queen Mother posted a hundred horsemen led by the Sieur de Cahuzac after them, fearing that they would encounter Monsieur. This disturbing escort descended upon the two ladies at Coulommiers, and proceeded to accompany them, not to Mantua but to a prison in the forests of Vincennes, where they remained for two months. Monsieur, thwarted and furious, withdrew to Orléans to play the sulky rebel, where he received a volley of angry letters from his brother. Worried, he then took refuge in Lorraine.

Peace was not restored to the royal family until January of 1630. Gaston made a rowdy return to Paris and spent his very first day in the company of his mistress with whom he stayed until midnight. Everyone was convinced that Mademoiselle de Nevers would become Madame, the future queen. But reasons of state interfered again. The Mantua affair was far from being settled, and Marie realized that a marriage contracted against the King's will might be the undoing of her father, Duke Charles. In the manner of a true princess, she sacrificed her personal sentiments to her filial duty. On January 28 after a heartrending scene, she and Gaston bid each other an eternal adieu.

Richelieu had never really wanted to persecute the young lovers. Their troubles sprang from the terrible Queen Mother, from the ancestral hatred of the Médicis for the Gonzagas, and from the King's sibling jealousy. The Cardinal was trying to ward off the crisis which finally exploded at the end of the year and which began a struggle to the death between him and his former protectoress. He had served the Queen Mother's designs in an attempt to mollify her rage.

Gaston and Marie, however, were unaware of the Cardinal's motives. Convinced that this cruel tyrant was exclusively responsible for all their misfortunes, they both hated him. Gaston became a devoted conspirator again, while Marie began gathering new recruits for the anti-Cardinal faction at Court.

Marie fell under suspicion, which was only aggravated by her friendship with Anne of Austria. Thus the age and opportunities for making an illustrious alliance passed her by. She was nearly twenty-six when her father died. Since Salic law applied to the fiefs of Mantua and Montferrat, they went not to her but to her young nephew. However, Rethel and Nevers legally reverted to the eldest Gonzaga. Marie was recognized Duchesse and solemnly entered Nevers on May 29, 1637. She inherited all her family's French possessions, which had been sorely depleted by Charles' recklessness. Determined to gain distinction and rule nobly, she refused to relinguish the minutest fraction of her inheritance to her two sisters, who were kept locked up in a convent. But the limited confines of her duchy, which she ruled personally without leaving the Court, were incommensurate with her ambitions.

The fruitless years continued to pass her by until Marie Gonzaga reached the age of twenty-nine. She still charmed men, though her beauty was now more majestic than seductive. The imperious Duchesse was still bent on attaining supreme achievements, but it seemed increasingly unlikely that her duchesse's diadem would ever become a royal crown.

Cinq-Mars had savored the pleasures proffered by Marion de Lorme, Mademoiselle de Chémerault, and various other lovely ladies of easy virtue—to such a point that he occasionally suffered from a mild case of amorous indigestion, and started to long for that sublime, illustrious love that poets and novelists exalted. Never had literary fashions imposed such refinement of sentiment and such heroic overtones on such a rough and thoroughly Rabelaisian society. *Le Cid* elaborated the rather insipid models set by Urfé and Scudéry. When Marion de Lorme applied her wit and skills to a crowd of admirers, she became more of a Greek-comedy courtesan than a true tragic heroine. Monsieur le Grand's reputation had now reached the stage where he demanded a mistress of greater stature.

Cinq-Mars had known Princesse Marie since he had come to court, as she was one of the Queen's retinue. She was one of a hundred noblewomen of exalted ancestry and "virtue" who boasted numerous suitors; none knew better how to mix haughty pride with subtle coquetry. The King's favorite admired her greatly.

We know little of how this admiration evolved. Their initial interest in each other probably sprang from their joint realization that they might well serve each other's ends. Cinq-Mars could dream of becoming a prince if he married the exalted Duchesse de Nevers. His increased status would fortify his position at Court, and moreover the marriage would certainly dazzle an astonished Court, the city, the Cardinal, and even the King himself. Marie, on the other hand, was an enemy of the Prime Minister. Her fortune was not enormous, and she was fast approaching thirty. She had also begun to realize that her exceptional fate might never materialize. If she conquered the charming gadfly who controlled Louis XIII, however; if she could induce him to gain complete control and even to govern in his name, such a fate would be truly fitting for a woman of her ancestry.

The Princesse and the favorite looked at each other through their respective illusions. Then nature took over. The charms and graces and even the fundamental frailties of the pretty boy moved the heart of this strong-minded woman, and Henri's fragile, unstable, even feminine side was ravished by her bold, courageous, authoritarian character. His mother had been just such a woman, and her maternal tyranny had disposed the young man to enjoy subjecting himself to a woman who was nine years his senior and who, at this juncture in his life, could give him the support and help he needed. Marie's beauty and her aura of queenly majesty toppled whatever other barriers remained.

The relationship was accepted as fact by September of 1640, when the King and Queen and their families were at Saint-Germain. Henri resumed his escapades to Paris to visit Marion and the dangerous society of the Marais, but this did not prevent him from becoming the Duchesse de Nevers' "lover." This word should not be misconstrued; it is used here as Corneille used it. Henri "committed his faith" to the Princesse. He "sighed" for her and proved his passion for her publicly and privately in a thousand ways. He swore to sacrifice "both his blood and his life" for her should the need arise. In return he was entitled to her "favors," to her smiles, ribbons, and token kisses.

This game produced remarkable results. Marie remained mistress of herself, despite her genuine feelings, but Cinq-Mars yielded himself up to the fury of a love such as he had never known.

This is how Cinq-Mars felt when he followed the King to Monceaux. Marie may have been responsible for his brief period of rational behavior which so delighted the King, but he was not capable of controlling himself for long. The life of a rustic Nimrod, which held such joys for the King, always bored the young man and now aggravated his distress at being so far from his beloved. Like a coquette or like a child, he took his restlessness out on the King by provoking gratuitous scenes. At such times Louis' letters show peculiar signs of weakness, unusual for a man who displayed such great physical and moral strength in the face of the most overwhelming odds.

> I would beg that you excuse me if this letter doesn't make too much sense [he wrote the Prime Minister]. I have been beside myself since one o'clock yesterday when it pleased Monsieur le Grand to quarrel with me and thus disturb my peace. Thank God I have witnesses who will prevent him from denying anything. Had he not received Monsieur de Noyer's letter, which he was obliged to bring me, I would not have seen him at all, as I have not done since three o'clock yesterday afternoon when he decided to keep to himself, as I fear he will continue to do. Monsieur de Noyers will tell you how I showed him all possible tenderness and friendship the evening before last. The more one shows him love and appreciation, the more he takes objection and is ill humored. I believe he will write to Monsieur de Noyers, but I would ask that you give

no credence to anything which you do not have directly from me in his presence and before Gordes, who witnessed all that happened. I was so angry that I did not sleep at all last night. I was quite out of humor. I will not continue to suffer his bad manners, for they have gone too far.

The King of France was made to endure the insolence of a poor subject and humble himself by pleading his case to the arbiter of conflicts. He lost sleep, he made himself ill, he swore he would tolerate it no longer. But the favorite's least gesture or smile were enough to gladden his heart. The evening of that distressing day, the two were reconciled once again, and another messenger set out for Rueil.

> I write this note out of fear that you may worry over what I wrote this morning. As soon as Monsieur le Grand decided to return to my company, I received him gladly, and now we are both happy together.

The King returned to Saint-Germain and Cinq-Mars to Marie. Their relationship was a fabulous romance in the Hôtel de Rambouillet style. Passions soared to an incredible pitch because the Princesse refused to allow them to violate the literary laws of chastity. The Court knew it and gossiped and commented and speculated, but remarkably, no one ever cast the slightest doubt on Her Highness' proud virtue. Tallemant shared this conviction: "He came to see her at night several times. Their respective positions at Court inevitably fostered a certain intimacy, but no one has ever said anything nasty about them."

"Their respective positions . . ." Henri naturally dreamed of a marriage which would join his desires and his ambition. Marie let him be the first to speak of this fantastic project. She smiled, gave him time to measure the light-years that divided an Effiat from the ruling Duchesse de Nevers. Then, when her suitor was in despair, she told him how he might span this distance. Monsieur de Luynes, the humble little falconer whom Louis XIII had loved as he loved

Monsieur le Grand, had managed to become a duc and peer, a constable and the Keeper of the Seal. Why should Cinq-Mars not also aspire to such promotions, and make himself worthy of the hand of a Gonzaga?

This artful suggestion set the hapless youth's mind racing. He began to plan feverishly. With a disarming naïveté, he hoped for the support of Richelieu, who in his eyes had remained the image of omnipotence. Their relations had deteriorated badly, however, since the favorite had refused to go to Rueil after the Arras affair despite the Cardinal's wrath and the warnings of his emissary, Saint-Aoust. Monsieur le Grand suddenly decided to listen to this mentor, and allowed himself to be persuaded to call on his former protector. He listened submissively to the inevitable dressing down, begged forgiveness, and promised he "would treat His Eminence in a more fitting manner."

Believing this token submission fortified his position with the Cardinal, he then decided to make peace with his mother, to whom he confided his intentions. Madame d'Effiat, pleasurably surprised, gave him a good deal of encouragement. None of his friends came forward to warn him. Ruvigny had too great a respect for the supreme rights of love, and the pious François de Thou and the cynical Fontrailles were delighted to see the frivolous boy finally embarking upon the right path.

Passion can cloud even the most lucid minds, let alone that of a twenty-year-old gadfly. Henri had decided to ask the King to make him a duc and a peer; and he thought he was being an artful strategist when he went to beg His Eminence not to oppose his desires.

Richelieu never ceased being astounded by this creature's incredible nerve. Cinq-Mars' request shocked and secretly worried him. He was aware of Marie Gonzaga's hatred of him and did not underestimate the intelligence, determination, and ambition of Gaston's ex-fiancée. All at once he saw the snare which was set to trap him and had no alternative but to destroy it at once. He did not waste his cunning skills on the young man, but dealt quite brutally with him, bluntly declaring that he could "not believe that Princesse Marie had so forgotten her birth and station that she would stoop to such a lowly companion.

"You must remember that you are but a mere gentleman raised by favor alone, and that the Marquis de Sourdis paid your brother [Martin] an inordinate honor when he gave him his daughter. I cannot think how you dare even think of such a union." Henri muttered that he had his mother's approval. "If what you say is true," thundered the Cardinal, beside himself with rage, "your mother is insane. And if Princesse Marie has entertained such a notion, she is an even greater fool than your mother."

Richelieu, like Napoleon after him, excelled himself in scenes of anger, sarcasm, and insults. Henri was devastated. He had great trouble in containing his tears and barely made it back to his carriage, gasping and choking. "When he returned home," G. de Pitaval notes, "someone noticed that the buttons down his doublet had burst."

Nine

THE ADVANTAGEOUS QUARREL

꿏 AFTER THAT SCENE, Cinq-Mars' for-
tunes began to bear on the fate of France and the world.

Henri did not have the strength to master his despair. He shut-
tled between depression and mania, imagined fantastic revenges—
withdrawing from the Court and its intrigues, and even from the
Princesse herself. He was too feminine, however, not to take his
disappointment out on a totally innocent victim. He wanted nothing of the King for the time being, and so made him his whipping
boy.

Louis was therefore subjected to a thousand capricious injustices.
He defended himself and rebelled, but he never thought of banishing
his dear tormenter. At times, Cinq-Mars deliberately sought to make
himself hateful and to provoke his own exile: "When he knew
that something would please His Majesty and that the alternative
would displease him, he always chose the alternative." But to no
avail. Incapable of subtle machinations, Cinq-Mars did not understand the human heart, which was just as well for him. His best
schemes were not schemes but instincts. Father Griffet betrays his
own lack of perception when he muses, "A favorite who behaves
so badly should not excite such fear." And he proves his lack of
subtlety when he adds, "The King's love for him was so strong
that all that should have destroyed it only increased it."

The sixteen-year-old Louis had declared, "I must prefer justice to pity"—well before Richelieu—and Richelieu later wrote to Louis, advising him that "Kings must be harsh and exacting to punish those who disrupt the order of their realms; they should never take pleasure in their destructive antics." But the implacable prince was a living paradox. The barbaric punishments inflicted on him as a child, his moral lassitude after his father's death, his mother's harshness and injustices, his Court's open disdain had all helped to make him the pitiless but masochistic man he was. The King who refused blessings and who signed the all-too-frequent death warrants may even have taken unconscious delight in doing so. It may have been his way of revenging himself on his terrible governess, Madame de Montglat, with her fearful disciplinary cane. And yet he had adored his tormentress, just as he adored his detestable mother.

The same monarch who ordered the erection of so many scaffolds experienced a profoundly voluptuous joy (as Marie de Hautefort had realized) in being snubbed and thwarted, bullied and martyred. Cinq-Mars' childishly tyrannical behavior only gained him even greater power over the King. These unintentional tactics served him more than he knew. Louis might grumble and groan while secretly enjoying his discomfort, but he was genuinely afflicted by his favorite's obvious suffering. Knowing the Cardinal was behind Cinq-Mars' unhappiness, he conceived a grudge against him.

It may only have been a slight grudge, a slight change of attitude, but when such a change came from the demiurge himself, it gained enormous significance. The Cardinal's faithful collaborators were the first to detect the winds of change. Chavigny wrote in code to Mazarin, who had been away for a few months on a mission, "The King, the Cardinal, and Cinq-Mars are exactly as you last saw them at Amiens, but for the fact that His Majesty has recently shown very ill will toward the Cardinal-Duc. I confess that I fear the outcome of it all, but Monsieur de Noyers continues to assure me that it isn't anything." Then on November 6 he insists, "I am on better terms than ever with His Eminence. He has told me of his feelings for that certain person whom you know well, whose insufficiency has greatly inconvenienced him. I cannot write in any greater detail, but I'm sure you will understand me." Eight days later a letter written in Italian informed Mazarin that His Eminence was anxious to find a solution to a most distressing situation and did not know where to turn.

A subterranean war was being waged, and the public was beginning to notice the first echoes. On the surface, the trouble appeared to be between the King and his favorite, who were making incredible scenes. When they left Saint-Germain, it deprived the young man of his Princesse and of the last of his self-control. On November 22 they were at Livry for a few days, and the King wrote to the Cardinal:

> I have kept my peace until now before writing to you, to see if Monsieur le Grand's ill humor might pass. But seeing that nothing has changed since I was last at Rueil, although I have been twice to his chamber to beg him to forget anything I may have said or done to displease him, he insists that I do not love him because, when he requests something which is unjust or contrary to justice or good usage, I refuse him. Also he wants me to inform him of my plans four or five or six days hence, when I myself do not know what I shall do an hour before I do it. These are the causes of his discontent. This is how he humors me when he knows that I am worried by my son's illness, and were it not for the long hours I spend hunting (for when I am at the lodge, I have to suffer his arrogant, aloof presence), I should have a fine time indeed! I can no longer stand his airs. He considers everything unworthy of him and refuses to see or talk to anyone. I would prefer not to importune you, but you are the only person I can wholly trust and to whom I can turn in my discontent. I bid you good day and hope you will take care of yourself.
>
> *Louis*

"He is as slothful and dilatory and negligent of his commitments as ever." Three weeks later another battle broke out at Versailles, and Henri stuck to his new strategy of "aloof arrogance," indifference, and offended dignity. On December 13, the King wrote to the

Cardinal, "I have no cause to complain of Monsieur le Grand, for since yesterday, he has uttered only commonplaces to me in everyone's presence. In his favor, he has shown me no anger; nor has he shown any sign of good spirits."

The young man may have been pining away, but he certainly did not deny himself any of the joys of life. The King continued to reproach him in vain for his extravagance and frivolity. Henri Arnauld wrote, "Monsieur le Grand has ordered some of the most beautiful furniture anyone has ever seen. The Court has never seen a table so magnificently laid and served." The King had a truly magnificent favorite. The Master of the Horse would escort the King in his own coach, which was more sumptuous than the Queen's. He resumed his visits to Marion, who furnished him with the pleasures of profane love while Marie Gonzaga proffered the nobler glories of sublime love.

If the Princesse would have him, Henri would become the envy of all France. But the Princesse had her pride, and she still insisted that her "lover" prove his worthiness. Cinq-Mars had no idea how to do so, and his plight reduced him to tears of frustration.

The New Year's festivities were peaceful enough, but a new clash broke out on January 5, 1641. This time the King decided to deal severely with him. He dispatched Cinq-Mars to Rueil with a letter instructing Richelieu to give him a thorough trouncing. The Cardinal did just that, lecturing and raving for a whole grueling hour. However, precisely because his recalcitrant protégé had become an adversary, His Eminence decided not to push things too far and to reinstate himself as peacemaker. He sent Henri back to Louis with a fairly mild letter which assured His Majesty of Monsieur le Grand's good resolutions. But Louis was not in a conciliatory mood when he received the missive. He wanted to escalate the quarrel and seized upon the first pretext that came to mind.

"Monsieur le Cardinal informs me that you wish to please me in all things, and yet you continue to persist in displeasing me on the one account I especially asked him to speak to you about: your laziness."

Henri had borne too many insults for one day and was at the end of his tether. "His Eminence did speak to me of this, but I cannot change, and I shall never be otherwise," he exploded.

The King was taken aback by Cinq-Mars' violence, and he tried to offer an olive branch without capitulating. "A man of your condition who dreams of commanding armies and who has expressed such a desire to me cannot afford to be slothful on any account."

"I have never had such a thought."

"To which," wrote the King in his account of the exchange to the Cardinal, "I replied that he had, but that I did not wish to dispute it further. You know what he is like." But Louis was definitely looking for a quarrel: "I then returned to the question of his sloth, saying that this vice rendered a man incapable of accomplishing anything good and that it was fitting only for the pleasure-seeking souls of the Marais where he had been weaned." The King became so excited with his own invective that he got carried away: "And if you want to continue living such a life, you'll have to go back there!"

"I am quite ready."

"If I were not wiser than you," Louis retorted, struggling to beat a dignified retreat, "I know what I should say to you about that." Then he added piteously, "In view of your obligations to me, you ought not to speak to me that way."

This had no effect at all on the insolent fellow; on the contrary: "I want none of your favors. I should like you to take every single one back and keep them. I can do very well without them. Furthermore, I would be just as happy to be Cinq-Mars as Monsieur le Grand, and as for altering my way of life, I cannot live any other way."

The outraged King left his room, crossed the gallery, and descended the palace steps. Cinq-Mars pursued him, and they continued quarreling loudly as they passed before the mocking eyes of the courtiers. When they reached the courtyard, Louis shouted, "Seeing that you are in such a mood, you will do me the pleasure of getting out of my sight."

"I'll do it quite willingly."

"I have not seen him since," the King noted sadly as he gave the Cardinal a detailed account of the whole squabble. He felt it necessary to emphasize: "All that I write took place in Gordes' [the Captain of the guards] presence." Then he added in a postscript, "I showed Gordes this note before sending it to you, and he agrees to its accuracy." [1] This was the absolute monarch who would have a man beheaded merely to justify a whim.

Cinq-Mars continued to play cat-and-mouse with him. The next day, at eight in the morning, Richelieu was informed of the following incident: "Last evening Monsieur le Grand asked Montespan to inquire if I should be glad to receive him. Then he changed his mind and sent word through Montespan to say he was unwell and could not come."

His Majesty was obsessed by the need to prove everything he said was true. "I ask you to refer to my two memoranda to Messieurs de Noyers, Comte de Guiche, Sénecterre, Bautru, and Saint-Aoust, who are his friends, so that you may ascertain which of us has been in the wrong and whether I did not speak to him for his own good and honor." But who was right and who was wrong altered nothing. Henri sulked, and Louis refused to make the first move. If the two people involved had not been His Most Christian Majesty and his Master of the Horse, one would be reminded of a pair of stage lovers.

On January 8 the King informed the Prime Minister of the gravity of the situation: "Since my quarrel with Monsieur le Grand on the fifth of this month, I have not heard from him. He expects me to go in search of him, which I refuse to do after the way he has treated me. Yesterday I said to his friends that I found it strange that he should make no attempt to speak to me and make peace, hoping that when he heard of this he would wish to do so. It was to no avail, however; he continues to be as stubborn and aloof as ever. I bring this to your attention now so that if he instructs his friends to tell you otherwise, you will know that all he says or has others say to you is false. I bid you good day."

---

[1] Published document in the Aubery collection.

An angry Cinq-Mars decided to seize this opportunity to break free—or so most historians have claimed. What probably happened, however, was that the Princesse advised Cinq-Mars to resort to that singularly astute maneuver which Richelieu himself had often used to such good effect. How many times had the Cardinal offered and threatened to leave his master in the knowledge and certainty that Louis could not possibly do without him! Monsieur le Grand duly wrote to the Prime Minister:

> Monsieur, I am much disturbed to see Your Eminence so frequently assailed with complaints about my person. A remedy must now be sought. Rather than give lengthy and useless excuses, I choose to admit full blame for I know not what. I would further entreat His Eminence to show no more of his kind disposition for me and to prefer his own peace to furthering my fortunes, and to support all that His Majesty's anger might demand. This is not a whim which I shall later regret. I have given the matter serious reflection, and I have concluded that I shall not fear the outcome providing that I am made exempt from the King's wrath. May His Eminence remember that I shall always be his most humble servant.

He sent another letter to de Noyers:

> The extremes to which you see me reduced will give you an indication of the state I am in. I implore you, in the name of the love you bear me, that you consent to help me end this miserable existence of mine. Go to His Eminence and ask him what I must do to break away while safeguarding myself against the King's wrath. This is all that I ask, all that I desire.

The Cardinal would have been delighted to take the young man at his word. But the King would not hear of it. He had been heroic enough to sacrifice Louise de La Fayette, and he had no intention of repeating the gesture and losing his "dear friend" four short years after being deprived of his "beautiful angel." His whole life was regulated by his terror of being brutally denied the solace of another loved one. Richelieu was put in the invidious position of seeking to mend a rift he would otherwise have welcomed.

Thus the young man who had been so viciously upbraided for his follies, and who had been threatened and humiliated and subjected to so many pearls of wisdom, had won a resounding victory. Superficial observers claim that his decline from favor dates from that month of January, when in fact the contrary was true. With the help and intelligence of his Egeria, Cinq-Mars had proved that his very indispensability to the King made him a free agent. Richelieu had used exactly these tactics when Marie de Médicis first launched her attack on him.

The Cardinal, therefore, was not hoodwinked, nor was Arnauld, who wrote to Barillon on January 13, "Monsieur le Grand is fully reinstated. The quarrel has been a foul and furious one. . . . It seems impossible that a real rupture will not eventually occur. . . ."

February 7, 1641, marked the apotheosis of the Cardinal-Duc. It was the day the King signed the marriage contract between the Cardinal's niece Mademoiselle de Brézé—the unhappy, half-witted twelve-year-old daughter of a totally mad mother—to the Duc d'Enghien, the son of the Prince de Condé, the noblest Prince of the Blood. It was a terrible union which the Prince de Condé had negotiated eagerly despite the protests and wishes of his brokenhearted young son who was in love with Mademoiselle de Vigean. The whole Court was shocked, but at the same time duly impressed with the exalted heights attained by the Queen Mother's former chaplain and with the pomp that surrounded the occasion.

Once the contract had been signed, the Cardinal's palace was transformed into a setting for a spectacle of unparalleled brilliance. A ballet of no less than thirty-six separate parts, subdivided into five acts, was performed, and the great ball that followed it lasted until dawn. "Never has His Eminence been in better sorts," remarked Henri Arnauld.

The ill-fated union was to have dire and unexpected consequences. It was to ruin the Condé line with Claire-Clémence de Brézé's congenital insanity. But more immediately, it linked the Duc d'Enghien to the Cardinal's faction, and won the future Grand Condé, as he was later known, the command of the French Army which won the battle of Rocroi.

Richelieu had his day of triumph, but the more perceptive courtiers had begun to detect the greatest peril which had threatened his existence since the near-fatal Day of Dupes.

Louis' quarrels with his favorite were not his only concern. He knew that the Cardinal was a very sick man and that he would soon have to find his successor. The King had started to see his favorite in a new light. He noticed that the boy had changed in the past few months, and was surprised by his intelligence, his informed opinions, and his new sterling ambitions. Louis began to wonder whether, after a suitable period of apprenticeship, Adonis might not reveal the qualities of a statesman. He was, however, unaware of the Princesse's influence. It was she who encouraged Henri to ask that he be given serious duties which would mitigate his frivolous reputation. He expressed his desire to enter the Council. The King finally authorized his entry, and Richelieu dared not object. Cinq-Mars thus brought himself a step closer to the Ministership.

Marie Gonzaga congratulated herself on her achievement. Her "lover" had climbed the first rung to power.

Ten

THE WIDENING ABYSS

ꣵ THE PRIME MINISTER'S dissatisfaction
with the favorite immediately roused the interests and the hopes of
the opposition. Fifteen years of abortive plots and futile civil wars
had not dulled their militant determination to get rid of the tyrant.

Besides the constant court intrigues, the last serious attempt on the
Cardinal's life had taken place at Amiens in 1636 during the campaign that regained Corbie and repelled the threat of invasion.
Gaston d'Orléans and his cousin the Comte de Soissons planned the
operation with the help of Gaston's favorite, Montrésor, and Sois-
son's factotum, Saint-Hibal (or Saint-Ibar). They had intended
killing the Cardinal during the commotion of the campaign when
he was less well protected than usual.

One day, the King left after a Council meeting at the Duc de
Chaulnes' house and Richelieu stayed behind in the courtyard of the
house to talk to Soissons. His bodyguards did not accompany him.
Gaston, Montrésor, and Saint-Hibal were present with three other
accomplices. Now they had their chance. The conspirators grouped
around the unprotected Richelieu and waited for the signal. Gaston
had only to flicker an eyelid, and their daggers would have been
drawn and the tyrant slain, while the others looked on enquiringly.
But His Highness hesitated. Under the weight of their inquiring
gaze, Gaston finally panicked and ran up the stairs to the first floor
of the Hôtel de Chaulnes. Montrésor followed his master and per-

suaded him to come back down, but the moment had passed. By the time the Prince had calmed his nerves, the Cardinal had left, unaware of his escape. Three days later they planned again to strike, but the opportunity never arose. The Cardinal's wary guards had not suspected anything, but Orléans and Soissons gave themselves away when they lost their nerve and fled. Orléans went to Blois and Soissons to Sedan, an independent town controlled by the Duc de Bouillon.

Monsieur eventually made a new peace with his brother, while the Comte remained at Sedan. He was a Bourbon and the head of a younger branch of the House of Condé. He was a gifted politician and soldier, and eventually became the leader of a large and powerful anti-Richelieu faction operating in France and abroad.

Richelieu's exiled victims became a veritable emigrant army, dangerously in league with France's international enemies. There were many illustrious exiles, such as the Queen Mother and the Duc de Guise, the Duchesse de Chevreuse, the Duc de Vendôme, and a host of lesser nobles, all plotting away in Holland, England, Loraine, and Germany. Even in the Bastille, prisoners like Maréchal de Vitry and Maréchal de Bassompierre conspired against him. Then outside the prisons there were those kept under close surveillance, and others like the octogenarian Duc d'Epernon and the young Abbé de Gondi de Retz, who were all prepared to take up arms and go into action. The most formidable of all was perhaps the Duc de Bouillon, whose citadel in Sedan became the retreat for the exiles and the headquarters for the active opposition.

This dissenting faction never missed an opportunity of asserting the nobility of their determination to rescue the King from evil counselors. When France was drawn into the Thirty Years War, her entry gave their cause and motives added weight. The greater nobility were not affected by the people's miserable plight, but the lesser nobility were directly affected. Since they derived their income from the revenues yielded by their estates, the peasants' horrible suffering at the hands of requisitioning soldiers and extortionate tax collectors threatened their very livelihoods.

In 1631, Gaston d'Orléans wrote a letter to the King that displays an unusually keen humanitarian concern for the poor. Richelieu could certainly never have written such a letter:

> Less than a third of your subjects eat ordinary bread. Another third eat oatmeal bread, and the remaining third are reduced to begging and languish in such an abject state that some literally die of hunger when they can no longer sustain themselves on a bestial diet of acorns and herbs. Those who complain least are the ones that feed on bran and the blood that trickles down a butcher's gutter.

By 1641, however, the situation was much worse, resulting in an almost annual peasants' revolt followed by ruthless reprisals. Louis XIII and Richelieu sacrificed the country to the interests of a foreign policy bent on making France the most powerful nation in Western Europe. But few believed in the success of their enterprise. The war was also unpopular among those Catholics who opposed the country's continual alliances with Protestants against the House of Austria, the champion of Catholicism. The conspiratorial opposition thus won support from all sides when it nobly declared that it stood for "peace among crowned heads and for the relief of the people's miseries." The leaders dubbed themselves Princes of Peace, and their claims and intentions did not fail to move the King, who immediately ordered his Minister to secure a decisive victory, an end to the disgraceful situation.

Cinq-Mars was first sounded out as early as 1640, when the Comte de Fiesque approached him on behalf of Soissons. They pointed out that his position was precarious, that the Cardinal was certain to contrive his downfall, and that he would have much to gain from joining forces with the opposition and helping them execute a successful conspiracy. He was even offered a royal marriage with Mademoiselle de Longueville, Marie Gonzaga's first cousin. At that time Henri had not yet fallen in love with the Duchesse de Nevers.

Troubled, Cinq-Mars asked Fontrailles for his expert conspiratorial advice. Fontrailles proved unusually circumspect. He told Cinq-Mars that it would be neither just nor profitable for a favorite to enter into dealings with a prince about to take up arms against the King and his Minister. Whereupon Monsieur le Grand spurned his tempters, "saying he could not conceive of any greater glory or contentment than that of serving his King." In reality, Fontrailles was completely devoted to Monsieur and, despite the connivance of the two princes, did not want to see Monsieur le Grand prematurely affiliated with Soissons.

When the news of the Arras affair reached Sedan, another conspirator, Alexandre de Campion, who was younger but more experienced than Fiesque, went to see Monsieur le Grand. He could not have chosen a better time. Cinq-Mars was furious with the Cardinal for accusing him of cowardice because he had refused to be his spy. He was more than ready to entertain offers from his persecutor's enemies. After being humiliated and belittled once, he was flattered to be treated as an influential power. The conspiracy itself and all the dangerous, secret midnight encounters appealed to a boy of his age.

On August 20, 1640, Campion wrote to Monsieur le Comte:

> Monsieur le Grand was pleased to receive your compliments
> and those of Monsieur de Bouillon. He has instructed me to
> make the best use we can of him and to assure you of his
> sincerity and loyal service. You can measure the sincerity of his
> intentions by his conviction that the Cardinal is determined
> to destroy him. . . . No one knows that I am seeing him,
> and if his increasing good fortune does not dull the keenness
> of his conviction, I think he may well undertake something of
> importance. In any case, it is good to secure the good faith of
> the King's intimate friend should you ever be in danger and
> thus in need of such protection. He has, moreover, a vested
> interest in helping to bring about the downfall of his dangerous
> detractor. I know that those who dislike him will accuse him
> of ingratitude, since the Cardinal has been his benefactor, but
> this need not concern you.

A Prince of the Blood had come to Cinq-Mars for protection. It was enough to make any young man dizzy with self-importance. Henri then became the slave of the Duchesse de Nevers. The months passed, and Cinq-Mars dreamed of seizing power while Richelieu won victory upon victory. Portugal rebelled against Spain. The Duc de Lorraine asked His Majesty to forgive him for having risen against him and restored a number of territories as a token of his capitulation.

The opposition felt it was time to act. In the spring, the Duc de Bouillon, as the Prince of Sedan, declared war on Louis. Soissons commanded an army soon reinforced by seven thousand Imperial troops. His proclaimed goal was to get to Paris and overthrow the tyrant. Hundreds of Frenchmen began to prepare for this happy eventuality. The Queen and Monsieur were anxiously awaiting the moment when they could reveal their true sympathies. The Cardinal was to be replaced by Monsieur le Comte, the King put under guard, power restored to the nobility, and foreign alliances would be reversed. Cinq-Mars did not actually play a part in these arrangements, but he knew all about them.

Toward the end of May the King went to Abbeville, following his usual route. He stayed for a month and left for Amiens and Corbie. He was in Péronne on July 3. The news from Roussillon was encouraging, as was that from Germany, where the Imperial Army had been routed at the battle of Wolfenbuttel. But the eastern prospects were bad. Maréchal de Châtillon's forces may have been stronger than the rebel army, but they were not strong enough to stop Soissons at the Meuse. On July 6 he faced Soissons at La Marfée and was crushed. The Royal Army had never been so completely defeated by a rebel force. Everyone was convinced that a wave of routs would follow and destroy all that had been accomplished since 1624, returning France to its old feudal structure. Richelieu believed himself lost, for unlike Louis, he always lost the courage of his convictions when he was confronted with a crisis. He had despaired in 1636 when the Spaniards took Corbie, and now he again failed to rise to the occasion.

Cinq-Mars was quick to notice Richelieu's total dejection. Despite his natural good nature, his foolishly benevolent reaction to his lifelong tormentor's distress was more probably dictated by vanity than by natural goodness. The misused pupil could score off his omnipotent master by offering him his protection. He was so delighted by the prospect of having Richelieu at his feet that he did not stop to consider the possible consequences of such a rash gesture. He went to His Eminence and, as Gaspard de Chavagnac recalls in his *Memoires,* told him "to have no fear, for he could stop [Soissons] himself. The Cardinal embraced him and said it would be the greatest service he could possibly render his King." Cinq-Mars was able to savor his revenge for three joyous hours before a messenger came from La Marfée with news that turned the tables. Monsieur le Comte de Soissons had been killed by a "pistol shot" as he was riding across the battlefield.

The Comte's providential death is still a mystery. The official account cited the Prince's foolhardy habit of lifting the visor of his helmet with the barrel of his own pistol. No one, however, believed this explanation. Some were convinced that he had been shot by one of the Cardinal's agents who had ridden alongside him; others preferred the rumor that he had been picked off by a straggler from the defeated army who had remained in ambush. Whatever actually happened, the opposition had to face the fact that a headless conspiracy could not possibly continue. His Eminence, saved again, immediately regained his composure and his omnipotence.

The rift had opened, and Monsieur le Grand suddenly found himself on the brink of a catastrophe. He despaired. The promised marriage was indefinitely postponed, but that was the least of his worries. Richelieu informed him of this decision as he embraced and thanked him for his concern. Henri finally regained his lucidity and realized the danger he was in. He cursed himself for his stupidity and wondered how and from where the fatal blow would be dealt.

Fontrailles returned from a long journey to be informed of his friend's mistake. He told Cinq-Mars what he thought of him, fanned his worst fears, and advised him to quit the Court. As Fontrailles himself remembered it, Cinq-Mars—or the Princesse—had the good sense to think otherwise and replied "that leaving would be no guarantee of future safety for him; the Cardinal was not a moderate man, and his absence would only give him the more latitude to destroy him. He had no other protector than the King, and if he remained, he could defend himself to Louis. The Cardinal would find it hard to impugn him since he had not written anything down and there could therefore be no concrete proof against him; witnesses would be far more reticent in his presence. He would be willing to entertain the most extreme measures to guard his safety."

Monsieur le Grand only spoke of entertaining "the most extreme measures" because he was excited and frightened, but the surprised hunchback took him at his word. There was no more talk of his leaving Court; Cinq-Mars' convictions might be put to some good use after all. The conspirator advised him to secure a loyal circle of friends and form a faction of his own.

De Thou highly approved of the project. "His Disquietude" did not show his usual indecision. He feared for Henri's life and even more for his Queen's, whose obedient knight he was. His mother's cousin, the eighty-seven-year-old Duc d'Epernon, had just been exiled to Loches despite his advanced age. De Thou sought the old man out and consulted him.

The meeting revived conspiratorial instincts and factional hopes in Henri III's aged *mignon*. He had been Henri IV's sworn enemy and had always loathed Richelieu. After preaching wisdom, he offered the conspirators the help of his own experience, which extended back to the Wars of Religion. Monsieur le Grand set about seeking support from his father's old friends. This was how he discovered another of the Cardinal's enemies, the Comte de Chavagnac, whom he asked to "give" him his younger son Gaspard.

In the meantime, the King and Richelieu seized their opportunity. The King took personal command of the army, recaptured Aisne and proceeded to the Meuse. On July 28 he called a meeting of his Council at Mézières. Cinq-Mars was setting out to attend the meeting when a gentleman, Monsieur de Sainction, came to inform him that the Cardinal "did not approve of the way he always tread on his toes before the King, nor that he concerned himself with matters which did not require his presence." Cinq-Mars was astounded and ran to complain to de Noyers. But he had scarcely opened his mouth when Richelieu, who had had him followed, appeared angrily before him. Without letting the young man say a word, the Cardinal "treated him with the insulting and authoritarian brutality he might use with his lesser servants. He disparaged his good fortune; he called him incompetent and worthless and then informed him in the most contemptuous way that the presence of such a man as he was a discredit to the Council as a whole in the eyes of the world. He concluded by forbidding him to enter the Council ever again and sent him back to the King to see if he did not concur with this opinion." [1]

In any other circumstances, the favorite would have taken Richelieu at his word. As it was, he had a guilty conscience and feared that Louis would throw his foolish avowals back in his face. Again he burst into tears and consoled himself with vengeful fantasies.[2]

The King crossed the Meuse, stormed Donchery, and besieged Sedan. The Duc de Bouillon was disillusioned by Spain's inertia and decided to negotiate for peace. He surrendered on August 5, eight short days after the Mézières incident.

Louis had not broached the subject with Cinq-Mars, nor had his affections diminished. Cinq-Mars was reassured and took further courage from the return of François de Thou. It was at this time that Mazarin was writing, "The Cardinal is paving the way for Monsieur le Grand's downfall." War had been declared. The favorite was easily persuaded to prepare himself for a surprise attack.

De Thou knew Monsieur de Bouillon very well. When the re-

---

[1] Fontrailles, *Memoires.*

[2] Montglat, Fontrailles, and Aubery give contradictory versions of this incident. It has been reconstructed here in what seems the most probable version.

bellious Duc went to the army headquarters to declare a formal end
to his rebellion, the young magistrate took him aside and talked to
him privately. He told him that Monsieur le Grand wished him to
know "that the King was very disgusted with the Cardinal and
that he did not know how to be rid of him." Cinq-Mars would
send word to the Prince de Sedan when the time came to destroy
the Minister.

The Duc was surprised and immediately suspected a trap. He
sang the Cardinal's praises and refused to believe that His Majesty
wanted to be rid of him. In any case, he added, Monsieur le Grand
would have to make the first move. Monsieur le Grand then realized he would have to prove the sincerity of his intentions and
demonstrate his good faith. He worked on the King to show Bouillon clemency, and Bouillon later admitted that "his good services
had not been in vain." The Sedan matter was soon concluded. Sedan
became a vassal state of the Crown, in return for which "His
Majesty, not doubting the sincerity of the aforesaid Duc's repentance, gave him a free pardon which he extended to all those gentlemen who participated in the same crime and might thereafter be
identified with it." Such generosity may have been a result of Cinq-
Mars' intervention, but it certainly shows the King's immense relief
at the failure of the rebellion. Louis had been really alarmed, and
he wanted at least posthumous revenge on Monsieur le Comte by
vilifying his name. Richelieu, who usually enjoyed being merciful
when mercy cost him nothing, was reluctant to intercede on behalf
of a Bourbon prince, even though he was safely dead.

On August 10 the Duc de Bouillon was received by His Majesty
at Mézières and then went on to dine with the Master of the Horse.
When Henri was escorting him back he said to Bouillon, "I was
pleased to hear from Monsieur de Thou that you wish to be among
my friends. I assure you that I shall not take any advantage of your
kindness until I have merited it by being of some service." He did
not understand men, but he admired the unscrupulous and astute
Prince. Cinq-Mars "was more at ease and satisfied" after their
meeting.

Fontrailles and de Thou did not allow him to become overconfident. They constantly reminded him that he was committed to contriving the Cardinal's downfall, and that if he did not break the Cardinal, the Cardinal would break him. This meant that it was necessary for him to approach the leader of the opposition, Monsieur, and come to an understanding with him. Gaston d'Orléans had suffered a setback at "Monsieur le Comte's misfortune, which had also been his own," but he had emerged from the situation unscathed despite the efforts of an *agent provocateur* to entrap him. On August 18 he went to see his brother at Amiens and was given an icy reception. He too was furious to find that he had been excluded from the Council. It was at that point that Fontrailles informed him that "His Highness can count on Monsieur le Grand's personal offer of service." The hunchback adventurer and the gallant mystic began hatching a new plot.

De Thou went to Sedan to persuade Monsieur de Bouillon to remain in his citadel and to trust the favorite, assuring Bouillon of Monsieur Le Grand's friendship and constancy. The Duc would be kept informed of all that happened at Court. Bouillon, delighted that the fires of rebellion had rekindled so quickly, responded with encouraging pleasantries.

Meanwhile Fontrailles arranged a secret meeting between Monsieur and the Master of the Horse at Amiens. This was the first time that the two men had ever met privately outside of the Court. Cinq-Mars was thus confronted by the same mirage that had proved fatal to Chalais, Montmorency, and so many other conspirators. The formidable hunchback had absolute confidence in his capacity to manipulate, control, and goad the two equally weak, unstable, impulsive, and seductive individuals. He so maneuvered the conversation as to extract a sighing admission from Monsieur: "Ah, how happy we would be if the Cardinal could die."

"Your Highness has only to give his consent and many would be pleased to oblige you," Fontrailles quickly replied. Contemporaries disagree as to whether it was Gaston or Cinq-Mars who objected to the proposal. In fact they were both terrified of the responsibility for an act which they had both envisaged and desired. The meeting came to an end on this timorous note. "Monsieur le Grand," Fontrailles was to write, "claimed that I was indiscreet and that he feared lest I had shocked Monsieur. This obliged me to tell him that, if that were indeed the case, it was well to know from the outset rather than be surprised by it once we had gone too far." The incautious Cinq-Mars was further from safety than he imagined.

At the end of September, Monsieur le Duc de Bouillon rejoined the King at Nesle. He had thought hard about the plot and finally assured Cinq-Mars "that he would be his friend against Monsieur le Cardinal and would come up to Paris whenever he wished."

The campaign continued for another month. By the time an exhausted Louis XIII retired to his winter quarters, victory was assured. He stayed at Chantilly for a short time and then went on to Saint-Germain where he arrived on November 5. Cinq-Mars was reunited with his dearly beloved Marie Gonzaga, whom he kept fully informed of all his various undertakings. She was not a woman to let their passionate commitment cool. Not only did she encourage him to pursue his fatal course, but she had also spoken to the Queen about him and his intentions. Anne of Austria had never stopped hating the Cardinal and continued to fear that he might take away her children. She was therefore delighted by the new cabal replacing that of Monsieur le Comte.

Henri was moved to have his beautiful Queen's confidence. He swore he would serve her and that he would never compromise her, come what might. Anne of Austria maternally encouraged him to woo and win his Princesse, who encouraged him with Corneille's enjoinder: "Be a victor in battle, for Chimène is the prize!"

Eleven

THE CONSPIRATORS' APPRENTICE

CINQ-MARS' FATE was determined in the decisive weeks between November and the January of 1642. He continued "sighing at his Princesse's feet," but the days of their idyll were numbered. The pure, lyrical, and almost literary romance they had created for themselves was becoming more and more a real-life Corneillian drama. His life was now entirely governed by his desire to deserve and win his lady. The proud Gonzaga had laid down her conditions, and it remained for him to achieve the goals she prescribed. The lady's motives for participating in this intense relationship are not as transparent. It is difficult to estimate the ratio of genuine emotion to ambition in her devotion to Cinq-Mars. They were an incongruous pair: the handsome, headstrong, resolute, and dominating young woman, and the pretty, graceful, but highstrung favorite.

In any case, they caused the Cardinal just as much anguish as the abscesses and festering sores that afflicted him. After Monsieur le Comte's uprising, Richelieu had changed his mind about Henri and decided to change his tactics. He stopped nagging a naughty boy and assumed his beguiling mask. He set about fanning and flattering Henri's insatiable vanity. Henri would certainly have fallen victim to these seductive ploys had not Marie been a powerful antidote. One day at Reuil, according to Avenel, the Cardinal astounded his courtiers by escorting the young man up the steps and saying, "As you see, I show you all the deference due to a great favorite. I am delighted to see you on such good terms with the King. Now that you are in a position to be of help to others, you no longer need my help as peacemaker. On the contrary, you can accommodate others."

But no one was fooled by these gestures. Henri Arnauld confided to Barillon that "there is definitely something gravely amiss between the Cardinal and Monsieur le Grand."

The real leaders of the cabal, the Princesse and Fontrailles, were not satisfied with the outcome of Cinq-Mars' first meeting with Monsieur. They wanted to force Monsieur to commit himself to a real alliance. At the end of November, Monsieur went to see his brother at Saint-Germain. Louis greeted him coolly but was not as reticent as usual. He discussed the affairs of state with his brother and told him of some of his worries and anxieties. He complained about the war and the ever-distant prospects of peace.

The interview encouraged the Duc d'Orléans to arrange a secret meeting with the Master of the Horse. Henri was thoroughly briefed by his mentors, who persuaded him to express a lot of uncertain assumptions with a great deal of conviction. He insisted to Monsieur that he was at the apex of royal favor and that the King had spent the last eighteen months urging him to break with the detested Cardinal. The quarrels they had were staged to mislead His Eminence. He also assured Monsieur that the King had sworn to protect him and anyone who would help him negotiate a peace with Spain.

Fontrailles was present and substantiated all these claims. Gaston was amazed, but he cautiously curbed his natural optimism and asked, "Have you proposed the ruin of Monsieur le Cardinal to the King?"

Henri riposted quickly, "I wanted to be sure of your protection before undertaking anything."

Monsieur did not haggle. He offered his protection, knowing that the favorite would in turn be his protector. He realized he had nothing to lose; if the plot worked, he might gain the throne, and if he failed, he would still be the King's brother.

Gaston decided to obtain the Queen's support, however, which would not only safeguard his involvement in the conspiracy but would also minimize the possibility of their becoming rivals for the Regency if the King died. They had been accomplices in the past, were still good friends, and still considered themselves victims of the same tyranny. Anne of Austria had a lot of influence over her brother-in-law. She may not have had a vast intelligence, but her instincts were excellent, and she was exceptionally subtle and cunning. She encouraged Gaston to trust Monsieur le Grand, assured him that none of them would take a single step without consulting him, and made him swear not to betray her if things went wrong. Anne was fully aware of Monsieur's history of broken promises, but the subtle lady knew that he would have to be discreet on this occasion. He would need her when the Regency began. Gaston was so busy concentrating on his own devious ends that he did not realize he was being used to serve her dream of becoming sole Regent.

Cinq-Mars thus became the pivot of an enormous faction, composed of a host of warring interests. The complexity of most of these interests were beyond his comprehension. Youth and love explain his candor, but his friend François de Thou proved equally naïve. Thinking he was serving the interests of his Queen and the desires of his friend, he was in fact being manipulated by both as a sacrificial pawn. Fontrailles had advised Henri to send the young counselor to Sedan to inform Bouillon of Monsieur's alliance and ask him to come to court. Bouillon was essential to the plot, as only he could guarantee them a place of refuge in Sedan if the need arose. Cinq-Mars suspected that "His Disquietude" would raise objections on the grounds of his principles; he therefore decided to give de Thou the letter for Bouillon without telling him about the implications of the contents. Fontrailles was indignant: "Monsieur le Thou will risk his life and his liberty. How can we leave him in the dark?"

"If I do tell him," Cinq-Mars answered cynically, "he will either refuse to go, or he will carry out the task with such reluctance and disgust that the mission will fail."

But Fontrailles was persistent. "Even if he doesn't want to take part in contriving the Cardinal's downfall, he is too loyal and honorable ever to betray anyone. He deserves your confidence." Cinq-Mars was convinced.

This discussion, as Fontrailles reports it, would certainly not have taken place had they not intended to assassinate Richelieu. We have it from Fontrailles himself that Cinq-Mars finally agreed to tell de Thou all about the mission but that, as soon as he began speaking, de Thou "interrupted him, declaring that he wanted nothing to do with the plan; he was against bloodshed on principle and he would never overthrow the Minister." And "Cinq-Mars said not a word more." Fontrailles then claims that he alone persuaded the young man to change his mind.

It seems unlikely, however, that de Thou should renounce his principles simply at the hunchback's eloquent request. But another voice was heard. The Queen had learned of the conspirators' ulterior motives from the Duchesse de Nevers. Without giving away details, she was able to persuade her faithful admirer to collaborate in an enterprise that would indeed determine her fate. He did not hesitate a moment longer and was soon galloping through the December snows to the depths of Périgord, for Bouillon had left Sedan for Périgord to stay in his château at Limeuil. When he met Bouillon, de Thou lost some of his resolution. He could not bear the idea of being mistaken for a hard-bitten professional conspirator. He therefore handed Bouillon the letter, telling the Duc he did not know why the favorite wanted him to go to Paris before the start of the next campaign. He even protested against the way they had kept him in the dark. Bouillon's suspicions were aroused, and he became defensive. He said he could not go to Paris because his wife was about to give birth. He also indicated that the King would regard his unexpected arrival at Court as unusual.

"In that case you should not go," de Thou concluded coolly. Before he left Bouillon, he tried to compensate for this deliberate diplomatic failure by praising Monsieur le Grand and by mentioning the important work being done by some of His Majesty's courtiers.

The Cardinal also made contact with Bouillon. Hoping to buy his loyalty, he wrote implying that Bouillon might be given the command of the French Army in Italy. This put the Duc in the strategic position of intermediary between the Cardinal and his adversaries and gave him the best reason in the world to go to Paris. Shortly after his arrival he accepted an invitation to visit the Master of the Horse. Their meeting was to have far-reaching results. Fontrailles and his friend d'Aubijoux stood guard in the antechamber while Bouillon and Cinq-Mars whispered animatedly in the favorite's bedroom.

Henri felt he was fighting for his love. This obsessive preoccupation lent his—or rather, Fontrailles'—arguments a convincing ring of urgency. The King was fast declining, Cinq-Mars explained; he would not live for long. Richelieu was planning to become Regent himself at the expense of the Queen and Monsieur. He had to be stopped at all costs. And because Monsieur had committed himself "to work for the Cardinal's downfall," the Duc de Bouillon should throw in his lot with the rest of them. Besides, His Eminence would eventually find some pretext for punishing Bouillon for his collaboration with Monsieur le Comte. The defenders of the Royal Family needed his alliance and his assurance that, if their plans miscarried, Sedan would harbor them until the King died.

The Duc was frank with Cinq-Mars, but raised one major objection: Sedan was not impregnable. At present it was surrounded by three royal armies, one under Monsieur de Guiche, another under Monsieur d'Harcourt, and a third under Monsieur de Guébriant. If the Cardinal ever suspected anything, the three armies would instantly occupy the hilltops, and all the troops in Europe would not be able to prevent disaster. Nothing could be done without raising an army such as they had had at La Marfée, which would be able to repulse any such attack. Of a French army there was no question, for since the death of Montmorency, feudal levies had become impossible to raise. They would have to turn to the King of Spain and negotiate with him.

The idea of negotiating an alliance with an enemy in wartime would be regarded as high treason today. Such ethical scruples did not deter the great seigneurs of Cinq-Mars' time. In the previous century, they had appealed twenty times for foreign support in their opposition to the French King, determined to defend their status and their religion at the expense of their country. But a lesser noble such as an Effiat, the son of a loyal servant of the Crown, should have experienced a twinge of conscience. Ruled by passion, however, Cinq-Mars saw the world through the eyes of a Gonzaga. He had no compunction whatever about accepting Bouillon's treacherous suggestion. He merely said he would have to refer the proposal to Monsieur. After the meeting Cinq-Mars assured Fontrailles and d'Aubijoux: "All went well, and Monsieur de Bouillon is agreeable to everything."

François de Brion, the Duc d'Orléans' first equerry, was one of the key figures of the conspiracy. He had a lodging in the residence of the Venetian ambassadors in the Marais. Cinq-Mars went to see Gaston there and informed him of Bouillon's proposal of the necessary treaty with Spain. The Prince had signed many such treaties before, and raised no objection to doing so again.

Caught up in the drama of the events, Henri was quite unaware of the enormous significance of what he was doing. He wanted his Princesse, he wanted power, and he wanted the destruction of his enemy. (The theory that he agreed to the treaty as a way of avoiding the need to assassinate Richelieu is quite unfounded.) He did not think he was in any particular danger in offering Richelieu's enemies their last chance to be rid of him. Blindly gambling away his marriage, his future, his life, Cinq-Mars was equally oblivious to the wider significance of his actions. If his conspiracy succeeded, if the opposition took control, France's policies would be reversed. France would lose her grip on Europe, her pre-eminence, and her absolute monarchy. She would return to a more pacific state on an international level but to a state of internal strife and constant faction. She would be open to foreign interference and liable to the sway of the Holy See.

Monsieur wanted exactly this. He was delighted by the prospect and went to notify the Queen. Anne gave her approval. She then informed de Thou that she knew all about the conspiracy and heartily endorsed it. Cinq-Mars was also delighted. Convinced he would triumph, he felt he had become the equal of Corneille's Rodrigue.

"You no longer need my help," Richelieu had said pointedly to Monsieur le Grand. Marie Gonzaga could be proud of her creation. Henri had devoted himself so completely to pleasing her that he was a definite contrast to the unruly young man who had delighted and tormented his King. He now had the manners and the graces of "a great favorite." Calm, dignified, controlled, and discreet, he had learned how to wield his seductive powers with consummate skill. This suited the King, who was worn by a thousand physical maladies and weakened by his physicians' treatments. He had lost his morbid appetite for masochistic rows and seemed to need to confide more and more in his favorite. Cinq-Mars, who a short time before would have avoided his master's endless complaints, now listened to him with infinite patience. The climate therefore changed between the two. Louis had become an exhausted old man of forty who saw his favorite less as a naughty little boy and more as his chosen confidant, to whom he could open his heart.

And Louis' heart was full of bitterness toward the Cardinal. He spent hours complaining bitterly about him to Cinq-Mars. Richelieu was himself a very sick man and feared he might die before the completion of his great tasks. He was working feverishly against time, had no patience for anything that might delay or interfere with the conclusion of his work, and was even more brutal and imperious. Louis reacted to the increased pressure by rebelling and denouncing Richelieu to Cinq-Mars as an evil priest who had obtained a dispensation from having to say Mass, an upstart who had wrested a vast income of three million livres (equivalent to tens of billions of francs today) for himself, which he lavished on his person to the outrage and dismay of the starving populace, a cantankerous despot, a tyrannical persecutor of the Royal Family, and a leader of spies. Henri would sigh hypocritically and recall the worst of the Cardinal's vices by referring to Richelieu's stubborn pursuit of a war

Louis loathed. Then, playing his role well, he would leap to the minister's defence, being delighted when Louis recriminated him the more.

One day Louis exclaimed, "I would give half my kingdom to rid you of the Cardinal. He has robbed me of all my friends, he even tried to take you away from me." Cinq-Mars affected a sad indignation, and Louis added, "His pressure is unbearable. I should like to see a party rise against him such as rose against Maréchal d'Ancre."

Cinq-Mars was astonished at the King's vehemence. He had never gone so far as to equate Richelieu with Concini, whom Louis had loathed so much when he was a young man and whom he had had slain on the drawbridge to the Louvre. The Master of the Horse jumped to hasty conclusions. He thought Louis intended to get Richelieu out of the way, which would vitiate the need for the conspiracy. The next day he discussed the situation at length with the Princesse and then reopened the matter with the King. When he saw that Louis had not changed his mind, he burned his bridges behind him: "Sire, you are the master. Why not get rid of the Cardinal?"

Despite their intimacy, Cinq-Mars did not understand the stoic aspect of the Monarch's character. In an instant the King's attitude changed. "Not so fast, Monsieur," Louis replied curtly. Cinq-Mars never realized how much Louis had sacrificed himself for the greater glory of France. Richelieu was a necessary if unpleasant burden, because he had proved to be the only artisan who could realize that great and glorious France within their lifetime. When he felt himself too weak, he abandoned his invisible armor and liked to take a beloved being as witness to his sacrifice. It did not mean he was giving up.

Cinq-Mars was only aware of the royal weaknesses, which gave him a distorted image of his King. Louis, however, realized that his favorite had interpreted his outburst as a desire to see a rash way out. "The Cardinal is the greatest servant the state has ever known," he said in his usual formula. "I don't know what I'd do without him. If he should ever openly declare himself against you, even I would not be able to save you." He then gave a dry commentary on the impetuousness of youth.

Cinq-Mars crumbled. Not only did his enemy remain as omnipotent as ever, but he realized that "even if the Cardinal died, His Majesty would continue to scorn the capabilities of people of his age. This meant that he might well have to suffer the disgrace of being forever excluded from participating in the affairs of state." [1]

This incident would have had a sobering and even beneficial effect on any other man. But the twenty-one-year-old Adonis chose to dismiss the warning. He knew Marie would despise him if he withdrew at this stage. He thus decided to keep the incident to himself and to rely on the effect of his charms. The conspiracy which depended heavily on the favorite's influence with the King should have shifted its emphasis at this point. It might even have been wiser if the conspirators had waited for a more favorable turn of events, or for the King's death. But Cinq-Mars did not want to wait. He did not think it would be hard to completely dominate a man who had so recently been a victim of his childish whims.

How could any boy who was less than a genius understand the soul of a Louis XIII? Cinq-Mars, like so many, thought that Louis was terrified of his Minister and that the "illustrious slave" would ultimately be grateful to him for liberating him of his scourge. He was also careful to say nothing to his associates.

The wheels of the conspiracy were thus set in motion. Monsieur and Bouillon had fallen out in 1632; the favorite undertook to reconcile them. One bitterly cold night de Thou agreed to drive Bouillon to the Hôtel de Venise, but he refused to enter and have anything to do with the meeting. "He was everywhere, but he didn't want to know anything." This persistent self-deception only served to intensify his risks. At the Hôtel de Venise, Gaston and the Seigneur of Sedan made their peace under the auspices of the Master of the Horse. That night, Cinq-Mars showed His Highness the draft of a treaty which Bouillon and Cinq-Mars were later to

---

[1] Fontrailles, *Memoires.*

accuse one another of making. The treaty was probably the product of considerably more experience than Cinq-Mars possessed. The treaty was not entirely satisfactory, however, and they decided to revise it after the New Year's Day festival and then submit it to the Queen.

Anne knew that she was at the crucial stage in her life. Up to this time she had been deprived of happiness and power, but she planned to obtain both. She was determined to direct the Regency and to keep her children. Her determination, coupled with her instinct for self-preservation, suddenly gave the lovely indolent Spanish princess the spirit of a Machiavelli. She not only encouraged the conspirators but recruited old experts to help them, making use of the unhappy François de Thou. La Rochefoucauld—whom she had once asked to take her home to Spain along with Madame de Chevreuse—wrote in his memoirs that Monsieur de Thou "came to see me on behalf of the Queen to inform me of her complicity with Monsieur le Grand and that she had assured him that I could be counted on. Monsieur de Thou also told me that Monsieur le Grand requested my services, and I found myself implicated in the affairs of a person I had hardly ever seen."

Once Anne of Austria had committed herself and her friends to the opposition, she calmly summoned one of the Cardinal's faithful agents, Father Carré. It was precisely this man whom Richelieu had entrusted with the task of disentangling the King from Mademoiselle de La Fayette. The Queen told the priest that she wanted him to plead Madame de Hautefort's case to the Cardinal. She praised His Eminence and assured him of her goodwill and intentions. She then proceeded to mention Cinq-Mars and subtly implied that she disapproved of the favorite's rank ingratitude toward his former protector. "I do not like him at all. If anything were to happen to him, I am sure no one would mind." Father Carré wrote off a long letter to the Cardinal and reported the whole conversation in detail.

Having thus betrayed both sides, the Queen then sat back peacefully and waited for the outbreak of hostilities. However, the King fell seriously ill, and everything remained in suspense.

Twelve

THE WAVERING BALANCE

꧁꧂ AT THE THRESHOLD of the new year,
the efforts of Louis XIII and Richelieu were magnificently rewarded. Alsace and then Artois were annexed, and war was carried beyond the borders of France to strike at the heart of the
Habsburg Empire. While France contained a powerful pro-Spanish
party, the Cardinal's agents were provoking separatist aspirations
within the Spanish kingdom. Portugal asserted her autonomy by
giving herself a national king, Don Juan of Braganca. The Catalans
followed this example and declared their intention of liberating
themselves from the tyranny of Philip IV. In the summer of 1641
their ambassadors had approached the Cardinal to suggest that
Catalonia become a vassal state of France. On September 19 they
knelt before Louis XIII at Péronne and swore him allegiance.
Louis accepted the titles of Count of Barcelona, Roussillon, and
Cerdagne, and promised to liberate those provinces. Now Louis
had only to keep his word and push the frontiers of France as far
as the Pyrenees, perhaps further. The next few weeks were spent
preparing the immense campaign and reinforcing the armies to the
north, on the Rhine, and in the Alps for the imminent offensives.

The great plan was on the brink of success when the Cardinal
again had to face the possibility of complete failure. The King was
taken seriously ill; Richelieu knew that if his master's worn constitution did not recover, his work and his life would be at an end.
Henri was equally worried—and mistakenly so, for had he been

endowed with foresight, he would have seen that the King's death, coming at this moment, was his only hope of salvation. While Louis lay critically ill for ten days, Europe held its breath and waited. Then Louis' natural resources of strength won through again, and a skeletal and waxen King returned to his tasks with undiminished resolution.

The King threw himself into preparing the Pyrenean expedition, delighted at the prospect of "the fracas we are planning to make in Spain." Maréchal de Brézé, now Viceroy of Catalonia, was already pushing on to Barcelona, and a strong army was to besiege Perpignan, the formidable key town of Roussillon. The siege was so crucial to success that Richelieu wanted Louis to conduct it in person. The favorite frowned upon the plan; it would be exceedingly difficult to control his conspiracy from such a remote outpost. He was also afraid that the campaign might prematurely kill the ailing King. Above all, it would mean leaving Paris and his love. Thus Henri protested loudly against the trip. His friends set about stirring up public feeling, claiming that the Minister's monstrous ambition was ruthlessly risking his King's life. The King, however, dismissed Henri's entreaties and his physical disadvantages as puny deterrents compared to the demands of duty and to the lure of battle. Louis would lead his army.

Richelieu tried to absolve himself of any responsibility for this decision and even make it appear against his better judgment. He made His Majesty sign a solemn declaration:

> I have told my cousin, Cardinal Richelieu, that I would much rather undertake the journey than remain at Saint-Germain . . . he was afraid that I should not have the strength to bear the strain of the campaign. Whereupon I begged him not to concern himself about my person. . . . I had no special preference for dying in one place over another. It is my duty to consider the wisdom of such matters and his to carry out my resolve. I have since become more and more convinced that I should undertake the journey, believing it is sure to bring me glorious rewards and being unable to stay at Saint-Germain rather than with my waiting armies.

Henri was thwarted and refused to conceal his resentment this time. His illness had made Louis even more irritable, and they soon had a row in which Henri "was so harshly reprimanded by the King that even his best friends believed his favor was on the wane." His enemies anticipated his downfall. The Master of the Horse tried to quash these rumors. He did not want them to reach the Duc de Bouillon, who had just been made Commander-in-Chief of the French Army in Italy, and who might well change sides if he lost confidence.

Cinq-Mars invited him to dinner with de Thou, but he was not an accomplished actor. "He wanted to communicate good cheer and was extraordinarily lively," Bouillon later remembered, "but his forced high spirits roused suspicion; it is most difficult to talk sensibly when one talks for fear of stopping."

But it proved to be a minor matter. Louis and his favorite were soon reconciled, and Cinq-Mars handled the situation so dexterously that everyone's faith in him was immediately restored.

The conspirators decided that time was running short and that they should settle the terms of the treaty as quickly as possible. They gathered together at the house of Monsieur de Mesmes, where Bouillon was staying, and drew up the final text. Monsieur was to receive from his brother-in-law, the Spanish King,[1] an army of twelve hundred infantry and six thousand cavalry and the necessary funds for their upkeep, in addition to which a further 400,000 écus would be provided for the levying of troops in France. Philip IV would also provide Sedan with a garrison which, of course, he would finance. His Highness would personally receive 150,000 écus, and the Duc de Bouillon and the Master of the Horse would get 40,000 each. The princes had everything to gain from such an agreement. Cinq-Mars agreed to everything. The Spanish Army would obey only Monsieur's commands, and he would keep whatever territories he won for himself. In exchange, the Duc d'Orléans would guarantee a "strong peace" between the two countries, and each would restore any conquered territories to the other. Monsieur

---

[1] Philip IV had married Elizabeth of France, daughter of Henri IV.

would also renounce France's heretic allies: Holland, Sweden, and the German Protestant princes.

The document stated, "We unanimously declare that we will do nothing prejudicial to His Most Christian Majesty and to his states, nor to the rights and authority of the Most Christian Reigning Queen; but on the contrary, that all will be done to uphold them." This hypocritical declaration was a necessary safeguard for the conspirators. It again asserted the nobility of their motives in regard to the King and absolved them in writing of treacherous intentions. On the other hand, homage paid to the Queen and her authority was not extended to her husband! Whatever Anne of Austria's apologists may wish to claim, the presence of that clause is conclusive evidence of her complicity.

The ink on the treaty was scarcely dry when an unexpected incident shook the hopes and confidence of its authors. Guébriant had just crushed an Imperial army at Kempen and taken prisoner its commander-in-chief, Lamboy. This gravely compromised the strategy of the conspirators. A disenchanted Bouillon went to see Monsieur at the Luxembourg Palace and said that "it was useless to count on the Spanish anymore. After Lamboy's defeat, far from contemplating a French offensive, they would be hard put to retain Flanders."

Experienced politicians would certainly have waited for more favorable circumstances, especially when the King was in such an unpredictable frame of mind. But they had gone so far that they knew that procrastination might mean shelving the plot permanently. The inexperienced Cinq-Mars would not hear of it. He was determined to become Constable of France and marry the Duchesse de Nevers before the end of the year. Bouillon allowed himself to be persuaded, in spite of having just been given the command of the army in Italy from the King and Richelieu. He did, however, refuse to give Cinq-Mars the letter which would guarantee him free entry into Sedan, asking to see the King of Spain's signature on the treaty first. Monsieur was his usual confident self. The die was cast.

On January 27 the King left Saint-Germain and spent the night at Chilly, Maréchal d'Effiat's enchanted castle. His visit indicated the extent of his favor toward Cinq-Mars, who returned the compliment by preparing his royal master a sumptuous welcome. Louis retired at his customary early hour, which left Cinq-Mars free to resume his normal activities. He called his friend Gaspard de Chavagnac.

"He asked me to follow him," Chavagnac was to write in his memoirs. "We took a hundred detours and finally reached a door at which he knocked. Monsieur, the King's brother, opened the door to him. He then asked me to stay and make sure no one came near. He spent the whole night within." Fontrailles and d'Aubijoux were there, but de Thou was not. It was a veritable hotbed of conspirators.

Cinq-Mars obtained His Highness' consent and requested Fontrailles to leave immediately for Spain with the signed treaty. The hunchback considered the procedure a bit hasty. He also took exception to being kept in the dark. Henri was charming and persuasive. Monsieur supported him, then retired. Fontrailles wanted to consider the proposition for a while and went into a huddle with d'Aubijoux. The two "agreed that they were involved in a sorry affair," but that they had gone too far to disentangle themselves. The Cardinal's agents were already suspicious, and Richelieu would eventually find a charge against them and make them pay for the follies of the Prince and the favorite. They had only one way out: to flee the country.

Henri was about to resign himself to Fontrailles' refusal when the hunchback told him he had decided to go. "He was visibly delighted." However, the Marquis posed one condition: that Monsieur le Grand saw to it that Monsieur and the Duc de Bouillon join the King at Lyon "to constrain His Highness to be present at the attempt on Monsieur le Cardinal's life."

Henri hesitated. The idea of assassinating the man who had had such a controlling influence on his childhood caused him a certain fear. He had learned to accept the idea with Marie's help and had himself wished Richelieu dead every time he had been humiliated by the man. But when it came down to the actual act, he shrank in horror. It was carrying out the murder, however, and not the act itself, which worried him.

Fontrailles had to bully the promise out of him. He pointed out that Bouillon's presence at Lyon was equally indispensable, as only he could provide the conspirators with the necessary refuge. The nobility of the Auvergne were extremely hostile to Richelieu, and they should also be invited to Lyon to take part.

The Master of the Horse finally acquiesced. He would also instruct Josué de Chavagnac, Gaspard's father, to stir up the Protestants in Cévennes and send de Thou as ambassador to the Duc de Mercoeur and Duc de Beaufort, the sons of the exiled Duc de Vendôme. The two young princes were bound to welcome the idea of making the Cardinal pay for all their father had been made to suffer at his hands. Once they had agreed to these procedures, the conspirators set about improvising traveling dress that would conceal the treaty. The three gentlemen unstitched Fontrailles' doublet and carefully sewed the treaty into the lining. They finished at dawn, whereupon Fontrailles said good-bye to his colleagues and set out on his dangerous expedition.

A few hours later the King started out on his own expedition. He stayed at Maison-Rouge that night and reached Fontainebleau the next day where the Court remained for five days. Henri spent most of his time with Marie. She tried to infuse him with her energy, and he swore he would return to her victoriously. As always, they had to wait until the King had gone to sleep before they could meet secretly. They would sit before an open brazier that protected them against the winter night, and they abandoned themselves to the chaste transports of legendary love. Louis must have known of the idyll, but there is no evidence that he disapproved of it. However, he never stopped loathing Marion de Lorme. He seems to have preferred the platonic love which kept his friend away from his old debauched habits and inspired him with soberer sentiments. Besides, an ambitious lady like the Duchesse de Nevers would naturally entreat the young man to please his master.

Jealousy, then, was not responsible for the King's curious moods. Louis' treatment of Cinq-Mars would often oscillate between tenderness and fury. He was affectionate one moment and rebuking him harshly the next. He would demand his beloved's presence and then send him away impatiently. These changes of mood were sometimes so sudden that Monsieur le Grand was forced to laugh the whole thing off. He who had once enjoyed provoking rows now had to conceal his displeasure for fear of incurring his Princesse's scorn and his partisans' distrust. The King's moods may have appeared groundless and irrational, but they were to have disastrous consequences. It may have been Louis' illness that was to blame, or Louis may have begun to realize that his favorite would never be the talented, gifted, virtuous disciple he had once hoped for but would remain a frivolous young man incapable of meriting his exalted status. Ironically it was precisely Cinq-Mars' lack of great ambitions that was to be his ruin. All the boy wanted was happiness, and happiness was not the patrimony of the great.

The Admiral Marquis de Brézé, the son of the Maréchal de Brézé, informed the Cardinal that he had walked in on a conversation in which His Majesty and Monsieur le Grand were "saying the most diabolical things" about the Cardinal. Richelieu's spies were everywhere. He must have known that something was afoot. One of his ablest agents, Rochefort, watched the favorite very closely and even had a key to a secret door of the Luxembourg Palace, which enabled him to spy on Monsieur as well. When Richelieu heard of "liaison between the two," he exclaimed, "The ingrate shall perish." But since he had no definite information or conclusive evidence as yet, he contained himself, reflected, and began to calculate the possible dangers. He was determined to avoid another rebellion such as had occurred the previous year during the great Roussillon campaign. The "four square feet of the King's desk" really did demand more of his time and attention than all his European political concerns. He cursed the day he ever introduced that dangerous child into the King's chambers.

The Cardinal hoped it was not too late. He was doubly gracious and flattering to the Master of the Horse and even asked the King to give him the governorship of Touraine. The masochistic King gave his consent, knowing that he would lose his beloved's presence. Louis offered Henri the honor at Fontainebleau.

Henri was struck dumb. Only a few weeks before he would have been transported at the opportunity of being more worthy of his Princesse. He had gone to some lengths to make it known that he wanted the post. In the present circumstances, however, he could not leave the King's side; the conspiracy demanded his continued presence. The way in which he refused reveals the constructive influence of his Egeria. He thanked His Majesty profusely for his kindness and then said that "such a reward should be reserved for those who have won distinction in his armies and that the Comte d'Harcourt merited the post far more than he." The poor King was astounded by his favorite's selfless consideration and above all, pleased that his friend would not leave his side.

Richelieu appreciated the artful parry and worried all the more. He tried to approach his ex-pupil personally. It was Cinq-Mars' turn to enjoy seeing the Cardinal squirm while he coolly stood his ground. The Cardinal was furious; he forgot his usual caution and openly attacked. He waited for February 2, and "thinking that on a day of devotion [Candlemas] he would find the timid and scrupulous Louis XIII in the right frame of mind, he delivered an indictment of the Master of the Horse, not omitting anything that might dispose Louis to send Cinq-Mars off to Touraine or elsewhere."[2] But the move proved ill-timed. The King happened to be particularly delighted by his favorite and tormented to see his Minister escalate hostilities when he would have preferred to declare a truce. The Cardinal was shattered by his master's violent reaction. Gassion saw His Eminence coming out of the King's chamber looking pale, crushed, and considerably older.

The court was soon agog with the news, and the young man was at the zenith of his career. It was the finest hour of the boy whose

---

[2] Le Vassor.

beauty was his ruin. "Everything conspired to intoxicate him. His daily rising ceremony was equal to that of the King and the Cardinal. Two hundred gentlemen accompanied him to the King, and he outshone all the courtiers with the magnificence of his attire, the nobility and charm of his person, and the grace of his manners. Women threw themselves at his head; ministers were at his service." [3]

Monsieur le Grand now had his own declared party. The gentlemen of his retinue relied on him for advancement, and their example influenced a sizable part of the army. Many of his old comrades from his days in the Royal Guard were sworn enemies of the Scarlet Courtier and swore him aggressive allegiance. The Master of the Horse was especially fond of Monsieur de Tréville and Monsieur de Tilladet, Monsieur La Salle and Monsieur des Essarts, who came to see him every day. Across the frontiers, well-informed exiles trembled for joy. The Queen Mother, it was said, even started planning her return.

In the meantime, however, the Cardinal's external policies continued their unfaltering course. The precarious balance of fate continued its seesaw, as Richelieu and Louis XIII, both half dead, set out on their last and most tragic voyage.

---

[3] Memoirs of Anne Gonzaga, Princess Palatine.

Thirteen

"Favorable Circumstances"

ON FEBRUARY 3 two immense caravans set out from Fontainebleau. His Majesty and Richelieu each had such a quantity of musketeeers, light cavalrymen, gentlemen, pages, servants, and guests in their respective trains that they were forced to travel separately for fear of provoking a famine.

The King went ahead, sustained by his usual martial enthusiasm, but he was too ill to be his old energetic self. The Cardinal followed at his own pace, wincing at every bump and jolt of his carriage. They joined forces at the major halts along the way. From miles and miles of dust clouds emerged processions of mounted soldiers in their blue-and-red helmets, brilliant livery, and glinting armor and weapons, courtiers in their lavishly worked doublets and lace trimmings.

As they traveled, Cinq-Mars commented on the miseries of the countryside, the direct result of the endless war. So many battles, casualties, and devastations had achieved little more than an illusion of glory. Peace was the only answer, but the Cardinal would never consent to such a measure, "as he would always find a way of deferring a treaty in order to preserve his indispensability." The unfortunate King found it hard to repudiate such an argument coming from such an individual. Louis fell prey to his constant anxiety. He was terrified of appearing before his Maker laden with the sin of this horrible conflict. But he was not convinced that Richelieu was acting out of self-interest.

133

Cinq-Mars did, however, believe just this. "Well," he said to Louis one day, "the only way to find out the truth in a matter of this importance is to ask a trustworthy person to write secretly to the King of Spain and find out how the peace negotiations are progressing. The reply will show you that only the Cardinal is opposed to peace."

"Whom could one safely ask to carry out such a request?" the King asked, somewhat taken aback.

The favorite hastened to put forward the name of François de Thou, who had originated the idea. The King consented. De Thou, a good lawyer, insisted on a written order from His Majesty. "The King gave two, one addressed to his favorite and the other to Monsieur de Thou, authorizing them to write to Rome and to Madrid in order to hasten the conclusion of the peace treaty." [1] The Counselor did write, but circumstances prevented him from following up on the inquiry.

This was the first time the King had tried to trap his Minister, the first time his confidence—which had never wavered in eighteen years—seemed ready to lapse. Cinq-Mars' impetuous friends encouraged him to take advantage of the King's uncertainty. If Richelieu was suddenly struck down, the King would surely not protest. "Favorable circumstances" presented themselves at Briare when the King's party joined up with the Cardinal's. The Cardinal and Louis worked alone together. The young officers of the guard planned to burst into the room and eliminate the Cardinal before the King, whose presence would guarantee their safety. Cinq-Mars did not want to risk anything without the King's explicit approval. He suggested "that the blow would be struck more safely at Lyon, where the Duc d'Orléans and the Duc de Bouillon would be present along with the nobility of the Auvergne." His cohorts agreed to wait. Cinq-Mars had some ten days in which to extract Louis' fateful words.

The caravans continued their journey through La Charité, Nevers,

---

[1] Father Griffet.

Saint-Pierre-le-Moustiers, and Moulins. Cinq-Mars had never been so gracious and considerate, and even seemed to shoulder some of the King's anxieties. The delighted King lent a willing ear to the intelligent proposals François de Thou had put in Cinq-Mars' mouth. The favorite was also helped by a minor squabble between the King and his Minister. That occurred during one of the halts. Cinq-Mars and Tréville were in the King's room when, somber and furious, Louis complained "of the slavery to which his Minister had reduced him."

"Get rid of him then," said Henri.

The King protested that it would not be easy to get rid of such a powerful man (his apparent concern with Richelieu's power, hardly in character, proves that Louis had no intention of carrying his complaints through to their logical conclusion). Cinq-Mars was being presumptuous but not perceptive. Tréville's presence compelled him to press the point and declare that "the easiest and surest way to have [Richelieu] assassinated was to surprise him when he came unguarded to [the King's] apartment." Montglat adds that Louis was "stunned," and it is necessary to take the word "étonner" in its seventeenth-century meaning and realize the King was evidencing profound emotion.

The fate of France was once again in the balance. The most significant facets of this dialogue are the emphasis given to certain words and Louis' pregnant silences. Concini's assassination was, after all, the result of such a mute order. The absence of objection could thus amount to approval. The King was silent for a long while, and then he said, "He is a priest and a Cardinal. I should be excommunicated."

Tréville immediately interjected "that if he had the King's consent, he would take the deed upon himself and then go to Rome to be absolved, where he was sure of being welcomed." [2] Again His Majesty did not answer.

It is difficult to ascertain the thought processes of such a man.

---

[2] Montglat.

Louis may have been tempted by the idea of unloading his burden once and for all, in which case his mild protestation could be interpreted as positive encouragement. On the other hand, he may have wanted to terminate the dangerous conversation with one of his macabre jokes. Many have chosen to believe the first hypothesis and have then judged his relationship with his favorite in the light of this complicity. The hypothesis seems almost credible when one considers that the merciless Louis would almost certainly have arrested his tempters had he disapproved of the assassination. There is, however, another possible interpretation. Louis could have wanted to prevent such a catastrophe but could not find the courage to lose the object of his passion.

The issue had been raised, however, and doubts remained. Tréville persuaded himself that no such doubts existed and that he had, in fact, obtained the necessary approval. Chavagnac and his son Tilladet and the other young men to whom he related the incident agreed with his interpretation [3] and tried to bring the unconvinced Cinq-Mars round to their way of thinking. They were sure that there was no longer anything to prevent them from striking "the blow" at Lyon, as Monsieur le Grand had once suggested.

Lyon had the honor of welcoming the King and the Cardinal on February 17. Monsieur de Guenitz, Guébriant's aide-de-camp, brought them a magnificent trophy, the Imperial banners seized at the victorious battle of Kempen. Richelieu and Louis worked feverishly throughout their brief stay, planning the campaign, while the conspiracy took shape around them. After they had extracted the King's supposed consent, the favorite's faction began to call themselves "Royalists" as opposed to "Cardinalists."

Cinq-Mars did his best to postpone the awful reckoning in the face of constant pressure from his friends. He finally yielded and played the part expected of him; as Chavagnac tells us, "having assembled us all, he informed us that he was on his way to the

---

[3] Chavagnac.

King and that he would rejoin us shortly." The young men gathered in the antechamber and waited for Cinq-Mars' order to strike. The Cardinal duly arrived, but his active intelligence network seems to have detected the danger. Contrary to usual custom, he was accompanied by de Bar, his Captain of the Guard, who entered the King's chamber with him. As Richelieu went in, Louis and Cinq-Mars were whispering excitedly, and they both seemed troubled at the sight of His Eminence. "They were both so embarrassed that the Cardinal realized they had been discussing something concerning him." The favorite, certainly, did not have the soul of a killer; he was not even an experienced conspirator. He lost his nerve in the Cardinal's terrible presence. "He could suffer Richelieu's presence no longer, left and told us to retire." Chavagnac goes on to say, "Many held him responsible for having lost the opportunity of killing him. Others have praised him for his prudence. In any case, he may have behaved like a good Christian; but he was certainly a poor politician." The opportunity never presented itself again.

On February 21 the King reviewed his troops in the Place Bellecour. The following day he attended a *Te Deum* in honor of the victory at Kempen. He then received the Catalan ambassadors, the Geneva delegation, and the Venetian ambassador. On February 23, "Royalists" and "Cardinalists," assassins and their hoped-for victims, Spanish allies and French soldiers all resumed their journey together.

At Valence the King solemnly presented the Cardinal's biretta to Mazarin, whose extreme humility was greatly noticed. Louis reached Narbonne on March 11, and the Cardinal two days later. "[Richelieu] had not seen His Majesty for ten or twelve days," wrote Henri Arnauld to Barillon. "This is supposed to demonstrate his lack of anxiety over the current rumor concerning Monsieur le Grand's power." Ever since Lyon, both the court and the general public sensed that the two rivals had drawn swords, but no one knew why. "Monsieur le Grand's affair puzzles even the most penetrating and experienced of observers," Arnauld records. Then a week later, he repeats, "The Monsieur le Grand affair continues to baffle the most experienced courtiers. . . . [Cinq-Mars] keeps telling his friends not to worry over him and that he is sure he has nothing to fear. . . ."

Monsieur le Grand's "court grew." Not at all unhappy at bottom that he had failed the assassination, he trusted in his charms and his cohorts, quite confident of his final victory and of the Cardinal's resulting ruin. Modesty and discretion seemed unnecessary in view of such certainty. He openly confessed to Monsieur la Luzerne one day "that he was not on good terms with the Cardinal, which affected and concerned him not at all and did not prevent him from having friends who would soon help him to achieve a remarkable feat . . . that he had so far only hinted at his intentions, but that he was on the point of announcing them in full." La Luzerne reported his statement to his friend Le Terrail, who in turn informed Maréchal de Brézé, who passed it on to Chavigny. A coup d'état in Spain's favor was thus anticipated while preparations were being made to launch a powerful offensive against her.

On March 12 the King sent Maréchal de La Meilleraye, the *Grand Maître* of the Artillery, to take Collioure. The Maréchal swiftly besieged the area and occupied Collioure within the week. His Majesty eagerly followed his progress, and this would have been a revelation to a perceptive observer. But Cinq-Mars had his head in the clouds and noticed nothing. He never understood that Louis may have longed for peace, but a glorious peace whose conditions he was to dictate a few months later. Louis XIII would never have consented to the kind of peace Fontrailles was arranging with Olivarès, Philip IV's Prime Minister.

When Fontrailles left Chilly, he galloped as far as Etampes where he caught the post coach. In his memoirs, Rochefort claims that he was accompanied at a distance "by a man often used for secret missions." The Cardinal's agents kept a close watch on this anonymous character, who is supposed to have hailed from Brussels, and thus, it is presumed, were put inadvertently on the conspirators' tracks. Rochefort mentions this "man from Brussels" several times and attributes a great deal of importance to him. When the fellow was captured, he promptly poisoned himself, whereupon Rochefort claims that he searched his corpse and found the original Spanish treaty. There is no factual evidence to corroborate this fantastic story, which is riddled with a number of gross inconsistencies. "The man from Brussels" was almost certainly a fantasy invented to conceal the real circumstances under which the treaty was seized.

We should therefore imagine Fontrailles and his valet setting off alone. Their journey was not without its dangers and misadventures, however. When Rochefort says that he was ordered "to find a convenient lookout post so I could observe those who entered Spain," he is probably telling the truth. The hunchback reached Limoges and met with the Duc de Bouillon, who was carefree. "The Spaniards," he said, "will give you more than you want."

Fontrailles asked him to be more careful, as all would be lost if the master of Sedan were arrested. The Duc shrugged and promised he would be cautious.

Fontrailles left Limoges and went to his home in Languedoc, where he asked d'Aubijoux to map out a route to Spain. D'Aubijoux proposed several alternatives, and Fontrailles finally chose to go via the "Aspe Valley and the so-called Caucasian port." Rochefort claims that he actually escorted him as far as Bayonne disguised as a messenger. In any event, the conspirator crossed the Pyrenees without more ado. He went to Huesca and then on to Saragossa, where the Viceroy was so angry at his secrecy that he made him leave without his valet at midnight. When he got to Madrid, Monsieur's letter of introduction gave him immediate access to the Count-Duke Olivarès. This haughty and portly favorite, whose portrait was painted by Velasquez, was an astute statesman, but in the long run he was completely outclassed by the Cardinal.

Fontrailles read him a long memorandum: "His Most Serene Highness the Duc d'Orléans and those who associate themselves with his cause promise to proffer a stronghold protected by a sizable army which they will use in their defense and in that of His Catholic Majesty should he enter France and need protection and refuge. . . . Monsieur le Duc d'Orléans will begin his offensive as soon as His Catholic Majesty's and His Imperial Majesty's armies have crossed the Rhine into France."

The Marquis was anxious to acquit himself like a great diplomat and withheld the vital names of Bouillon, Cinq-Mars, and Sedan until the clauses of the treaty had been accepted, which explains his archconvolutions. His efforts intensely irritated the hidalgo. "We have often been deceived, and we will agree to nothing that is not accompanied by full guarantees."

And since Fontrailles would not yield, Olivarès responded by coolly offering him his pass back to France. Fontrailles was forced to give in. Olivarès seemed pleasantly surprised at the extent of the conspiracy. His pleasure did not prevent him from haggling over all the conditions of the treaty for four whole days. Finally exasperated, Fontrailles proclaimed, "I am not surprised that your affairs are in such a bad state. Here you are amusing yourself over insignificant details while Perpignan is at stake. If Perpignan falls, you will lose Catalonia forever." Olivarès was amazed at his impertinence, but he did not "amuse" himself any longer.

The treaty was secretly signed on March 13. Fontrailles was then accorded the singular honor of being presented to His Catholic Majesty. The treaty was resewn into the lining of his doublet along with a letter from Philip IV to Gaston d'Orléans:

> My good brother, I received with deep joy the proposals made in Your Highness' name for the general good, for the peace of Christendom; in a word, for the establishment of a solid peace. . . . It is essential that solidarity underline this undertaking and that all parties concerned be prudent and single-minded and that your good intentions and resolve be enlisted in service of God and the general good, two causes which have been ill-served in our lifetime.

When Fontrailles reached Huesca, this time in the company of several people, he found waiting for him his Béarn guide who had conducted him across the mountains. The man informed Fontrailles that he had been followed and would certainly be arrested should he return by the same route. The hunchback made for "the port of Benasque [Venasque]." There were no unpleasant incidents, and he returned to Languedoc safe and sound, where d'Aubijoux was awaiting him. The two then set out for Narbonne to report to Monsieur le Grand.

We have no way of knowing how much Richelieu knew by the end of March. One of his agents had trailed Fontrailles as far as the border, but had not intercepted him coming back. A letter from the Nuncio in Madrid informed him "that a certain Frenchman was seen for two or three days in the Count-Duke's antechamber, and he had a long meeting with the Minister," but no name was mentioned.

The Cardinal did not act on this information, however. Three explanations are possible: He may not have known the precise identity of the conspirators' emissary and did not want to hazard a wild guess; he may have been reluctant to cause a scandal at a time when his relations with the King were so poor; or his agent may have been unusually incompetent and had lost track of Fontrailles' movements.

Fontrailles had a secret meeting with Cinq-Mars and informed him of the successful outcome of his trip. He was more terrified than proud of the whole business, however; he had had the unpleasant sensation of being trailed since he left Huesca. The Master of the Horse, still sure of his good luck, tried to dissipate Fontrailles' fears. Their roles were ironically reversed.

They agreed to send a reliable gentleman, Monsieur de Montmort, to inform Monsieur. D'Aubijoux would take him the treaty when they were positive that the coast was clear. Fontrailles then requested permission to go to England. He did not dare to reappear at Court, "because Monsieur le Cardinal was capable of having him arrested on the slightest pretext and, given his great authority, of having him put to the question [tortured]. . . . He did not know how he would bear up under such pressures." [4] Cinq-Mars pro-

---

tested. "He replied that, now that I had begun to risk so much, I should follow the matter through to the end, but he agreed that I should not return to Court."

Fontrailles and d'Aubijoux left for Toulouse. They saw de Thou at Carcassonne, who told them that his mission to Mercoeur and Beaufort had failed. They shared their separate disillusionments and then parted.

In the midst of all this gloom, another "favorable circumstance" presented itself. Paradoxically, a Spanish defeat served the cause of the Spanish allies. At the beginning of April, Monsieur de la Mothe-Houdancourt routed the Spanish forces which were to reinforce Collioure, which fell soon afterward. This victory paved the way for the siege of Perpignan. Louis was eager to conduct the campaign personally.

At this vital hour Richelieu suffered an attack of malaria, and a cruel abscess appeared on his right arm, preventing him from accompanying the King and participating in a siege which promised to be as glorious and as crucial as that of La Rochelle. Richelieu's indisposition thus left the field open to his young rival. Henri was overjoyed and relished the prospect of having the King to himself while his enemy languished. When they set out from Narbonne, everyone believed in his ultimate triumph.

Fourteen

"If He Had Let Himself Be Bored. . ."

HENRI WAS SO certain of success that he
was not afraid of, in his words, "lifting the mask," and before they
left Narbonne, he declared himself the head of the party. Richelieu
took Henri's temerity seriously, and the two antagonists started
gathering allies in preparation for the trial of strength ahead.

The Cardinal was the first to score. He succeeded in gaining
maréchal's batons for two of his loyal supporters, Guébriant and La
Mothe-Houdancourt. This success was followed by an unexpected reverse which lost him the ground he had won. Maréchal
de Schomberg, son of the Schomberg who had defeated the great
Montmorency, was generally regarded as a "Cardinalist." He was
given joint command of the French army at Perpignan, although
La Meilleraye, the cardinal's nephew and Montmorency's co-com-
mander, was offended by this action. Schomberg immediately joined
the army at the head of five hundred gentlemen and declared himself in favor of Monsieur le Grand. This was a victory for Cinq-
Mars, who now had a partisan to share the command of the army
with his mortal enemy and brother-in-law La Meilleraye.

Richelieu received the bad news on his sickbed and retaliated by
asking the King to give Gassion a command in the Roussillon army.
The King decided to send Gassion to Flanders. The letter which
the worthy Gassion received from de Noyers at the time is most
revealing:

The time has come for you to declare yourself; here we are
distinguishing friend from foe. . . . His Eminence has asked
me to write to you and assure you of his good will. . . .
Among his regrets, not the least is that you are no longer near
him. . . . Don't fail to express your gratitude to him because
right now one compliment carries the weight of two. Do not
take public rumors too seriously; court gossip seems to be
deceiving even the sharpest of wits.[1]

Despite this last phrase, the Cardinal felt seriously threatened
and hurried off an unctuous letter to Maréchal Schomberg's wife
in an attempt to regain her husband's loyalties. The generals and
the courtiers were now expected to choose sides and pledge allegiance to Richelieu or the Master of the Horse. The younger generation declared themselves promptly and aggressively. Twenty-two
royal guardsmen were unequivocally Cinq-Mars' men. Cinq-Mars
cockily dubbed them "My Twenty-Two" after Henri III's "My
Forty-Five."

Cinq-Mars knew that the Queen's backing would cause a number
of valuable people to join him. He would entrust de Thou with the
task of approaching Anne. He sent word to de Thou and asked him
to join him immediately near Perpignan.

De Thou returned to Paris and went to see the Comte de Brienne,
a relative of his, who also belonged to Anne's House of Austria.
He asked him to obtain blank sheets of paper which bore the
Queen's signature. These would then be transformed into letters to
various officers requesting their support. Brienne, a moderate and
cautious man, was horrified by the demand. He refused, then re-
considered because he feared the matter might fall into less trustworthy hands.

He approached Anne, and to his amazement she immediately
agreed. "I had scarcely opened my mouth on the subject when Her
Majesty consented. I then said to her, 'Her Majesty should be wary

[1] Archives des Affaires Étrangères.

of entrusting such papers to anyone, even to me; for although I know I could not abuse them, they could fall into such hands as would give you cause to be sorry.'"

Brienne also tried to dissuade de Thou from his complicity with Cinq-Mars, "telling him that far from being as fond of Cinq-Mars as he used to be, the King had started having his doubts about him and even found him insufferable." But de Thou did not listen. "I know," Brienne continues, "that my arguments would not conquer his blind devotion. I went down on my knees to him to beg him to have more faith in my words, and finally I predicted that his attachment to the Master of the Horse would eventually destroy him."

De Thou was disturbed by Brienne's conviction, but he would not abandon his friend. The Queen asked him to dispel any reservations he may have had. She received him and, according to Fontrailles, told him that the Spanish Treaty had been signed. Monsieur had been as good as his word and had just informed her. He then sent her a copy of the explosive document. François was shocked by the news, since it was the first he had heard of an agreement with the King of Spain. He continued to have a poor opinion of the whole business.

The Cardinal was an excellent propagandist. His agents started circulating the rumor that Monsieur le Grand had lost the King's favor. The rumor sounded credible, considering the King's variable moods, but at that juncture, the rumor was absolutely false.

De Thou soon heard the rumor, and he did not dismiss it. He was naturally an anxious sort of man, and Brienne's warnings and the Queen's revelations had shaken his faith. He had felt the plot was being mismanaged and that Cinq-Mars was being too flippant. Before leaving, he expressed his doubts to the Queen and begged her to be careful.

On his way south he met with Fontrailles, whose recent mission had drastically reduced his old audacity and confidence. The two discussed the whole situation at length. The hunchback was staggered to learn that, despite Monsieur's formal orders, de Thou knew of the treaty. He was doubly shocked to hear that the Queen had been the informant. These "slips" augered ill. Fontrailles decided to take his apprehensions to the Duc d'Orléans at Chambord.

Gaston was also uneasy. He sent the Comte de Brion to the King begging to be excused "that his poor health prevented him from coming to celebrate the victory at Catalonia." Brion also took a letter to Cinq-Mars to hand to the King. The letter, an indictment of the Cardinal, was Monsieur's way of evaluating Cinq-Mars' power.

Richelieu quickly reacted to Brion's arrival in spite of his indisposition. Much to Louis' annoyance, Richelieu had begun to dispense with his usual formalities toward him. Now he sent the King a curt message which Louis felt was little short of an order: "His Majesty will please disregard Monsieur de Brion and dismiss him as promptly as possible. . . . I enclose the answer His Majesty should make to Monsieur's letter, although I have not yet seen it."

There is no way of knowing whether Cinq-Mars withstood Monsieur's test. The Cardinal continued to pretend that Cinq-Mars had no power whatever, while his actions proved that he actually believed the contrary to be true. The worried Minister spent sleepless nights plotting his course of action. As soon as he received Father Carré's long letter, he instructed Baron de Brassac, the Queen's Master of the Household, and his wife, a lady in waiting, to watch Anne of Austria closely. Despite their proximity to the Queen, the Brassacs proved ineffectual spies and detected nothing unusual in her conduct. Richelieu knew nonetheless that the Spanish lady was an artful intriguer. On the eve of an imminent crisis, he thought it impolitic that she should have the future of France in her power. If anything happened to the King, she would obviously use her children to bargain for her survival.

Historians have speculated endlessly on the reasons for Louis' apparently "inexplicable decision" to send his wife to Fontainebleau and threaten to remove her children from her keeping. They had parted on good terms in February, and then in April, on the eve of the Perpignan siege, Louis suddenly attacked her. It is the timing of the incident, rather than the incident itself, which has given rise to the confusion. Louis had always toyed with the idea of removing his children from the care of a woman he regarded as worthless. Many have favored the theory that Cinq-Mars was responsible, but this is obviously absurd. The favorite depended on the Queen's support and could not afford to indulge in such a folly. Anne could easily ruin him.

The Cardinal is the most likely culprit. The tortuousness of the maneuver, calculated to intimidate Anne of Austria, is typical of Richelieu's manipulation of people and events for his own ends. Without intervening in person, all Richelieu had to do was to re-awaken Louis' own fears, and the King would react according to plan.

He succeeded beyond his hopes. On April 30, Anne wrote Richelieu a letter: "Having my children removed from me at such a tender age is unbearably painful to me. . . ." Richelieu did not reply. "Has Monsieur le Cardinal abandoned me?" Anne sobbed to Monsieur de Brassac. Anne was left with the sword of Damocles hanging over her.

Richelieu won another round and lost no time in securing further success. He acquired the services of the Duc de Bouillon's young brother, the Vicomte de Turenne. He also had the loyalty of the Prince de Condé, who commanded Paris. This removed another worry from the Cardinal's list. Richelieu continued to devote himself to his greater tasks, drawing in the vast net he had cast over Europe.

His health deteriorated steadily. "A new abscess has formed on my arm," he wrote to de Noyers. "And the old ulcer which God and nature opened is suppurating pus in quantity. My physicians, to console me, talk of playing with their knives again. I do not have the strength or the courage to face such torment at present. I pray that God will help me obey His will." His body wracked him, but even worse was the terrible anxiety that heightened his fever. He became increasingly depressed and dispirited. His two faithful secretaries of state, Chavigny and de Noyers, were his lifeline to the King, but he realized he was losing his hold over Louis. Seeing the King in the clutches of his rival, the powerless Cardinal must have felt like the inventor who sees his creation destroyed by inexperienced hands, like the father who witnesses the ruin of his son by a worthless hussy. On the eve of a crucial siege, Richelieu's work, welfare, and future depended upon the emotional relationship between a King with one foot in the grave and a boy who was gathering rosebuds.

The siege of Perpignan is a perfect example of courtly war. Before Louis invaded the area, he suggested that the governor send a messenger to Philip IV to ask for help. The governer refused. Later, when the Spaniard ran out of money, Louis entreated him not to touch his church treasuries. The governor protested "that he had never even contemplated such a notion." These gentlemanly exchanges were punctuated with cannonades and fierce battles.

The soldiers flourished on the yields of the fertile lands. Louis installed himself in Jan Pouquet's farm and followed the operations with his usual military lust. Around him, intrigues and rivalries ran rampant. The army was clearly divided into "Royalists" and "Cardinalists." The King's immediate entourage was convinced that the favorite would triumph. Montglat observed that "he was so certain of his victory that everyone hung about him in such droves that one was crushed by the crowd whenever one tried to get near him."

Henri was delighted by his popularity, which he encouraged with gifts. He later denied his generosity, but he did relieve himself of a good sixteen hundred pistoles. Monsieur de Campis, a lieutenant colonel, received three hundred. Where money failed to buy his allegiance, he tried seduction. There was one captain of the French guards, Abraham Fabert, whom he had failed to entice. Fabert was an excellent soldier whom Louis liked and respected despite his humble origins. One day when the army halted to rest, Monsieur le Grand approached Fabert and asked him to join him in a game of quoits. The captain accepted, and the two men dismounted and left the company of the royal escort.

Cinq-Mars ingenuously blurted out his intentions. He was so sure of the excellence of his cause that he thought the upright soldier would instantly come into his camp. But he was brutally reproved: According to Tallemant, Fabert declared, "I have made it my motto to become involved in my friends' interests and never in their passions. Any man who insults me by asking me to dishonor myself releases me from bestowing on him the regard and consideration I would otherwise owe him."

This affront did not really disillusion Cinq-Mars. He was reassured by another incident. The King had stopped sending a messenger to inquire after his Minister's progress, which further upset the ailing Cardinal. Cinq-Mars' friends adopted Richelieu's own tactics and started circulating the rumor that the Cardinal was finished. Richelieu steeled himself against the inevitable stab in the back. Then the Duc d'Enghien, who had never forgiven the Cardinal for making him his nephew but who hated Cinq-Mars far worse for his impertinence at Arras, offered to kill the favorite for Richelieu. "The Marquis de Pienne heard about the proposal and told Ruvigny who in turn told Monsieur le Grand and advised him to inform the King. The next day Cinq-Mars told Ruvigny that 'the King said, "Dear friend, take some of my guards for yourself."' . . . Ruvigny looked him in the eye and asked, 'Why have you not done so? You are not telling the truth.' Cinq-Mars blushed. 'At least,' Ruvigny added, 'Why don't you call upon Monsieur le Duc with two or three friends and show him that you are not in the least afraid of him?'"

Henri was piqued, but he took his friend's advice. He and Ruvigny paid Enghien a visit and found him playing cards. The young prince either had changed his mind or thought the occasion inopportune. He received Monsieur le Grand with manifest delight and was extremely jovial. Cinq-Mars was convinced he had won him over.

He would have been wiser to devote more of his time and energies to his King. Louis, among so many cares and physical miseries,
was delighted at the chance of enjoying several weeks of his
friend's company without the constant intervention of the Cardinal.
He had no idea of supporting any kind of coup d'état, but like
many others he prayed that he would soon be released by Richelieu's timely death.

If Louis had not been so repressed and inscrutable, he would
have averted a number of misfortunes. If Cinq-Mars had been
more patient and perceptive and had dissembled more, he would
eventually have achieved all his desires. Unhappily, Louis was
uncommunicative, and Henri had little self-control. In Marie's absence, he seemed incapable of being all that she had trained him to
be. At the very same time when he should have been doubly
thoughtful, kind, and pleasing, he relapsed into his capricious, impertinent, freedom-loving ways.

Monsieur le Grand had become the idol of the younger generation, the head of a faction that robbed His Eminence of peace of
mind; and since this image did not tally with an ingratiating and
anxious favorite, he rejected his royal duties. Tallemant reports:
"He resumed his former behavior toward the King, and the more
the King wished him to be at his side, the more he sought to be
away. When his friends counseled him to be more loyal to his King,
he thanked them for their advice but told them he could no longer
bear the King's evil-smelling breath . . . or his ridiculous way of
life."

He went out of his way to be as defiant and insolent as possible in
spite of the austere King's disapproval. One day, as the short de
Noyers approached His Majesty in full military regalia, his sword
trailing on the ground, Cinq-Mars burst out laughing. He openly
tried to pick a quarrel with La Meilleraye and finally succeeded in
having a fierce argument with him over some military question.
The King finally took advantage of the opportunity and said, "It is
very like you to argue with a man who has years of military experience behind him, when you have none."

"But, Sire," protested the *enfant terrible,* "if one has good judgment and sharp wit, one knows things without having seen them." Then he fell back on his old trick and sulked. "In spite of what Ruvigny said to him," Tallemant reports, "he never made any attempt to reconcile himself to the King."

When de Noyers arrived at court, he was surprised by what he found. He immediately informed the Cardinal: "I arrived yesterday, the twenty-eighth [of April], to find that the Pyrenean fogs have settled over the Court itself. If only that sun [Richelieu] which has in the past dispelled such gloom and confusion were strong enough to appear now and make everything bright and clear again! . . ." It is significant that Richelieu was worried by the news. He was so afraid of the favorite that his one concern was to prevent La Meilleraye's disgrace. He wrote back to de Noyers, "If it is true that Monsieur le Grand and La Meilleraye have quarreled . . . see to it that they be reconciled at the King's command so that all goes smoothly."

Henri, however, refused to salvage the situation. Despite the cautioning words of de Thou and Ruvigny, he decided to give himself up to a totally debauched life. Marie was farther away than ever. If Henri had been asked to account for his behavior, he would have glibly answered that his former tactics with the King hadn't produced such bad results. Times had changed, however. Louis XIII was engaged in a pathetic struggle against his illness and had no taste for his former masochistic pleasures. He needed to be comforted and tended with affection, not with quarrels and lovers' jealousies. Cinq-Mars was foolhardy enough to ignore the King's displeasure. He prolonged the row and provoked several other unpleasant incidents, without taking the King's mounting exasperation into account.

In the past their differences had only been known to a select few. Now suddenly they became common knowledge. Once, as Fabert was informing the King on the progress of the siege, Cinq-Mars, who had not forgiven Fabert, kept interrupting him. Louis' resentment exploded. "Monsieur le Grand, you are wrong. You have no experience to justify your contradicting a man of experience. No doubt you spent the whole night inspecting our fortifications because you speak of them so wisely! Go away! You are unbearable. I know you like to give the impression that you have stayed up helping me run the affairs of the kingdom, and you spend your evenings in my wardrobe reading novels with my valets!"

"Your Majesty will do me the favor of explaining what he means by that," Cinq-Mars retorted, wounded to the quick. He turned to leave, and as he passed Fabert, snapped, "I thank you, Monsieur Fabert."

"What's that?" Louis demanded. "Did he threaten you?"

"No, Sire," Fabert replied calmly. "One does not make threats in Your Majesty's presence, nor would any be tolerated."

Louis could not hold his tongue. "I must tell you, Monsieur Fabert! No man is more corrupt and displeasing! He is the world's greatest ingrate. He has kept me waiting whole hours in my carriage while he indulged in some despicable vice. An entire kingdom could not finance his extravagance. He has some three hundred pairs of boots at this moment. I have been sick of him these past six months." [2]

This last sentence, so often cited, has led many historians astray. They have concluded that the King had ceased to love his favorite, have thought to have discovered the reason for his future conduct, and sometimes have thought that the conspiracy had no solid foundation.

If Louis had really been "sick and tired" of Cinq-Mars for the last six months, all that had happened during that time—Richelieu's panic, the Lyon affair—would be incomprehensible. When Louis spoke thus to Fabert, he was exasperated by his favorite's "despicable vices" and by his rank "ingratitude." His anger, his obvious hurt feelings, his scorn ("three hundred pairs of boots") are all indicative of his involved concern. They do not express the waning of an affection, which is still patently strong and binding. If he had

---

[2] Tallemant and Father Barre, *Vie de Fabert.*

become indifferent to Henri, he would have had no compunction whatever about getting rid of him as he had Baradas, Saint-Simon, and Marie de Hautefort.

Cinq-Mars, however, was finally shaken. He was so alarmed by the incident that he went to see de Noyers, whom he had insulted the previous day. He asked the Secretary of State to be peacemaker, but de Noyers refused and immediately wrote to Chavigny:

> N . . . came to see me about ten o'clock this evening and spent three quarters of an hour with me. He was friendly rather than indifferent. He told me that he had suffered three blasts from His Majesty's bad mood in the past two days and that he had endured them peaceably because of the King's indisposition. But if the King were in better health, he assured me he would speak out. I didn't get into details and passed the time in civilities and jokes. I believe he had his reasons for coming and had hoped I might effect a reconciliation, but I did not react to the suggestion for obvious reasons.[3]

The following day he wrote again: "Everything continues to be as I have already described. It has been a very good day. The cold and unpleasantness has [*sic*] lasted six days and warmth has not returned." The old warmth never really returned. The Princesse's absence may have had an enormous effect on Cinq-Mars. As it was, he did not have the courage or stamina to play the part required of him. He refused to do violence to himself and control his impetuousness, withdrew from the struggle by sulking and bickering, lost his ground, and gave way. Anne of Austria later wrote, "One wonders what might have happened if only Monsieur le Grand had let himself be bored for a few hours."

---

[3] Letter of May 14, Archives des Affaires Étrangères.

Fifteen

Two Dying Men and the Queen

"EVEN THE MOST adept courtiers are reduced to waiting to see what this intrigue is all about," Henri Arnauld wrote to Barillon. In both factions, confusion reigned.

On May 20, Fontrailles finally arrived at Chambord after many comings and goings, to find Gaston d'Orléans calm and quite confident that he would soon hear of the Cardinal's death. The Marquis soon dampened his spirits. Still in the grip of a strange panic, he told His Highness that the Cardinal was merely pretending to be dying, that Monsieur le Grand "had lost the King's favor." The conspiracy was doomed, and "that it was now necessary to safeguard his person and that of those who had served him!"

Monsieur was alarmed, but he did not lose his nerve. He was concerned that Bouillon had not yet given them their passes into Sedan. D'Aubijoux was dispatched to the Duc to obtain them. At Cinq-Mars' first signal, everyone was to meet. They chose an "inn at Moulins where a trustworthy man would be on the constant alert to receive Monsieur le Grand's messenger." In the meantime, the Prince would make it known that he would soon be going to Bourbon-l'Archambault to take the waters, so as to get near Moulins without rousing anyone's suspicions.

Once he had seen to these arrangements, Fontrailles made for the royal encampment to which he had only recently sworn he would never return; he had gone as far as staging a mock duel to give himself a good pretext for disappearing. The unstable Cinq-Mars was alternating between temerity and depression. He was not the man to change the course of history. The Master of the Horse had some 30,000 francs sent from Paris to a Lyon banker and carried out a strange transaction with one of his friends, Monsieur de Gué, who was Treasurer of France at Lyon: "I am sending you this courier with a bill of exchange, which I would ask you to cash into Spanish pistoles, since louis are not in current use down here. I would ask you to keep them for me until I let you know how I want them transferred to me safely." He also sought to safeguard himself with "fifty gentlemen kept in readiness in the Auvergne."[1]

While the conspirators thus began to prepare for defeat, their enemy was convinced of his own imminent downfall. On May 23, the Cardinal drafted his will, in which he distributed vast sums of money. He could not even sign it, as his right arm was paralyzed. He was given two days to live. But the two days elapsed, and the steely wizard bounded back and got to work on a counteroffensive. He told de Noyers to approach Father Sirmond, the King's confessor, and invite him to put pressure on the august penitent. Then he sent Daridol, one of Chavigny's adjuncts, to Holland to obtain a practically preworded letter from the Prince of Orange. The Prince was asked to write "that his confidence in my [the Cardinal's] capacities is what binds him to France's interests and dissuades him from accepting the offers made him by Spain." Father Sirmond agreed immediately, but the Prince of Orange kept a discreet silence.[2] Richelieu must have really thought he was in terrible danger to humiliate himself before a prince whom he was already subsidizing heavily.

He used very different tactics with the Queen. He saw through her motives and knew where her sympathies were. François de Thou was away, and Anne had no way of knowing what was

---

[1] Henri Arnauld.
[2] He answered on July 18 when circumstances had changed.

happening. Brassac was ordered to aggravate her anxieties about her children.

All these maneuvers were of no comfort to the worried Minister. He could not decide whether there really was a new plot to kill him or whether the opposition was merely frightening him and intimidating him as he was Anne. In any case, his obsession that he was being threatened with extermination was communicated to his entourage.

His niece, the Duchesse d'Aiguillon, received an anonymous letter in Paris which said, "You would be wise to warn His Eminence to be careful of his person, because it is known that his enemies are trying to persuade the King to have him arrested as soon as he is well, and they are taking every step to arrive at this." The Duchesse alerted Chavigny.

The Cardinal no longer felt safe. He instructed his doctors to inform Louis that the climate of Narbonne was detrimental to his health. Louis did not object to his departure. Richelieu left Narbonne immediately, but Montglat is wrong when he says that "he departed without taking leave of the King, without knowing where he was going." The Cardinal had, in fact, decided to go to the fortress at Tarascon, where he could easily defend himself against an attack. He did not rule out the possibility of being forced to withdraw to the papal refuge at Avignon as the last resort. He did not budge from Narbonne before taking a thousand precautions and filling a mountain of blank paper. His mind was incredibly agile for such a very sick man.

First of all he wrote a carefully worded letter to the King. "I am leaving, following Your Majesty's counsel, which cannot but be good coming as it does from such a good master. . . . With the help of God's grace I shall accept whatever change He may give my malady. I shall be happy as long as I know that Your Majesty is well and that he has taken Perpignan."

He handed his Secretaries of State a volume of instructions which mapped out the positions they were to take and the lines they should adopt.

It is certain that my innocence is under attack. Silence only gives the wicked a means of achieving their ends. We will use the most innocent means of defense to prevail upon the King to undo the evil plans. . . .

The Brussels and Cologne newspapers, the Queen Mother's preparations to terminate her exile, all the purchases of vehicles and transport mules, Madame de Chevreuse's revealing communications, all the correspondence traversing the whole country, all the reports from every court in Italy, the rumors that stir the armies, the hopes nourished by the Spaniards . . . Monsieur's decision to stay away, contrary to his promises, perhaps waiting for lightning to strike . . . all these things have persuaded me to inform the King about it all so that he may restore such order as pleases him and counteract the rumors which are fast destroying his affairs.

. . . Monsieur de Thou and Monsieur de Chavagnac must be sent away. I believe Monsieur de Chavigny and Monsieur de Noyers can be frank with Monsieur de Schomberg when he approaches them, and should tell him that he must declare himself openly and not remain an amphibian in the opinion of the public.

After many more such instructions, Richelieu, carried away by his own energy, addressed a moving exhortation to the King. "Had God called me, Your Majesty would now be calculating his loss. The loss would be the worse if my life were taken at your behest, as Your Majesty would then himself lose all the trust and confidence that he has won."

Chavigny's and de Noyers' blind devotion to their patron had already made Louis wary of them both. Richelieu began to look for a spokesman who could double as informer and was not suspected of partiality. He was fortunate in finding such a man in the First Gentleman of the Bedchamber, Gabriel de Rochechouart, Marquis de Mortemart (father of the future Madame de Montespan), whom Louis was fond of. Richelieu always called him "the faithful Mortemart."

He was certain he had provided for all contingencies, and yet he was as anxious as ever when he set off on his enormous red litter. However, his friends in Paris, the Prince de Condé, Chancellor Séguier, and the Duchesse d'Aiguillon, appeared perfectly calm and spread the news of His Eminence's excellent relations with the King, of his ease and contentment, and of his restored health and energies. Richelieu was nonetheless fleeing. The formidable Cardinal, the object of universal admiration and terror, still master of the kingdom, had been routed by a love-sick youngster. He was a shattered, insecure, and anxious man who trembled in anticipation of the future.

On May 27, torrential rain pelted down on Perpignan, severing communications and toppling the French Army's tents. The rain lasted three days. An attack from the besieged was feared, but the city was paralyzed by famine. According to one prisoner, the Governor was seen to share a cat with his noble guests. The King was suffering from hemorrhoids, and his health was affected by the rains. It was rumored that Monsieur le Grand was going to take him back to Saint-Germain or Fontainebleau. The Cardinal was deeply disturbed. Louis' departure would remove him from his sphere of influence and leave the field open to the favorite. On his way through Béziers, Adge, and Saint-Privas, the Minister wrote to the King every day trying to elicit his sympathy. "I do not need evidence," he wrote on June 4, "of His Majesty's affection because it has always been constant, even when great efforts were made to remove it." [3] Louis reacted to the entreaty by reverting to the tone of their best days. "Despite the groundless rumors that are abroad, I love you more than ever. We have been together too long ever to be separated."

In fact, the King was furious with Monsieur le Grand. Henri missed his Princesse too much and began to detest Louis more and more. Henri would finish their unpleasant scenes by wishing for

---

[3] Archives des Affaires Etrangères.

his freedom, though he knew he would only be free if his tyrannical benefactor died. Someone asked him how the King was, and he replied, "Oh, he is dragging along."

Louis sensed Henri's revulsion and felt humiliated by the realization that he was nothing more than a tottering old man for the magnificent youth. He would dearly have loved to be able to dazzle him with reports of his former exploits, but he was no longer the hero of 1629 who turned to his despairing generals and proudly said, "I will not send my soldiers to the slaughter, but I will lead them myself." [4]

On June 4, the Cardinal sent His Majesty a sentimental letter. Chavigny had just arrived at the camp, and the Duc d'Enghien wrote, "Monsieur de Chavigny has returned and has not as much as mentioned Monsieur le Grand to the King since he has found everything so well disposed that he has not believed it necessary to say anything. First off, the King and Monsieur le Grand are at odds. Moreover, the King is well disposed and even indescribably tender toward the Cardinal."

Louis was ill from the fourth to the eighth of June and kept to his rooms. Henri could easily have reinstated himself in Louis' affections with a single word, a gesture, a smile. But he seems not to have wanted to do so. He may have found himself incapable of going against his instincts, or he may have nourished the hope that Louis would soon die. Louis seemed to recover on June 8, but then two days later he felt "somewhat unwell" again. His doctors ordered him to take the waters. He decided to leave the encampment and go first to Narbonne, which he reached on the evening of June 11. Cinq-Mars met Fontrailles there, who was carrying a message from Monsieur. Fontrailles informed him of Gaston's arrangements. He also received a letter from Marie, which said, "All your plans are as much common knowledge here in Paris as it is that the Seine passes beneath the Pont-Neuf."

When Fontrailles read this, he panicked and advised the favorite

---

[4] Spoken at the Battle of the Pas de Suze, when the cavalry attacked the enemy's cannons.

to withdraw immediately to Sedan. Henri hesitated, almost gave in, and then drew back. "I thought I had settled the matter," the hunchback wrote later, "when he turned and asked if I had informed Monsieur that he would soon be joining him. To which I answered that I had not done so since he had not asked me to."

"In that case," Cinq-Mars said, "I shall send Montmort to get him to set a date when we can arrive in Sedan together."

Fontrailles begged him "not to risk his life for the sake of custom." But the Master of the Horse would not listen. This time he was not wrong to ignore the advice. If he had arrived at Sedan alone, he would have been reduced to the sad role of a fugitive, losing all hope of success and his Princesse as well. If he arrived in the company of the King's brother, however, his position would be vastly different. Moreover, he could not afford to act precipitately at this juncture. Marie Gonzaga knew nothing of the Spanish Treaty because Henri had not wanted to involve her in such a dangerous secret.[5] The "plans" she referred to were his plottings against the Cardinal. His greater ambitions still had a chance of success if Richelieu or Louis XIII died or if he tried to make amends with the King. Henri still believed he held the trump card in reserve, and it never occurred to him that the treaty had been discovered. He wrote a reassuring letter to his beloved. It was to be his last letter to her.

The Baron de Brassac understood the importance of his mission. His every action proves his devotion to the Cardinal. He continued to fan Anne of Austria's anxieties. By the beginning of June, Anne was convinced by his insinuations and by the King's and the Cardinal's silence that her children were about to be taken away from her.

The conspiracy seemed to be marking time; the Cardinal lived on, and the Perpignan campaign was drawing to a successful conclusion. Richelieu was obviously not as slow and weak as his enemies. Anne, disappointed by the conspiracy which had shown no results

---

[5] Avenel.

whatever, began to think that by the restoration of the half-dead Minister she might well avoid a catastrophe, save her position, and gain herself a bit of time. This last consideration was of paramount importance to the vigorous woman who had so much to gain from the two invalids whose inheritance she intended to receive. In these circumstances, it is not surprising that she wasted no sleep over her feelings for Marie Gonzaga, the devotion of de Thou, and her alliance with Monsieur. She could not afford to have a conscience. The princes of the time, even the most devout, placed themselves above the moral considerations of mere mortals.

On June 7, the Queen instructed Brassac to inform the Cardinal that she had firmly decided "to be of his party, knowing that His Eminence would return the compliment and not abandon her." Brassac's next letter to Richelieu the following day contains a significant incident: "Her Majesty has sent word to Chavigny through Monsieur de Gras." The Queen's precise message is unknown, but it seems likely that she not only told him of the existence of the conspiracy but even sent him the text of the Spanish treaty. We know from Madame de Motteville that several copies of the treaty were passing from hand to hand.

All manner of attempts were immediately made to conceal the identity of the real informant. The names of Schomberg, Béthune, Abbé de La Rivière, who was Monsieur's confidant, and the Duchesse de Chevreuse, an enemy of Bouillon, were bandied about. Tallemant, whose authority we do not question any more than Avenel's,[6] was not taken in, however. "They claim," writes Tallemant, "that a messenger who missed [Richelieu] at Narbonne arrived with a packet from the Maréchal de Brézé, viceroy of Catalonia, who in four lines informed him that they had found Monsieur le Grand's—or rather Monsieur's—treaty with Spain on a shipwrecked vessel along the coast, and that he enclosed it. This is the rumor that is going around, but it is not the truth, and those who have believed it are overly credulous."

---

[6] Cf. Antoine Adam.

Researchers have discovered an obscure French agent in Madrid, a certain Pujols, who may have sent the document—or so Monsieur de Termes claims. But the anonymous commentator of Monsieur de Termes' memoirs then writes, "I remember that when Monsieur de Fabert told me about this matter in 1659, he said, 'I should like to be able to name the person who gave Cinq-Mars' treaty to the Cardinal. But I cannot satisfy you until two persons have died.'" The following year, Gaston d'Orléans died and the commentator reports, "Fabert told me on another occasion, 'Only one person has to die now before I can tell you who it was that handed in the treaty.' And I believe the person that M. de Fabert meant was Queen Anne of Austria."

Voiture once tried to make Chavigny confess: "You insist on safeguarding this secret, yet Monsieur le Prince has whispered it abroad."

"Monsieur does not know it," said Chavigny, "and when he does he will never dare reveal it." [7]

Brienne is enigmatic: "Monsieur was not betrayed, as it was rumored, but the mystery was revealed by a totally unexpected source." Even La Rochefoucauld, who was so devoted to the Queen, does not rush to exonerate her in his memoirs. "It seems best," he says, "to give credence to the most harmless opinion and believe that the treaty was truly found in the Spanish courier's bag, which is usually searched when couriers pass through Paris."

There may be no formal proof, but there is little doubt that Anne of Austria, believing she was in a trap, saved herself by sacrificing the friends whom she had encouraged to undertake the dangerous conspiracy. These ruthless sacrifices enabled her both to keep her children and to prepare for her Regency. It is interesting to speculate whether the devout Spanish matron lived to regret her actions and whether they were included in the penances which she imposed on herself toward the end of her life and which finally killed her.

---

[7] Tallemant.

Sixteen

"Marvelous Discoveries"

PARIS WAS IN a state of anxiety. The defeat
of the French Army at Honnecourt inspired the fear of another
invasion. This fear was aggravated by new troop levies and by the
order issued to civil militia colonels to have their companies in
readiness. Some evidence suggests, however, that these emergency
measures were not taken against any Spanish advance but against
a threatened coup d'état.

Richelieu had entrusted the capital to completely reliable men
who saw to it that no disquieting news was released and who
vigorously disseminated optimistic opinions. However, the public
did have a confused inkling of the Cardinal's illness, of the pre-
cariousness of his position, and of some of the favorite's activities.
A thousand incredible tales moved about the city. There was a
general feeling that nothing was impossible: The King and the
Minister might die; there could well be a civil war, or an enemy
invasion. Frightened and wary, people woke up surprised to find
that nothing remarkable had happened during the night.

The Cardinal was no less fearful when he arrived at Arles on
June 9. His physical maladies continued to exacerbate his torment,
and he felt everything was lost. He was in one of his lethal depres-
sions when a savior presented himself. Historians have been unable to
identify this mysterious guardian angel, but we believe him to be
Monsieur le Gras, who left the Queen on June 7 to deliver a mes-

sage from her to Chavigny. It is known that he was carrying a crucial document. Whatever it was, it produced a literal resurrection. No sooner had he read it than the Cardinal dismissed everyone from his presence except Charpentier, his first secretary, whom he then asked, "Bring me an enema, for I am upset." Having given the enema, Charpentier bolted the door behind him. He was amazed to see His Eminence lifting his arms to heaven and exulting, "O God, Thou must have a great interest in the Kingdom and my person." Then he added more calmly, "Read this and make copies of it."

The sick man, who had recently lain on his deathbed, now proceeded to exhaust his staff. Throughout the next two days he dictated dispatches to enlighten the King and to destroy his enemies. He had to tread cautiously, for he knew that despite all the clouds that had come between the King and his "dear friend," it was no easy task to destroy the suspicious King's incredibly strong attachment. Richelieu accomplished this enormous task without interrupting his journey. He still felt the need to be surrounded by the stout walls of Tarascon. Chavigny, called to come at top speed, joined him at Tarascon and was dispatched to His Majesty with the papers that determined France's fate.

"Monsieur le Jeune," as he was affectionately known, left by coach for Narbonne on June 11 as the Cardinal wrote to de Noyers. "The purpose of Monsieur de Chavigny's journey will astound you. God has come to the King's aid with marvelous discoveries!" The rest of the letter deals with a host of different matters. Then: "His constant lucidity reflects the orderliness of his mind, or rather his incredible capacity to appear calm even in the midst of the most violent emotions." [1]

Chavigny reached Narbonne at dawn on June 12. The King had arrived the previous evening. Chavigny went straight to de Noyers, and they prepared a plan of action. They then attended the King's *lever.*

---

[1] Avenel.

Monsieur le Grand was there. Louis spoke to him and more amiably than he had in the last few days. Chavigny did not hesitate to enter into the conversation. At the first propitious moment, "he tugged at the King's hem, which was the custom when one wanted to say something to him in private." Louis, ever a conscientious servant of his country, immediately agreed to withdraw to the adjacent room. Cinq-Mars started to follow him, but Chavigny barred his way. "Monsieur le Grand, I have something to tell the King." Whereupon "the other, like a good boy, left them alone together."[2] But the incident frightened him, and he went off in search of Fontrailles. They both waited nervously for Chavigny to emerge and were further perturbed that de Noyers had been summoned in to the closed meeting. Their wait was a long one.

When Fontrailles realized that Cinq-Mars was going to be excluded from the discussion, he panicked. "Monsieur, all is lost. We must withdraw [to Sedan]." But Henri would not hear of it. The hunchback lost his temper and snapped, "You will still be of a pretty height when they take your head off your shoulders. But I am too short to risk that." Then he changed his tone and added in a trembling voice: "Alas, I shan't ever see you again." He left, donned his Capuchin habit—which had disguised him on his journey to Spain—and vanished. Had Henri followed him, he would certainly have had a long life ahead of him. A Maltese astrologer had once predicted that if he survived his twenty-second year, he would be the happiest man alive. But pride or indolence or his blind confidence in his power over the King made him prefer to face his fate.

Louis was hardly prepared for the shattering revelation of Cinq-Mars' treachery. The violence of his reaction to the news refutes many claims that his passion for his favorite had died. Beside himself with rage, he ranted and he raved that this was another of the Cardinal's inventions and that he was not going to be taken in.

---

[2] Tallemant.

Chavigny and de Noyers remained undaunted, as Richelieu himself had prepared them for this reaction. "The King will tell you at first that it is all untrue, but persuade him to have Cinq-Mars arrested, and that afterward he can easily be set free if the charge is false. But once the enemy has taken refuge in Champagne, it won't be easy to get him back."

The two Ministers did not find their task a very easy one. The luckless King was once again forced into a Corneillian dilemma. His whole life seemed to be dogged by the conflict between his sense of duty and his personal inclinations. He had already had to sacrifice his mother, Louise de La Fayette, and many others to his royal duties. And now his greedy political Moloch demanded his cruel, impossible, but adored boy. He was being asked to renounce his last joy on earth.

Another king might have rebelled and even executed the messengers of such unhappy news, as the ancient kings had done. Exposed, Cinq-Mars was no longer dangerous; a forgiven Cinq-Mars would be eternally indebted and finally submissive to Louis' will. But Jeanne d'Albret's grandson never considered such a compromise. His rigid principles were outraged by what he read: "It is agreed that neither of the contracting parties shall approach the French Crown without the consent of both contracting parties. . . . After the war, Spain shall recover all the strongholds, provinces, and kingdoms which His Most Christian Majesty has already seized or which he shall have seized." No two ways about it: The Master of the Horse had committed high treason. Louis was submerged in chagrin and disgust. He finally mastered his immense sorrow and resigned himself.

When the Lord's Anointed, the guardian of France, accepted the news, he submitted totally to the Minister's demands. Messieurs de Cinq-Mars, de Thou, de Chavagnac the elder, and the Duc de Bouillon's gentleman d'Ossonville were to be arrested, and Monsieur de Castelan was to be sent to Casal to arrange the arrest of the Duc de Bouillon, who was surrounded by his troops. Louis also agreed to the Cardinal's Machiavellian plan against Monsieur.

As soon as the Secretaries of State emerged from the royal chambers at ten o'clock that morning, they sent a triumphant message back to Richelieu:

> Monsieur de Chavigny arrived this morning, an hour before the King's rising. He and Monsieur de Noyers conferred together and then went to see His Majesty to give him a detailed account of the matter. His Majesty duly read all the relative documents. Everything has conformed with His Eminence's wish. Orders will be dispatched this evening without fail. The King has approved Monsieur de Castelan's voyage to Piedmont.
> Signed: *Chavigny*
> *de Noyers*

The matter was kept secret, and nothing happened that day. Chavagnac claims that the favorite was warned, but it seems unlikely. Fontrailles had already fled, and if Cinq-Mars had really known that he had been exposed, he would certainly not have dined so calmly with Monsieur de Beaumont, governor of Saint-Germain, who was his guest that evening. The dinner took place at an inn called The Three Nurses because of the caryatids that decorated its facade. One of the King's valets interrupted the dinner to inform him that His Majesty "was retiring." Protocol required that the Master of the Horse be present at the King's retirement—which, it seemed, was at least an hour early this evening. According to his statement at his trial, Henri left the inn immediately and hurried to the Archbishop's palace, where the King was staying. When he arrived, he was accosted by an unknown person who handed him a note.

"What is it?" Cinq-Mars asked.

"Read it and find out," came the reply from the vanishing messenger.

In the doorway of the Archbishop's palace, Henri deciphered the hastily written scrawl: "You are in danger."

He retraced his steps, profoundly troubled, wondering who had sent the message. Some historians claim that it was a ruse of Chavigny's, who later declared that "Monsieur le Grand's flight proved his guilt." But the claim lacks substance. "Monsieur le Jeune" would never have dared take such a risk. Chavigny would have incurred Richelieu's fury if he had put his principal victim to flight. On the other hand, nor would de Noyers have exposed himself to such a danger. There were only three people who knew of the decision to arrest Cinq-Mars.

The third person was, of course, Louis. One can only conclude this was the first and last time he allowed personal sentiment to take precedence over the interests of state. The man who had exiled his own mother gave a treacherous but beloved conspirator a last chance.

Henri hesitated for a moment and then made for one of the gates, but found it closed. The precise whereabouts of his final place of refuge are not known. He may have gone to the house of Burgos, whose daughter he knew, or to the father of one of his valet's mistresses, or to that of the goldsmith who lived opposite the garden of the Archbishop's palace. The most convincing suggestion is that he took cover at Monsieur Siouzac's in the rue du Tribunal. There is reason to believe he had an affair with Madame Siouzac during his first visit to Narbonne. The lady would not have turned him away if he asked her help.

While Cinq-Mars went into hiding, the King ordered the Comte de Charost to arrest the conspirators. Charost first knocked on the door of Monsieur le Grand. He arrested his servants, seized his papers and his caskets, which Monsieur des Yveteaux was instructed to open.

"My faith," exclaimed a valet to the military gentlemen, "you are going to find in there what you are not looking for."

"They were letters from his mistress!" [3]

Ceton, a lieutenant in the Scottish Guard, arrested de Thou and gallantly allowed him to burn his papers.

---

[3] Tallemant.

Charost went to tell His Majesty that the bird had flown. The King ordered the consuls of Narbonne to keep the city gates shut and instructed Charost to search every single house in the city as soon as dawn broke. Somehow the King learned of his friend's whereabouts. The honest Father Griffet writes, "At three in the morning a valet whom he [Cinq-Mars] did not recognize knocked at the door of the house where he was staying and informed him of the King's order." Henri's surprising reaction was to turn jovially to his valet Belet and say, "Go and see if by chance there is any gate of the city left open."

One of the city gates had in fact been left open to allow La Meilleraye's retinue to enter the city that night. The King must have known about this and probably hoped that Cinq-Mars would slip away unnoticed. Unfortunately, however, Belet was as negligent as his master. Convinced that all the gates would be closed, he did not take the trouble to check.

The King awoke at his usual early hour and asked for news of Monsieur le Grand. When he heard that there was none, he thought Cinq-Mars was safe. He therefore continued to act out his part and ordered the public pronouncement of the death penalty for anyone who attempted to hide him. He then set off immediately for Béziers without waiting for any results.

Claude de Rébé, Archbishop of Narbonne and an agent of the Cardinal, hastened to reinforce the King's commands by offering a reward of ten thousand écus to anyone who handed over Monsieur le Grand. When Madame de Siouzac heard the town heralds broadcast the offer, she panicked. She told her husband "that a nice young gentleman had asked her for shelter and that she had taken pity on him and not turned him away." Siouzac did not hesitate. Cinq-Mars had drifted off into a troubled sleep and was lying fully dressed on a bed with the poster curtains drawn when the fracas of armed troops entering the house woke him with a start. He rose and "calmly and resolutely" presented himself to the soldiers. Ricardelle, Charost's lieutenant, asked for his sword. Cinq-Mars "asked permission to keep his sword, as he had no greatcoat

and did not want to appear in the streets like a common criminal."
The permission was granted.

Chavagnac's father had also been arrested. His son and many of
Cinq-Mars' other friends ran to the Archbishop's palace. They
talked to Cinq-Mars and planned an escape. Their plans were
foiled by Jean Ceton's arrival at the head of forty Scottish guardsmen. Ceton's guards were soon reinforced by the Champagne Regi-
ment, which Richelieu did not feel was disproportionate to the
importance of the prisoner. He was obviously taking no risks. The
Master of the Horse still had a great many friends. Richelieu was
particularly afraid of what Tréville, Ruvigny, and Chavagnac's son
might do. Ruvigny nobly announced to La Meilleraye, "I am loyal to
Monsieur le Grand. Even if I were to see the Spanish treaty with my
own eyes, I should not believe it."

Henri was taken to Montpellier prison. Sobered by his solitude
and by the loss of his Princesse's moral support, he soon came to
realize the folly of his ways. As he crossed the drawbridge to the
fortress, he was heard to say, "Must I really die at twenty-two! Did
I have to conspire against my country at such an early age?"

The King was consumed with anger toward Monsieur, without
whom the Spanish Treaty could never have existed. He raised no
objection whatever to Richelieu's cunning trap. On June 13, he
sent Monsieur two letters dated from Béziers. The first one announced the arrest of the Master of the Horse for fictitious reasons:
"The excessive insolence he has committed in my presence," he
wrote, "has forced my hand. I am certain that you will approve of
the punishment meted out to those who do not pay us due respect."
The second letter appointed the Duc d'Orléans Commander-in-
Chief of the Army in Champagne. The army had recently been
defeated at Honnecourt, and it was now being hastily re-formed
to repulse the threatened invasion. The King was thus making
Gaston defend the frontier against his secret allies, the Spaniards.
The Cardinal calculated that Monsieur would need superhuman
nerve to resist the temptation of fleeing to the enemy camp.

Gaston was amazed, but he did not see the trap. On June 17, he wrote the Cardinal a letter which really debases the son of Henri IV. "My cousin—the King my master has done me the honor of writing to tell me of the consequences of Monsieur le Grand's ungrateful behavior. He must be the most contemptible man alive to have displeased you who have done so much for him. The King's favoritism has always made me wary of him and of his artifices. . . . You, my cousin, continue to have my regard and sincere friendship." The Prince was anxious to demonstrate his gratitude for the honor bestowed on him. He spent so much time trying to ingratiate himself that he lost the few days during which Richelieu made his flight impossible.

Louis XIII had decided to take the waters at Montfrin and stop on his way at Tarascon. The discovery of conspiracy and Cinq-Mars' arrest had exhausted him. He performed his duties like a robot and traveled from one town to the next under the sharp eyes of Chavigny and de Noyers. His thoughts returned constantly to the prisoner whom he had tried to save without failing his duty.

On June 15, de Noyers showed him the document which had been attached to the original treaty containing a list of the conspirators. When the King read Cinq-Mars' name, he asked miserably, "Could it be that his name was put there in place of another?" De Noyers was upset by the suggestion and dismissed it sharply, but His Majesty remained "in a profound reverie." De Noyers sought to shake him out of his dejection by referring to a number of state affairs, but Louis turned a deaf ear. Suddenly he said, "What a fall Monsieur le Grand has taken." And he kept repeating his lament.

"True, Sire," said de Noyers, "but the greatest fall a subject can take is that of disloyalty."

Louis refused to listen. He had always accepted such pronouncements as sacred, but he now realized that they had dug innumerable graves and finally brought him to the most horrible loneliness. How could this dark little man understand his feelings? He was only the tool of a man who was a genius at reaping personal vengeance in the holy name of the state. De Noyers' sole concern was to prevent Louis the Just from choosing happiness over cruel justice, from pardoning a guilty child whom he longed to clasp once again.

But Louis was too ruthless with himself to yield to any such temptations. Cinq-Mars was not entitled to gentler treatment than Montmorency, the idol of the Languedoc, or than Marillac, the valiant old soldier. He could not afford to unleash a series of similar rebellions and throw away all the positive results of his iron rule with one weak gesture. He could not be permissive. He could only die of chagrin.

De Noyers did understand Louis' internal conflict, however. He described the incident to Richelieu in two long dispatches. "I think the earlier Monseigneur le Cardinal Mazarin can come here, the better. His Majesty is truly in need of consolation, for he is heartbroken." But Richelieu had another mission for Mazarin. He left the restoration of the King's spirits to the wily Marquis de Mortemart.

The King's health deteriorated as a result of his grief, and this deeply worried His Eminence. His letters are full of concern.

> I beseech Your Majesty to take great care of your person, for the welfare of France and perhaps of all Christendom depends upon your well-being. . . . I also entreat you not to torment yourself. . . . I again beg Your Majesty to take care of your health and not to torture yourself with all the weighty problems which have once again assailed you, daring to assure you that as long as you are of good health, you will be victorious.

Shortly after this, the Cardinal learned that Louis had burned a good many letters following Cinq-Mars' arrest. We cannot know what these letters contained or what secrets Adonis and the Stoic shared. Richelieu was concerned and ordered his agents "to impress upon the King that he should never tell anyone he burned the papers." Other documents continued to disappear in the same way, however.

On the night of June 17, a messenger from the Duc d'Enghien informed Marie Gonzaga of what had happened at Narbonne. The Princesse was shaken, but immediately thought of the "terrible quantity of letters" which must have been seized from Cinq-Mars' apartment and which could irrevocably ruin her. She begged her friend Mademoiselle de Rambouillet to approach the Duchesse d'Aiguillon, Richelieu's much-cherished niece. The Duchesse was staying at the Cardinal's palace in order to guarantee her own security. Mademoiselle de Rambouillet called on her and then took Marie to her. The proud Gonzaga fully confessed her worries and no doubt her regrets. She hastened to add "that the letters dealt only with their marriage."

The former Madame de Combalet was the widow of a minor gentleman, and she had once been chased away from the court by the jealous Marie de Médicis. She was therefore delighted at the opportunity of having the sovereign Duchesse de Nevers at her feet. According to Tallemant, "She received her in the kindest way, and immediately had all her letters returned to her." As these letters were hastily destroyed, we have no firsthand account of Cinq-Mars' fatal love affair, nor of those aspects of his relations with Louis XIII which the King concealed from Richelieu. If ashes could speak, history might be very different.[4]

The announcement of the discovery of the plot in Renaudot's *Gazette* of June 21 dejected most of the court, the Hôtel de Rambouillet, and the Marais. Marion, who was still being called Madame la Grande, wept bitter tears. Many a sensitive soul, most of Richelieu's enemies, and a number of eminently sane and distinguished individuals who took exception to the Cardinal's political conduct were genuinely distressed.

But at Saint-Germain, the Queen was delighted, having been re-

---

[4] The history of Louis XIV's reign would have to be rewritten if we had Madame de Maintenon's voluminous correspondence.

warded with "the thing she most desired in the world." The King had written an almost affectionate letter on June 15, asking her to keep the children with her. Brassac informed the Cardinal of Her Majesty's gratitude and assured him of her loyalty—as if any such assurances from her carried any weight. "Nothing in the world can make her change." Anne of Austria had taken a decisive step toward reaching the goal of becoming Regent, which she was to attain the following year.

Seventeen

THE SOLEMN PROMISE OF A SON
OF FRANCE

꿈 MONSIEUR HAD NO idea that his sister-in-law had won such a resounding victory. His suspicions were not aroused even when Chavigny came to see him at Moulins and presented him with the proof of his treason. "Monsieur le Jeune"'s voice wavered as he concluded his mission. "Your Highness' crime is so great that you are beyond His Eminence's help. Your very life is in jeopardy, for you have committed a crime that human clemency cannot absolve."

The Prince finally broke down. "Chavigny, I must find a way out. You have twice before interceded on my behalf with His Eminence. I assure you that this will be the last time I shall ever make such a request."

"Your only hope is to confess the full extent of the error you have committed."

Gaston understood that what Richelieu wanted of him was enough material evidence to discredit him and hang Cinq-Mars. Before replying, he sent his favorite, the Abbé de La Rivière, who knew nothing of the Spanish Treaty, to the King and the Cardinal to see how serious the situation really was. The Abbé was "the most infamous, wealthiest and best paid traitor in the kingdom [who] knew better than anyone his master's value, having sold him so many times." This time, however, the Abbé was loyal. When Richelieu knew of his departure, he sent Louis strict instructions on

177

how to receive him. Louis passively acquiesced. He nourished an implacable bitterness toward his brother; and his despair made him generally indifferent.

Louis was slowly approaching Tarascon, where Richelieu was waiting to upbraid him for failing in his duties for the first time. Before he reached Tarascon he learned of the Duc de Bouillon's arrest at Casal. The ruler of Sedan had suffered the indignity of being surprised while amorously engaged in a hayloft, among bales of hay. Louis then revealed his true sympathies, "saying that Monsieur de Bouillon had spoiled him [Cinq-Mars] and that it was he alone that should die." But the Cardinal had no such sympathies.

At this stage he was less concerned with saving the kingdom from traitors, who had in any case ceased to represent any real danger, than with personally avenging himself. He had raised this youth from obscurity, only to escape being his victim by a hairbreadth. After his earlier physical and political recovery, his body once again rebelled against the overexcitement and frenetic overwork. He was forced back to his sickbed, from where he directed the capture of his enemies and conducted the Thirty Years' War. Several floors beneath his sickroom, locked in the depths of the fortress, de Thou and Chavagnac patiently awaited their fates.

The King was in no better health than the Cardinal. The sudden news that Marie de Médicis was seriously ill at Cologne aggravated his condition. He had not seen his proscribed mother for eleven years, and he still winced at her exile. "No son ever loved or honored his mother more," he once wrote her on the occasion of one of their reconciliations. It was true, despite the fact that he had never managed to move the hardhearted woman who had never once embraced her son in the seven years of her Regency. Louis had been forced to spend his life fighting her while he yearned to demonstrate his unworthy affection for her. Now he was faced with the torment of letting the mother of the King of France, of the Queens of Spain and England, die miserably in exile, bereft of the blessing that he longed to bestow on her that could wipe out the past.

On June 28, the Marquis de Brézé's fleet defeated Ciudad-Real's Spanish fleet. France was thus master of the Mediterranean, which robbed Perpignan of its last hope. The King arrived at Tarascon on the day of the sea victory. The Cardinal dreaded their meeting after three tragic months just as much as the King, and neither had the energy to see the other immediately.

The two collaborators, whose first serious misunderstanding had nearly changed the course of history, finally met stretched out side by side like two marble effigies under their baldachins, two invalid travelers who were nearing the end of their lives. The two litters draped with rugs were placed side by side in a beautiful room overlooking the Rhône that lapped peacefully at the walls of the fortress. To their mutual relief there were no recriminations, no bitter undertones, even though their conversation inevitably revolved around unhappy incidents. The Cardinal, too clever to complain, thanked His Majesty for not paying attention to the adverse rumors that the wicked had circulated about him. Louis was reassured by the Cardinal's consideration and treated him with his old deference. His meeting with the implacable genius whom he still admired, hated, and to whom he was so indebted had the effect of calming him and removing his persecuting demons. He regained his self-confidence; and his doubts, if not his pain, began to dissipate. At one point in their conversation, the exhausted King's thought started to stray. "My Cousin," he said, "you are so near the Rhône. It's sad to hear the monotonous sound of the waves."

They came to no decisions before they parted, but Richelieu had won. He had regained the King's confidence, which alone had enabled him to rule France for eighteen years against her people's will. The following day, the King set out for Lyon, and sent Richelieu a reassuring note. "I never fail to benefit by seeing you. I feel much better since yesterday. . . . I hope that, with God's help, all will be well." He was tired of sitting in judgment over his fellowmen, however, and of executing justice. He wanted to withdraw to his beloved refuge in the forests of the Ile-de-France where he might regain his will to live. From Bagnols, he gave the Cardinal full legal powers as lieutenant general of the provinces south of the Loire and appointed him to deal with the conspiracy as he thought best and to arrange the conquest of Roussillon. He had shifted the burden, but it did not have the desired effect of reducing his torments.

Rebuffed by the Cardinal, the Abbé de La Rivière dashed off to the King, who received him rudely. "Do not tell me of my brother's loyalty! Everyone knows he never had any." The King then showed the Abbé a copy of the treaty. La Rivière was ruffled but still had the courage to plead his master's cause by shifting the blame to others. The King asked him to put his imputations down in writing, which the Abbé bravely refused to do. Louis, at first taken aback, concluded the interview with an attempt to intimidate La Rivière. "Those who have given my brother bad counsel cannot expect from me anything but the rigors of justice. If my brother agrees to give me a complete account of all his actions, he will benefit from the effects of my goodness as he has in the past."

As soon as he left the King's audience, the Abbé was seized by Chavigny, who threatened to have him arrested. The luckless emissary "was so terrified that he almost fainted and then proceeded to throw a nervous fit which was cured only by reassurances." While reassuring him, the Minister suggested that "he undertake to persuade Monsieur to confess openly everything he did in a document which he would send to the King. Then once he had seen His Majesty, he would leave the kingdom for a time."

Richelieu then invited the Abbé to see him and put extra pressure on him. Richelieu was less confident than he seemed. If Monsieur refused to release the original treaty, his efforts might well prove useless. A duplicate of the treaty would not serve as proof at a trial. "Monsieur has committed an action unworthy of a Son of France," the Cardinal declared. "He deserves death. However, if he obeys His Majesty's commands, he will be given leave to withdraw to Venice." He gave the Abbé a letter for Monsieur in which he urged him once again to have "recourse to an honest and full confession." Richelieu was still uneasy, but once the Abbé had left, Chavigny reassured him. "Fear is the most likely agent to persuade Monsieur."

Fear was, in fact, the ruin of Gaston and his entourage. Vincent Voiture wrote to Mademoiselle de Rambouillet, "Monsieur is lost, and so are all of his friends and to my mind their ruin is inevitable and definite." The Prince's servants did not acquit themselves very well. "If you could see the anger and despair which has seized his household, you would be sorry for him," wrote Du Boulay, one of the less cowardly, to Chavigny. Gaston feared arrest and took refuge in the mountains of the Auvergne, "and kept on the move to avoid the peril that menaced him."

Richelieu grew impatient. Cinq-Mars and de Thou had both resolutely denied everything during their preliminary interrogations. The Cardinal instructed Chavigny to offer Henry IV's son as much money as would buy a confession from him. But this proved unnecessary. The horror of exile and his friend's pressure had already spared Monsieur the supreme dishonor of selling his friends for money. On July 7, His Highness wrote to Richelieu from Aigueperse in the Auvergne, expressing his "extreme regret at his past relations and correspondence with his [Richelieu's] enemies," and swore innocence of any plot to assassinate him. "I would rather have died than lend an ear to the least proposition that might have caused Your Eminence harm." There followed a long "Declaration to the King," in which Monsieur revealed "all that he had been guilty of," which in fact did reveal a good part of the conspiracy. He did not mention the Queen and defended de Thou: "He never mentioned the Spanish matter at all in the two conversations I had with him. . . . I know he condemned it to the Comte de Brion, to whom he said that he would rather go to Rome than become involved." He vented all his anger on the favorite, whom he accused of tricking him—despite his solemn word to Cinq-Mars that he would never expose him. Henri had given his word in return to Monsieur, and when he learned of Monsieur's betrayal, he exclaimed: "If I must die, I shall die an honorable man without compromising anyone." But the Son of France did not attach such sanctity to his own word of honor. He begged Chavigny to spare him having "to leave the state" and added, "There is nothing I will refuse to do to avoid this." A hundred and fifty years later, another Duc d'Orléans was to comment after voting for Louis XVI's death, "I could not avoid doing what I did." Gaston was not being asked to commit regicide, he was merely sending to the scaffold a foolish youngster who believed in a prince's solemn promise.

The Marquis de Mortemart had succeeded in becoming Louis XIII's needed confidant, as Richelieu had wished. The stoic may have resigned himself to being unhappy, but he had to communicate his miseries. Mortemart took devilish advantage of his position, aided and abetted as he was by the Duc d'Enghien and other gentlemen who wanted to dissociate themselves from the Master of the Horse. No opportunity was lost to remind the King of his prisoner's insolence, faults, indiscreet love affairs. Louis was being prepared for the blow that would eventually be dealt by the Cardinal and his agents. Mortemart repeated the heartless quip Cinq-Mars had given during the King's illness at Roussillon: "Oh, he is dragging along." The unhappy King was cut to the quick. Louis nourished the very normal hope that despite everything, the object of his love felt something for him, even if it was only friendship. The man whom Louis had loved more than anyone else and who had —albeit briefly—taken precedence over his royal duty had wished him dead for the sake of an evil ambition and a woman's influence. Louis also had a nagging suspicion that Cinq-Mars had wished to rid himself of the unpleasant company of an invalid who revolted him.

Louis' future reactions would be hard to explain unless we give this revelation its real importance. Despite his anger, humiliation, and grief, his affections refused to dwindle. To lessen his attachment and overcome the weakness he despised, he tried to force himself to hate Cinq-Mars. He took to repeating, "The wicked wretch wished me dead" ten times a day. He talked of nothing else and encouraged everyone to express their loathing of "the worst villain and the worst traitor that has ever lived." One day when two Jesuits at Privas denounced the hopes nurtured by the Protestants because the conspirator Chavagnac was a Protestant, Louis exclaimed to de Noyers, "Monsieur le Grand would have been capable of becoming a Huguenot!"

"He would have become a Turk," the little man replied, "if it would have enabled him to wrest from His Majesty what God so legitimately gave him."

"I believe so," was Louis' incredible reply.

One evening he summoned Fabert to discuss his only topic of conversation—Monsieur le Grand. "He was so incredibly extravagant," he exclaimed, "that he has forty-three suits. He had a German cabinet made for him in Paris worked with gold and gems, which cost a hundred thousand livres. Such extravagance makes me suspect that he had other sources of income besides myself. I know how much I gave him in the last two years, which could not possibly have covered his expenditures. Now that I have seen the Spanish treaty, I know that my suspicions were fully justified."

The King knew that Henri was hopelessly in debt, however, and did not really believe that he had received bribes. He may have thought Fabert could give him some evidence that would convince him, but Fabert, who was no particular friend of Cinq-Mars, said nothing. On July 6, Chavigny wrote to the Cardinal, "His Majesty is now so incensed with the traitor that it would be harder to make him clement than ruthless."

Then a number of people directly or indirectly involved with the conspiracy decided to buy their safety by revealing the failed attempt on the Cardinal's life at Lyon. When Cinq-Mars himself, questioned about the attempt, declared that "he had done nothing which the King had not approved," Richelieu was rightfully horrified. It had never occurred to him that Louis would ever consent to his assassination. He had, at the time, explained away Tréville's presence in the royal antechamber as part of his guard duties.

Richelieu dealt with the matter in a consummately cunning way. He instructed Mortemart to tell His Majesty about the whole thing as if it had only just been brought to the Marquis' attention and as if the Cardinal did not yet know about it.

It was Louis' turn to be shocked. What had he really meant by his ambiguous opposition to Cinq-Mars and by his silence to Tréville's rash suggestion? Had he ever realized what had happened when Cinq-Mars decided against taking advantage of that occasion? He could understand how his manner might have been interpreted as it was, and he shuddered to think what might have happened. His detractors have accused him of cowardice and compared him to his brother, but the comparison is odious. They could not have been more dissimilar: The one was a dedicated king, a martyr to his duty, and the other an unprincipled prince who thought nothing of sacrificing his friends to save himself from a distasteful exile.

Louis feared the outcome of such a revelation and resented Cinq-Mars all the more for implicating him. This hardened him and made him all the crueler toward his "dear friend." But he was not afraid of his Minister, whom he could strip of power with a single word. On the contrary, it was Richelieu who feared his King, as the deviousness of his tactics demonstrates. At a time when victory was about to reward all his years of blood and tears, Louis was loath to publicize his brief flirtation with a notion which would certainly have jeopardized his and his country's chances of success. If he let the rumor of his ambivalence toward Richelieu, all his sacrifices—including the suppression of his feelings toward his mother, who had just died—would have been in vain. He could not afford the luxury of superfluous and dangerous gestures. He was too upset to be wily and simply trusted Mortemart to play a simplistic trick on Richelieu and inform him of the horrible plot which had fortunately miscarried.

The King was being naïve, but Richelieu kept up the pretense by writing him a naïve letter:

Monsieur de Chavigny has informed me of the latest discovery concerning Monsieur le Grand's plot against me at Lyon and of His Majesty's indignation, for which I cannot hide my gratitude. I confess that Monsieur le Grand could easily have executed his plan on my unsuspecting person. I would never have believed he was capable of sullying himself with the blood of a cardinal who, by the grace of God, has happily served his master for twenty-five years and who would gladly serve him a thousand lives if he had them to live. The more evil that miserable soul reveals, the greater appears His Majesty's goodness. Reason demands that kings protect those who serve them, but His Majesty has always protected me with his innate natural goodness.

This letter reveals the Cardinal's extraordinary cunning, his hypocrisy, and his belief in the necessity of flattering the sorely injured King. Richelieu did not even consider verifying the facts of the case. His fever helped convince him that he had narrowly escaped the fate of Concini, that the King had, in fact, given the Master of the Horse his consent to kill him. He began to resent the King from this moment, and his hatred and his fear of Louis were to dominate the last weeks of his life. His conviction is attested by his coded letter to Chavigny dated July 14:

> The darkest mysteries are slowly explaining themselves. The traitor [Cinq-Mars] was aware [confessed] not that he plotted against the life of Monsieur Amadeau [Richelieu], but that his plans were known to du Chesne [the King] and had his consent. . . . It will be hard for you to calm Monsieur Amadeau, who knowing of du Chesne's consent, will certainly be wary of walking abroad to those places where he would be in danger of succumbing to that which he once narrowly escaped, especially when such people who were present at the attempt [Tréville] are still abroad.

Even if Louis forgave Cinq-Mars for wishing him dead, he could no longer afford to be interested in his welfare. Many historians have criticized him for doing away with his "dear friend" after inciting him to do the same to Richelieu. But the King had no choice but to endure his martyrdom. His leniency would be taken as proof of his complicity and would doubtless have had the effect of encouraging the Master of the Horse's accomplices to renew the assassination attempt. This is why he dismissed the dangerous topic with a declaration that Cinq-Mars "was the worst liar in the world" and that "he must be made to submit to the full rigors of justice." He ordered that Cinq-Mars be locked up in his cell to prevent him from escaping and asked His Eminence "to reinforce his guard." He constantly spoke of the "enormity of the conspirators' crime and the punishments that would be meted out to them." He declared that "Sedan should get a reprieve [he wished to show mercy to Bouillon], but that he would never pardon Monsieur le Grand." He eventually dispatched two letters to the magistrates, ordering them to condemn to death the boy to whom he had "given his heart," promising "to share it with none other."

On July 13, the King wrote to his brother before leaving Lyon for Fontainebleau. The Cardinal was not satisfied with Gaston's "Declaration" and wanted to arrange a confrontation between Monsieur and his accomplices. The letter in which Richelieu expresses his intention to his ministers is a masterpiece of duplicity and can only provoke our pity for an individual so unworthy of such efforts. The meeting was to be suggested to the Duc d'Orléans as an "act of goodness by a prince trying to save those who have served him." The meeting was the price Monsieur would have to pay to earn his reprieve from exile. The Cardinal's ministers were to be careful not to let him suspect that he would then be deprived of all his rights and privileges.

Gaston had managed to reach his sister, the Duchesse de Savoie, who was alarmed by his visit. He continued to excuse and lower himself in Richelieu's eyes. He was base enough to write this astonishing phrase: "If you could only see my sincerity, I know that you would not be reluctant to add to your glory the further glory of helping a needy Son of France." But he refused to agree to the meeting. "I despair that I cannot consent to the King's expressed desires. You know what a toll my actions have already borne upon my honor, and I could never live with myself or show my face to the world again if I consented to this as well." Gaston was more afraid of appearing before his victims than he was of incurring the Cardinal's anger. He appeared openly indignant and refused to "act as accuser or witness against a man who had undertaken to act as he had only because he had received his [Monsieur's] word of honor that he would not be betrayed." He directed La Rivière to tell the King that he preferred "to go wandering and begging throughout the world."

Mazarin decided to be far-sighted, and intervened on Gaston's behalf. Chancellor Séguier discovered that in 1574, the Duc d'Alençon had not been confronted with the condemned La Mole and Coconnas. This precedent made Richelieu relent. He wrote to Gaston and expressed his pleasure at seeing him choose "the only way out of his miseries and crimes." Then the Cardinal and the King's brother both signed an agreement by which Monsieur would regain his privileges in exchange for his confirmation of the conspiracy and of the Spanish Treaty. Since he had burned the original, he agreed to certify a copy. He would also make a solemn deposition before the Chancellor of France.

Gaston was forced to submit to another indignity, however. He was asked to change his evidence and state that, although de Thou had not actively participated in the plot, he had at least known of the "agreement between Monsieur, Monsieur le Grand, and Monsieur de Bouillon and of his proposed escape to Sedan." But the Cardinal was not satisfied, and persecuted the Counsellor with inexplicable hatred. Nevertheless, he was hard put to find any real evidence with which to prosecute. He even set a spy, the agent Crombis, on de Thou's heels, but to no avail. The Cardinal tried to extract a confession from the Duc de Beaufort, who defended himself brilliantly but nonetheless decided to join his father who had taken refuge in England.

Mazarin was asked to work on the Duc de Bouillon. "He negotiated so adroitly that Monsieur de Bouillon has said enough to
make our evidence complete," the Cardinal exclaimed triumphantly.
The Duc felt the dismal proximity of the scaffold and broke his
word of honor just as Gaston d'Orléans had done. Richelieu and
Mazarin instructed him to deny having been a party to the Spanish
treaty and maintain that he had promised Monsieur free entry
into Sedan only "in the event of the King's death." The full blame
for the entire conspiracy was pushed on to the shoulders of Monsieur le Grand, who had been its moving force. It was further estab-
lished that Monsieur de Thou had known nothing.

Bouillon saved his own life, but he lost Sedan. Thus the two
mortal enemies concluded their monstrous agreement to transform
a misguided child into a vile and dangerous criminal while the real
villains of the piece, Orléans and Bouillon, preserved nearly all
their deadly power.

Eighteen

THE CITADEL OF MONTPELLIER

𝕰𝕰 IN A FLASH, Cinq-Mars had fallen from the
splendor of a court favorite to the miserable condition of a convict.
He pined away in Montpellier prison, veering among despair, fear,
resignation and rebellion. He would "rant and rave" and then become touchingly docile. At first he banked on the King's affection,
but when he realized that he could expect nothing of him—that he
had in fact been abandoned and betrayed by everyone—he became
disillusioned and embittered toward the human race.

He was also suddenly overtaken by grief. He had always been
sure that he had never loved the King, whom he had treated like a
toy with total disregard to his wounded sensibilities. He had even
scorned and deprecated his jealous, cantankerous, sententious tyrant, whose trying inconsistencies had bored and exasperated him.
He was sure that he had never felt anything, and yet the residual
effects of Louis' passion had left their mark on him. Henri suddenly discovered how accustomed he had become to Louis' smother-
ing affections, how much he had unwittingly come to depend on
the King for help and support. His three years of involvement in
the King's emotional life had made Louis an essential component of
Henri's own life. He was so grieved and indignant at his rejection
that one would think he had shared those feelings he himself had
so often rejected.

He blamed the King for his plight, maintaining that he had been far too young and too inexperienced to know that Louis had wanted only to confide his frustration in him and had never wanted him to remove the source of his anxieties.

Father Robert, the chaplain of the fortress, tried to calm Cinq-Mars and persuade him to resign himself to his fate. Henri was greatly comforted by the priest, whom he soon began to win over. "He [Father Robert] could not extol too much the virtues and rich qualities he saw in him." [1]

The eminently seductive captive also managed to charm his jailer, Ceton, that rough and ready lieutenant of the Scottish Guard. Ceton was sixty-six years old and a reliable, loyal, and obedient servant of the Crown. This proverbial bear of a man was so affected by his prisoner's charm that he actually shed tears over him while discussing him with the president of the Grenoble Parlement. He allowed Henri to take short walks and to buy books; he was as lenient as he could afford to be. But after the Master of the Horse was imprudent enough to mention the "evil designs" which "the King had approved," the Cardinal ordered that he not be allowed to speak to anyone.

Father Robert's comforting and Ceton's indulgence did not make prison life acceptable, however. Cinq-Mars decided to escape.

He was still permitted visits by his bootmaker and his launderer, through whom he made contact with Prugues and Siougeac, two of his more constant and loyal friends. He then set about winning over several of his guards. Prugues and Siougeac rounded up a few reliable men. The plan was that one night the accommodating guards would open the prisoner's door. Monsieur le Grand would then slide down the bastions into the moat, meet his friends beyond, and ride away with them.

Almost on the eve of the escape, unfortunately, a letter was intercepted, and the plot was exposed. The Cardinal flew into a rage when the news reached him. He scolded Ceton, but did not dare replace him because he knew him to be exceptionally dutiful. Fifty soldiers were sent to reinforce the Montpellier garrison, and Mon-

---

[1] L. Guiraud, *Notre-Dame de Montaigu à Montpellier.*

sieur le Grand's friends were pursued. Siougeac managed to escape, but Prugues was captured. Rodes, the bootmaker, and Carpentier, the launderer, were promptly hanged. Cinq-Mars was put "in a dungeon where he could scarcely see the light of day." [2] There he stayed for two dark, silent, and stifling summer months.

Ceton naïvely sought to persuade him to save himself by making a full confession.

Henri would reply, "I once knew a song that went, 'I would rather die than tell.' They have no proof against me. They want me to give myself away."

"But you must confess the truth," the old officer would repeat tirelessly.

"Do you really not know that one is hanged for telling the truth?" Cinq-Mars would say. "If they guaranteed me my freedom, then I would tell them what I would not otherwise. I have been asked to confess, but I have not been given any assurances."

The two pathetically naïve men argued day after day. Ceton really believed that a sincere repentance would win him a pardon. Cinq-Mars was convinced of the loyalty of his princes and therefore that they would never obtain substantial evidence against him. He therefore tried to obtain what could only be false assurances of his future safety.

"If they would pardon me," he once said when he was feeling particularly sorry for himself, "I would be happy to be spared. I would gladly submit to all manner of deprivations."

He rebelled against the idea of dying before he had had the chance to live. Ceton was shocked by the humility of his desire. "If all you want is to save your life, you deserve to lose it," he snapped. Then he added, "Everyone is talking about your crimes, and you are fully aware of what you have done."

But the old soldier was touched when Cinq-Mars said, "I shall say nothing, I shall accuse no one, and if I must die, I shall die an honorable man."

Ceton decided to set caution and discretion aside when he sug-

---

[2] Vittorio Siri.

gested, "Monsieur may well have confessed everything to His Majesty."

Cinq-Mars refused to believe him. "I have a great respect for Monsieur. But should he say anything against me, I shall contradict his claims to his face and to that of all my detractors with the exception of His Majesty."

These futile dialogues continued for weeks. We know of them from Ceton's statement at the trial. The officer continued to urge Cinq-Mars to seek a royal pardon, and Cinq-Mars would answer with the same refrain, "I have been asked to confess, but I have been promised nothing." Henri fell sick as a result of his living conditions, his grief, and the loss of his beloved. Although he dwelt morbidly on his approaching death, he retained his confidence that his guilt and complicity could never be proved.

Richelieu was still toiling away on the completion of his great tasks, but he found the time and energy to devote himself feverishly to the preparation of the trial or, rather, the condemnation of his former protégé. A letter of Henri Arnauld's indicates how the Cardinal spent his time:

> He works and dictates from seven [in the morning] until eight. From eight until nine, his health is attended to. From nine to ten he gives audiences to those who have come to see him. From ten until eleven he works again. He then hears Mass and dines. He talks with Monsieur le Cardinal Mazarin and others until two o'clock. Then from two to four he works, and then he gives further audiences.

The Cardinal was unpleasantly determined to take no chances over the trial's outcome. After a few hesitations, he chose Police Superintendent Chazé to conduct the interrogation of Cinq-Mars and tested him out on de Thou. "If Monsieur de Chazé proves efficient," he wrote to Chavigny, "we will give him the president of the Grenoble Parlement who is biased in our favor, as [his] assistant in order to make the proceedings seem more authentic. . . .

It is essential that the case be dealt with by such people, as we [the Cardinal, Chavigny, and de Noyers] all know that the traitor will say a good many things which will have to be suppressed."

The interrogations began on July 22. Henri obstinately denied everything. He kept his word of honor to the Ducs d'Orléans and de Bouillon and refused to say what had transpired between them. Richelieu was annoyed, but he saw that there was some advantage in Cinq-Mars' reticence: "The good thing is that Monsieur le Grand, not having said anything against Monsieur, Gaston won't know enough to give him any useful reproaches."

He was worried to hear from the president of Grenoble that Ceton was so well-disposed toward his prisoner. Mazarin and La Vrillère were asked to inspect Montpellier. Mazarin confirmed Ceton's "genuine affection." At first Ceton refused to repeat any of the conversations he had had with the Master of the Horse, but then Mazarin used his Italian wiles to trick him into divulging parts of their exchanges, notably Ceton's ill-advised reference to Monsieur's confession. Mazarin reproached him for this, and Ceton objected to the reproof. He had to be cajoled all over again. The ingenuous officer then thought to help his protégé by saying, "If Monsieur le Grand were guaranteed his liberty and his position, I think he would speak. If you want me to give him such assurances, I think he'll talk."

On August 6 at Fontainebleau, the King signed a long declaration to the Parlements, to the commanders of the armies, and to the guilds. It was an account of recent events and an indictment of Cinq-Mars. The document was something of a humiliation for the King, as Louis had to admit to having given his favorite great freedom of speech and action in order to discover the true extent of the deep designs of this "bad spirit" of whom "it was easy to see that God was not in his heart."

Richelieu expended a good deal of energy on the conviction of de Thou, whom he wanted out of the way. He even interrogated de Thou himself, on the pretext that the King had asked Richelieu to proceed with the peace negotiations with Spain. De Thou saw the trap, however, and said rather that the King had ordered him to see to the negotiations, and that the signed documents were in safekeeping until such time as they were required. The Cardinal preferred not to dwell on this aspect, as it constituted the one and only crucial breach of confidence between himself and Louis.

The young Counselor kept his head and effectively thwarted the spy Crombis and all the commissioners who were ordered to make him speak. Monsieur de Thou had never suspected his friends Cinq-Mars and Fontrailles of any involvement in reprehensible projects. He gave irrefutable explanations and alibis for all his trips. He had never heard any mention of conspiracies or any particular plots. De Thou had other reasons than his own safety and loyalty to his friends: He knew a great deal about the Queen and would have endured the worst tortures rather than expose her. He would have been deeply shocked had he known that his idol had been the first to speak, but he was never to be disillusioned.

The Cardinal decided that his presence at the trial at Lyon would intimidate the judges in his favor. He wanted to see Monsieur Séguier, the Chancellor of France, conduct the trial in person. He asked the King for his consent, and Louis wrote a letter which was a virtual carte blanche:

> My Cousin—I have ordered the Chancellor to go to Lyon, and if you think right, to advise and assist you with his knowledge and long experience of such matters, which may help this one achieve the outcome I desire. I pray you to examine everything that can be justly done, and do anything which you believe will benefit my person. I shall leave the whole matter eventually to your judgment. I have always been too content with the results of my unreserved confidence in you to withhold you full powers on this occasion.

Louis wrote Richelieu this empowering letter from Fontainebleau, at a sufficient distance from his bedridden mentor at Tarascon. He was not pressured, therefore, into ceding such power. Louis had finally succeeded in controlling his own impulses and had sacrificed his friend for the great political scheme, which the least pity would have endangered.

On August 17, Richelieu left Tarascon. His illness and his constant fear of assassination made the journey troublesome. He took special precautions: Spectators were allowed to admire his enormous escort only from a safe distance. He traveled down the Rhône on a sumptuous barge, his cabin hung with crimson and gold brocaded silk, and he never left his bed of purple taffeta. He was preceded by a frigate and another ship manned by harquebusiers. De Thou, twelve guards, and a guards officer were towed in a closed boat behind his barge. There were also barges for bishops, abbots, and gentlemen and cargo boats bearing His Eminence's silver and a part of his treasury.

A philosopher might have mused at the spectacle of this dying man, so elaborately protecting himself against a violent death so that he could inflict one on his enemies.

A few days later, Monsieur le Grand was also conducted to Lyon. He made a last attempt to remove his head from the noose. An officer at the fortress, a Monsieur de La Bonaudière, admired Cinq-Mars in the way that young people admire famous men. He jumped enthusiastically at the opportunity of risking his life for his prisoner, bribed a guard, and planned a fresh escape.

The plan was a daring and dangerous one, but appeared not to be beyond the abilities of a twenty-two-year-old. On the chosen night, La Bonaudière opened the window of Cinq-Mars' cell and helped him along to a chimney ledge which served as a rampart. According to Delort's *Memoires sur Montpellier,* Henri "had only to hang by his hands over the edge of the slate roof, which would leave him suspended two or three feet above his landing step. He was then to descend nine or ten steps and inch along twelve or fifteen paces before reaching the bastion of the parapet, where a rope ladder had previously been attached with thick knots on which to rest his hands and feet. Had he had the self-confidence to do all this, he would be saved. His path of escape had been made easier since the only sentry that could possibly have detected his movements had been bribed. But he had to execute what he had to do promptly."

Speed was essential, in fact. Father Robert saw a man pass overhead and ran to rouse the warden, while one of the guards who had not been bribed discovered the empty cell and sounded the alarm. A second later the citadel was alive with shouts and clanging. Cinq-Mars had a few minutes' grace in which to get himself down to the steps and reach the parapet. A vigorous and determined man could have made it, but his dungeon existence had not only affected his health but undermined his mental resolution. At the crucial moment of his drop, his strength and his will deserted him. He clung miserably to the chimney ledge, paralyzed by the din of the search and the glare which suddenly illuminated the fortress.

He was soon discovered. La Bonaudière was thrown into a cell and Henri was returned to his, where he was locked in all the more securely. All he could do was lament his irreparable misfortune. Shortly afterward he was put into the carriage which was to take him to Lyon. He was given an enormous escort: four armed bodyguards inside the carriage with him, a hundred of the Cardinal's own guards, and around him marched five hundred other guards, including two hundred Catalans. His carriage was left open throughout the journey, and as they approached Lyon, Cinq-Mars asked that it be closed. Ceton refused. The former fashion setter of France was allowed to wear his finest clothes, however. He chose to face the worst ordeal of his life as a beautifully dressed dandy. The citizens of Lyon were not disappointed. Monsieur le Grand wore a musk-colored Dutch doublet covered in gold lace and a scarlet cape trimmed with large silver buttons, looking more like a prince visiting one of his cities amid his guards than a convict on trial. He smiled continually, nodded to those he recognized, called them by name, and even leaned out of the carriage to exchange a few friendly words.

It was a very long ride, and curious onlookers kept mingling with the escort and delaying their progress. During one of the halts, a little Catalan footman adroitly threw him a little wax ball. Henri opened it without alerting his guards' attention and found Princesse Marie's last message to him.

He was feeling dejected when the carriage finally halted before the formidable castle of Pierre Encize. He thought they would take him to the forests of Vincennes. He had even asked—for he retained a naïve hope despite his distress—to be allowed to go hunting one last time. But he was ordered to get out of the carriage and enter the castle on horseback.

"Here, then, is the last ride I shall make," he sighed.

He was given a room at the foot of the castle's great tower. Ceton and four guards shared the room with him, and its two tiny windows overlooked a garden crammed with a host of more guards. It almost appeared that the fate of France depended on the security of this ailing youth.

Henri had been ill ever since Montpellier. He suffered from a "looseness of the bowels" which he had not had time to cure. The intense heat and the lack of sleep imposed by his close quarters with five other men only aggravated his condition. When Richelieu's brother, the Cardinal of Lyon, visited him the following day, he found a "very pale and weak" young man lying in bed under a pink damask spread.

"Do you mind being sent someone with whom you can divert yourself?" His Eminence said.

"I should be delighted, but I do not deserve such attentions."

A Jesuit, Father Malavalette, paid him a good deal of attention and managed to "enter the soul" of the boy. During his brief stay at Pierre Encize, Henri asked for this confessor every morning and night. Richelieu had wanted to attach a spy to Cinq-Mars, but the Jesuit turned out to be Monsieur le Grand's most fitting source of consolation.

Nineteen

"The More Dead, the Fewer Enemies"

LEBRUN'S PORTRAIT OF Nicolas Séguier, Chancellor of France, is perhaps one of the finest paintings of the "realist" school. The gold-clad Chancellor walks under a parasol in Queen Maria-Theresa's retinue, but his face breathes neither the infatuation nor the solemnity which his almost oriental costume might have induced in him. His sharp, astute eyes, the ironical curl of his lips, his calm, almost contemptuous self-confidence reveal the cool and clever lawyer beneath his magnificent attire. Ever since Richelieu's rise to power, Séguier had suppressed the arrogant and frivolous sides of his nature to suit the weight of his office. He looks the man he was: a courtier and an opportunist supremely indifferent to everything that did not advance his own fortunes. This was the parlementarian who had sent thousands to their deaths at his superior's orders, who had seen to the slaughter of the Norman rebels, and who had once dared search the Queen of France's corsage for a compromising document. Now he was charged with handling Cinq-Mars' case according to the Cardinal's will.

Séguier was a personal friend of François de Thou, and he felt eager to protect the interests of one of his subordinate counselors of state. He wrote to Richelieu "that it will be difficult to condemn him to death, since to all appearances, we haven't the least evidence against him." But his effort was in vain. Richelieu merely responded, "Say what you will, Monsieur de Thou must die."

Séguier could not disobey. He left Paris on August 28, accompanied by six counselors or examining magistrates: Messieurs de Laubardemont, de Miromesnil, de Marca, de Chazé, de Paris, de Champigny. On the following day they arrived at Villefranche-en-Beaujolais, where they interrogated Gaston d'Orléans at length and made him sign a twenty-article declaration embracing the whole of the conspiracy. It compromised everyone, including his intimate friends Brion and d'Aubijoux. Anne of Austria was spared by omission.

Monsieur also certified the copy of the treaty, but he was so unperturbed by his actions and their inevitable consequences that he boisterously threw a lavish dinner to celebrate the occasion—the guests including the Chancellor and his judges.

Séguier left Villefranche for Lyon, where he proceeded to examine the Duc de Bouillon on August 31. Bouillon knew his lines, and the interrogation was soon concluded. The Cardinal joined them with vengeance in his heart. There is something distinctly unpleasant about this distinguished Prince of the Church's avid determination to send the two young men to death when he knew he would soon be dead himself.

Séguier made another bid for de Thou's life and was foiled by his colleague Laubardemont. The overzealous courtier, magistrate, and opportunist exhumed an accommodating ordinance from Louis XI's reign, which Richelieu brandished at Séguier. "Whosoever has known of any conspiracy," read the old ordinance, "shall suffer the same punishment as the principal conspirators if he does not immediately make his intelligence known to the King or to the judges of the country in which he is resident." Séguier was thwarted and defended himself, saying "that it [the ordinance] had never risen or been used in the Parlement at Paris where he had always practiced." It was now his duty to obtain proof that François de Thou had known about the conspiracy, in order to condemn him and satisfy the Cardinal.

On September 6, there was a dramatic confrontation between the

Duc de Bouillon and the Master of the Horse. One of the magistrates read the statements of the Duc and of Monsieur le Grand, and Monsieur's certified copy of the treaty was produced. Henri was thunderstruck; the conspiracy was revealed in its entirety. The two Princes had ignominiously betrayed him and broken their sacred word of honor.

Cinq-Mars lashed out at Bouillon, "After so many fine promises and assurances, I should never have suspected such an action from a nobleman praised for his courage and generosity. I would sooner be tortured to death than betray a friend, but now that you have broken faith so easily, I have no desire to quibble vainly over my life."

But his instinct of self-preservation and his concern for de Thou soon returned. He then tried to deny his outburst which amounted to a confession. His friendship for the Duc de Bouillon had not been motivated by any desire to harm His Majesty. Monsieur's declaration was "false to the last article" and "having not had any part in [the treaty] and having never seen the original, he could not know whether the copy was accurate or forged." They were unable to drag any more out of him. If Orléans and Bouillon had not been cowards, the lawyers would not have had a case.

The following day de Thou was summoned. Séguier reminded him of his oath as counselor of state and asked him, "If he did not feel he had committed the crime when he failed to inform the King about the treaty with Spain and their lordships' plans to take refuge in Sedan." De Thou protested that he had never known about either project. He was then confronted by Bouillon and his statement. This confrontation differed vastly from the earlier one with Cinq-Mars, as the Duc was no match for the trained lawyer, who ran legal circles round him. De Thou stood his ground and forced Bouillon to declare "that he had never spoken of any conspiracy to the said Monsieur de Thou."

The investigation was not proceeding to Richelieu's satisfaction. Then a letter from the King altered the whole complexion of the trial. The supreme judge of France lowered himself before his Chancellor in order to facilitate the conviction of his former favorite.

> Monsieur le Chancelier, [wrote His Majesty] I learned from the dispositions of Monsieur de Ceton and from Monsieur du Ripaire and his brother the Abbé that Monsieur de Cinq-Mars pretends, insinuates, and maintains that his wicked designs on Cardinal Richelieu's life were known and approved by myself. I am sending you this letter to inform you that I have long known Monsieur de Cinq-Mars to be a vile imposter, liar, and slanderer, as many have often heard me say; that he believes this conduct to be just and that he will defend his lies with conviction. It is true that Monsieur de Cinq-Mars has indeed heard me express dissatisfaction with my cousin Cardinal Richelieu when I learned that he would prevent me from conducting the siege of Perpignan in person or persuade me to return from the front because of my health and other similar complaints. But Monsieur de Cinq-Mars should not forget all his efforts to antagonize me against my cousin which I tolerated . . . [until] he surpassed the bounds of moderation by proposing to rid me of my cousin himself. I was horrified by this evil notion, which I rejected, and if my word is insufficient proof, one need only consider that had the said Monsieur de Cinq-Mars indeed won my consent to his evil notion, he would not have sought the King of Spain's alliance against my person and my government, for fear of not accomplishing his desires. I want you to convey this letter to all those of the company over whom you preside, so that they may be advised of the truth.

It is difficult to understand what induced the proud and angry monarch to write such a letter. He must have had a guilty conscience over his part in the Lyon affair, and have thought it a convenient way of proving that he no longer loved Cinq-Mars. But these seem insufficient motives for such an action. If, on the other hand, Louis feared that certain intimate secrets which had no direct bearing on the matter in question were in danger of being revealed, his willful humiliation would make sense.

When Séguier read this, he exclaimed, "The Cinq-Mars case is clear and closed. . . . But I don't know what we'll do about Monsieur de Thou." Richelieu felt the letter was doubly incriminating, for he interpreted the King's protestations as proof of his own complicity, and he began to hate his master.

The Chancellor and the young favorite had been friends once, not so long before, and Henri had done Séguier a number of favors. When the Cardinal ordered Séguier "to do everything to induce Monsieur le Grand to admit his guilt and name his accomplices," Séguier decided to use their former friendship as an instrument of persuasion. He visited Cinq-Mars alone and told him in a paternal voice that he had come as a friend and not as a magistrate. Séguier assured him that there would be no transcript of the conversation; therefore it could not be used against him.

Cinq-Mars' defenses began to tumble, and Séguier pressed his advantage. "The King loves you too dearly to let you die. He will take pity on your youth, but you must merit his mercy by confessing everything that's happened. Comply with them and you will never regret it."[1] Henri was ill and confused and tempted to trust a man whom he believed benevolent. Dissimilation weighs on spontaneous and impulsive personalities. He made Séguier promise that his confidences would be respected and not go beyond the Cardinal's ears. Séguier agreed, and Cinq-Mars recounted the entire story from the very first day that his protector became his enemy. He described all the ill-treatment and all the painful humiliations to which Richelieu had subjected him and confessed "that he had conceived an aversion for him which he had been unable to conquer or moderate."

Séguier asked if de Thou shared this aversion, and Henri "was indiscreet enough to reply that [de Thou] hated the Cardinal

---

[1] Father Griffet.

personally, and that if he were ever released from prison, he would have to be watched." He withheld nothing except the Queen's participation. That remote deity escaped again. He also admitted that de Thou had known about the treaty. The trusting boy was naïve enough to think that the same man he had just denounced as a villainous tyrant, the man who had exterminated Chalais and Boutteville, would be satisfied at having learned the truth and reward Cinq-Mars with clemency in return!

But Richelieu was hardly satisfied when Séguier reported to him. He angrily dismissed the confession as useless, as it revealed nothing new and would prove nothing in court. The Cardinal grumbled that he would have to see to the matter himself and lower himself to performing the functions of a magistrate in order to ensure that his interests would be adequately represented at every level of the proceedings.

In Avenel's words, "What a strange spectacle—Europe's foremost statesman, who held the fate of nations in his hands, who fought and was defeating Spain and the Empire with diplomacy and war . . . busy arranging the future destiny of Europe and drafting his great Peace of Westphalia, which Mazarin would conclude according to his dictates . . . was here dividing his precious time between the crucial duties of a statesman and the base concerns of a jailer."

Séguier tried to appease His Eminence by suggesting that Cinq-Mars, who had responded to his affectionate assurances only a few hours before, be put to torture. Richelieu angrily dismissed this suggestion. He would have been delighted to torture Cinq-Mars, but he was afraid of the King's probable reactions to his friend's mutilation. He may also have feared that Cinq-Mars would say too much.

The Attorney-General demanded that "Monsieur le Grand be found guilty in fact and in law of the crime of high treason, and that prior to execution he be subjected to torture in order to learn the identity of his accomplices, and that any further action against Messieurs de Bouillon and de Thou be suspended until such a

time." Richelieu ignored the procedure and proceeded to give Séguier his orders as if no trial were about to take place. When Richelieu had achieved his ends and Cinq-Mars had been condemned,
he coolly informed the King that "Two days before Monsieur le
Grand's conviction, Monsieur le Chancelier and I decided to declare
that he would suffer torture, when he would be subjected only to
the declaration and not to the fact." They also decided on capital
punishment and ordered the erection of a scaffold on September 11.

By this date, however, they still did not have enough evidence to
convict de Thou. Mazarin doubted that the counselor had known
of the treaty, and had written, "No one worked more tirelessly for
His Eminence's ruin than he, all the time without violence." This
was why the Attorney-General had sought to suspend further action
against his young colleague. Séguier wrote to Chavigny, "Tomor-
row, Friday, the trial should produce a conviction, but the trials
of Messieurs de Bouillon and de Thou will be deferred. I shall
have to remain here until the conclusion of the trials and do not
expect I shall leave until the beginning of next month."

But Richelieu knew that his own days were numbered and had
no intention of extending those of his enemies. He had no compunction about resorting to tricks that defiled his holy office, his
reputation, and even his life's work. He lost patience with his incompetent Chancellor and summoned Laubardemont, who agreed
to play the trick which was permanently to sully his name and
reputation.

Laubardemont's sartorial elegance, officious manners, and courtly
pomp disguised an unscrupulous opportunist. He went to see
Cinq-Mars on September 10 and came straight to the point: "If you
wish to be pardoned in your present situation, you have no alternative but to make a full confession. Monsieur de Thou has revealed
everything he knows. It would be astonishing for you to persist in
protecting a man who has betrayed you at the expense of your
own life. Your avowals to the Chancellor are legally ineffectual.
The King and the Cardinal require you to make a legitimate written
declaration. If you continue to refuse, not only will you die but be

subjected to interrogation and torture. If you declare the whole truth, however, you will spare yourself both calamities." He then added; "I give you my word of honor, if you do this, you will come to no harm."

Laubardemont played his role to perfection. De Thou had said nothing, of course, and Richelieu never considered clemency, but Henri was confused, heartbroken, and terrified. A more experienced and self-confident man would have sensed the trap and recalled the innumerable times that judges resorted to such tactics and that Richelieu was not a compassionate soul. But once again, Cinq-Mars was too young, too impetuous, and even too generous to harbor such suspicions. "He repeated everything he had told the Chancellor and promised to make a full and honest declaration at his interrogation." He had successfully acquitted himself as an honorable gentleman for months, only to yield to the temptation of venting on his innocent friend all his anger and disillusion with his real betrayers. Laubardemont rushed off a transcript, which Cinq-Mars duly signed.

Laubardemont left Cinq-Mars' company a triumphant but dishonored man. "A judge cowardly betrays his duty," Father Griffet wrote, "when he makes promises to an accused which he cannot keep. The trick is the more despicable when the promise is false."

There seems to be no satisfactory explanation for Richelieu's excessive dislike of de Thou. The Cardinal's obsession was such that he was prepared to diminish his own renown in order to see the man die. Avenel rejects a number of hypotheses and suggests that the mystery is best solved by Chavigny's formula: "The more dead, the fewer enemies."

The trial opened at Lyon's High Court of Justice at seven o'clock on the morning of September 11. Laubardemont read the "trial brief," which the Prime Minister himself had written. "The Cardinal's style and personality were recognized throughout," noted Father Griffet. The passage that refers to de Thou is particularly revealing: "The crime of high treason, be it only through conclusive conjecture, is justly punishable nonetheless. I say this with conviction, as its legality has been authorized by several eminent doctors in law who have based the assertion on the reasoning that the State, which must at all costs be preserved and constantly guarded, would be endangered and perhaps destroyed if crimes aimed against her required definite evidence to substantiate individual details, thus ruling out the possibility of averting such dangers by convicting such criminals on conclusive conjecture." The twentieth century has reinstated this notion, which was then regarded as outrageously untenable.

"Monsieur le Grand," the brief continues, "has been charged not only as an accomplice to this conspiracy but as its originator and its promoter. Monsieur le Grand is guilty of having poisoned the mind of Monsieur with illusory fears. This is in itself a crime. Then in order to make these fears come true, he persuaded Monsieur to form a factional party within the State; this is his third. He induced him to contrive Monsieur le Cardinal's ruin and removal from office, which is a fourth. He tried to make him rise up against France during the siege of Perpignan to weaken the defenses of the state; that is the fifth. He then drafted the treaty with Spain; that is a sixth. He suggested that Monsieur send Fontrailles and Monsieur le Comte d'Aubijoux to Spain with the treaty. The consequences of this mission combine all the previous crimes and are considered to constitute a seventh crime. All are those of high treason."

The indictment wrongly imputes Monsieur's and Bouillon's betrayal to Cinq-Mars. Cinq-Mars was indeed politically guilty and fully deserved to die in spite of Laubardemont's promises to the contrary. Historical hindsight condemns his enterprises, which would seriously have threatened France's grandeur and unity. But if a dispassionate court had confronted this confused twenty-two-year-old, it would surely have had to find extenuating circumstances. Henri d'Effiat was forcibly drawn out of adolescence and thrust unprepared into the midst of Court intrigues. Against his will, he was made the object of the immoderate affections of a neurotic and inscrutable King. For refusing to spy on the friend who had been foisted upon him, he incurred the hatred of his protector. He was made to pay the price for the King's favors, which he never wanted and which he always wished he could refuse. He was led to believe that his master would always help him. Then he fell in love, which confused his sense of values, which had remained those of an adolescent.

Despite his many faults, Cinq-Mars deserved greater clemency than most hardened conspirators. Nor was his death indispensable to the "preservation of the state." For eighteen years the Cardinal's enemies had proliferated, undeterred by the probability of punishment, and a lovesick boy was unlikely to change the course of history now that he had fallen from favor.

But the implacable Cardinal had no time for such considerations. He left Lyon on his scarlet litter just as the judges began their examination. The incorrigible schemer who had once exulted at having discovered Cinq-Mars' handsome head, now reveled at the certainty of its imminent separation from Henri's body.

Twenty

Justice and Vengeance

THE GENTLEMAN OF the watch fetched Monsieur le Grand at eight o'clock in the morning. "He [Cinq-Mars] was extremely pale and drawn as a result of his indisposition. Passing through the streets, he often waved to the crowds that gathered to see him." When he arrived at the Palace he asked where he was going and then climbed the steps "with great resolution." He entered the courtroom, and leaned over to whisper to Séguier. We presume that he reminded the Chancellor of Laubardemont's promises. Richelieu, however, claims that he also leaned over to "mention his master. Monsieur le Chancelier put him down so strongly that he stopped." The reprimand did not worry Cinq-Mars because he was so confident of receiving the promised pardon. Tallemant recalls that he answered all the questions fired at him "in the unruffled manner worthy of a true gentleman."

When he was called to accuse his supposedly treacherous friend, he was calm and candid. "Asked if Monsieur de Thou had known about his Spanish Treaty and about the liaison between Monsieur and the Duc de Bouillon. Answered that the said Monsieur de Thou had known of both the relationship and the Treaty. . . . Asked who had told Monsieur de Thou about the negotiations and when he had first learned of them. Answered that the King himself had indicated to Monsieur de Thou that he knew of the decision to approach the King of Spain." The judges let the matter drop, and again the Queen was saved by omission.

The only accusation Cinq-Mars persistently denied was his intention to assassinate Richelieu. He maintained that Fontrailles had suggested such a plot to him, "but that he had always rejected such propositions as infamous." The Chancellor did not press the charge; he had more than sufficient evidence against the accused. His main concern was to satisfy the Cardinal's demand—that is, to finish with de Thou the same day.

Cinq-Mars' stomach was giving him a good deal of trouble. He asked to be given leave to return to Pierre-Encize "to take the medicine that had been prepared for him." He was so elated by his belief that he had been acquitted, that when he was offered food, Tallemant records, "he said, 'I do not wish to eat. I need to be purged and must take the pills I have been given.'"

He was exasperated by the long adjournment and paced about the courtroom impatiently. At one point he made for an antechamber which looked out over the Saône, but his terrified guards stopped him before he reached the window. If Henri had looked out, he would have witnessed the magnificent spectacle of the Cardinal's departure from Lyon. He would never again see the man who had thrown him into history. "My God, will this never be finished?" he complained.

De Thou arrived about half past nine, and Cinq-Mars was taken into a small side room. Séguier asked him about the treaty, and again François denied all knowledge of its existence. Then Henri was summoned into the courtroom. The Chancellor turned to de Thou and said, "Have you any reproach to make to Monsieur le Grand?"

"I have none. I know Monsieur le Grand to be a gentleman who cannot have said anything but the truth." Cinq-Mars' face fell. Then de Thou turned to Henri and blurted out, "Is it really true that you told them all I have just had to read?"

Henri was crestfallen and confused. He began to stammer, "Be patient . . . no, I can explain. . . ."

De Thou cut him short because "he was afraid that he might say something which would further endanger his friends"—that is, the

Queen. "Messieurs," he said to the magistrates, "I shall give you a brief but honest summary of my involvement in this affair, which may well prove better than the Master of the Horse's account." Too late, Cinq-Mars realized he had been the victim of a dreadful trick. François proceeded to admit his complicity. He also asked the said "Monsieur le Grand to verify that he had entreated him daily to desist from participation in the Treaty. Monsieur de Thou added that he had not admitted this previously because he had not felt in a position to do so." This account of the trial may have been "arranged." Such a practice was traditional and has given de Thou's statement the heroic dignity of Plutarch.

"Messieurs," the young magistrate is supposed to have stated, "that only proof you have of my guilt is Monsieur de Cinq-Mars' testimony. I have never written or talked about [the conspiracy] to anyone. One accused man cannot validly accuse another. The death sentence demands the testimony of two irreproachable witnesses. I can either save my life or choose to condemn myself with my own words. However, Messieurs, I admit I knew about the conspiracy. I have two reasons for confessing this: During my three months of imprisonment, I have clearly envisioned both life and death and understood that whatever life I could enjoy would only be sad and boring. Death is much more advantageous to me. . . . I have prepared myself for death, and I will not again find myself so disposed. I therefore take the opportunity of my present health. My crime may be punishable by death, but it is neither heinous nor grave. Messieurs, I knew of the conspiracy, but I also did all in my power to deter Monsieur de Cinq-Mars. He considered me his only faithful friend, and I did not wish to betray him. This is why I deserve to die, and why I condemn myself."

Richelieu's enemies insisted on the validity of this sublime statement, but it has its inconsistencies: It was precisely de Thou who originally gave Cinq-Mars the ideas that inevitably drew him into the conspiracy. We also know that de Thou later declared that he would much rather die than suffer torture and life imprisonment.

The proceedings were adjourned while Séguier argued with Du

Faure, the Attorney-General. Du Faure doubted whether they could find de Thou guilty of a capital crime. "See to your summing up, and leave the rest to me," snapped the Chancellor.

Before reconvening, Séguier set about "arranging the judges so that his opinion would prevail." Monsieur de Miromesnil, known to be partial to de Thou, was seated "in such a way as to be the last to pass judgment, so as to prevent him from influencing anyone with his eloquence."

The Attorney-General asked the court to declare the accused "guilty of the crime of high treason." The Chancellor turned to the judges for their verdict. Cinq-Mars was unanimously condemned to death after having been put to the question. De Thou was condemned to death without torture by eleven out of thirteen judges. Monsieur de Sautereau suggested he be sent to the galleys for life, but Monsieur de Miromesnil defended his young colleague so eloquently that he disturbed the tribunal.

Séguier replied with a long discourse against de Thou. He resorted to a weighted, if not altogether judicial, argument. "Think, Messieurs," cried the Lord Chief Justice of France, "how the King will judge you for condemning his very own confidant, his very own favorite, and for saving the life of your colleague." François-Auguste de Thou's fate was sealed.

The verdict was agreed, pronounced, and hastily signed by Séguier, who immediately dispatched it to the Cardinal. The courier Picaut handed His Eminence the document at Lentilly, two leagues from Lyon.

The Minister was delighted at the news, which capped a series of crucial victories. He had just heard that the Spanish troops had withdrawn from Perpignan on September 9 following the formal capitulation of the province on August 29. The Duc d'Enghien was now occupying the defeated city. Richelieu was striking down his enemies even as he endowed France with a new province. He was particularly pleased that de Thou had been convicted: "The good Chancellor has delivered me of a great burden." Then he grew moody again. His prodigious memory, which did not let any detail escape, prompted the recollection that the Lyon executioner had recently broken his leg. "But Picaut said they have no executioner." "The courier assured him that they would find a replacement." The same inconvenient mishap had befallen the Chalais affair and had transformed the execution into a butchery. But Richelieu did not choose to remember the gory precedent. He wrote Chavigny a quick note full of predatory satisfaction. "These three words will inform you that Perpignan is in the King's hands and that Messieurs le Grand and de Thou are on their way to the next world, where I pray God they will be happy." Then according to Father Griffet, he briefed the King, "Sire, your enemies are dead and your armies are in Perpignan."

But Richelieu was not that succinct nor that kind. His letter to Louis reads, "Your Majesty shall have two quite different pieces of news. The first is that the rich and beautiful Perpignan has been won for France. The other is the condemnation and execution of Monsieur le Grand and Monsieur de Thou, who were [they had not yet, in fact, been executed] found so guilty in the judgment of all their judges that the judges found no difficulty in condemning them to death [*sic*]. These two incidents prove how well God loves Your Majesty." These last words were undoubtedly Richelieu's cruelest thrust at Louis XIII.

The Chancellor also chose to be viciously ironic. He ordered Counselor Saint-Germain and Laubardemont personally to inform the two condemned men of their sentence and to dispose them "to prepare themselves for a Christian death." The indignant magistrate had to face the very victim of his felony and inform him of his impending death. Despite his previous hopes, Cinq-Mars took the shock heroically. "It was a harsh and unexpected blow," Tallemant writes, "but he did not show the least surprise."

Cinq-Mars could not forgive himself, however, for betraying his friend. His guilt made him look upon death as a form of deliverance.

De Thou was no less gallant. He turned to Henri and "gently" said, "Ah, well. Monsieur, I could complain about you—you have accused me and sent me to my death. But God knows how much I love you. Let us die bravely, Monsieur, and merit heaven." Cinq-Mars threw his arms around him. "They embraced with great tenderness and agreed that they would find great comfort in dying together after having been such good friends during their life."

Four more judges came in, accompanied by Pallerue, the clerk of the court, who interrupted their exchanges to read the final verdicts. He asked the prisoners to kneel and hear their sentences.

"Friend," cried Cinq-Mars to his companion, "you have no need to worry." De Thou knelt, reciting some verses from the Bible. The Master of the Horse knelt on one knee and clasped his hat to his breast with his left hand "in a cavalier fashion." Pallerue began to read, but de Thou objected to the words "conspiracies" and "adventures." "These words do not apply to me," he protested.

Henri subsequently learned of the thorough interrogations he was supposed to undergo. He could not know that it was only to be a mock torture and was horrified. "Is there no mercy?" he pleaded. When he had regained his self-control, he turned to the magistrates and said, "Messieurs, I think this is too brutal. A person of my age and station should not be subjected to such formalities. . . . I have told everything, and I am willing to do so again. I am prepared to meet my death in my own way and with a good heart and think the rest unnecessary. I confess my weaknesses and beg that I be spared such treatment." Henri feared for his soul as much as for his body, because he knew that the condemned were forbidden confession and absolution before undergoing torture. He dreaded dying unabsolved in the throes of agony.

The magistrates may have felt tempted to reassure him, but they had been sworn to secrecy. The night before the trial Séguier had taken the precaution of writing to Chavigny, "I am informing you of the mock torture trial so that you can tell the King the truth, should he hear about it." Cinq-Mars was not to be tortured, but the Cardinal wanted to make him go through agonies of expectation. He also hoped that this would frighten Cinq-Mars into proffering testimony against the young officers who had conspired to assassinate Richelieu at Lyon. Richelieu later tried to scare Louis XIII by claiming that Cinq-Mars had actually threatened "to spare no one if he were pressed beyond endurance and had no hopes left."

Weeping bitterly, Cinq-Mars confided his fears to Father Malavalette, whom he was allowed to see when the judges withdrew. Father Malavalette rushed off to the magistrates to plead for mercy. Two of the magistrates told him the truth and begged him not to share their confidence. The priest ignored their request and returned to Cinq-Mars. "Are you capable of keeping an important secret?" he asked.

"Father, I assure you that I have never broken faith with anyone, except God."

"Well, you are not to be tortured. I shall accompany you to the chamber to remind you of your promise."

But after so many lies and false promises, Henri was not prepared to believe Malavalette. He bravely faced Ceton, who came to escort them to Thomé, the Provost-Marshal of Lyon. As they were leaving, Cinq-Mars turned to de Thou as if to apologize again. "Monsieur, we are both condemned to death, but I am less fortunate than you since I am going to have to suffer torture as well."

Ceton was unable to conceal his grief in taking leave of the prisoners. Even the guards in attendance had tears in their eyes. Monsieur le Grand tried to comfort them. "Do not cry, my friends. Pray to God for me and be assured that death has never frightened me."

Laubardemont, followed by the clerk of the court, led him to the interrogation. The sometime royal favorite was led past reeking dungeons crammed with prisoners of low estate. He discovered the existence of an underworld he never knew existed. "My God, where are you taking me? How bad it smells here!"

The "torture chamber" was a small cell lighted by three candles. Amidst the horrifying apparatus, Laubardemont questioned Cinq-Mars "on his conspiracy against the life of the Cardinal." But for a man on the verge of fainting away from fear, Henri was astonishingly self-possessed and controlled. He insisted "that he had always considered the assassination as a preposterous fantasy."

"You will not receive absolution for your sins if you withhold the name of your accomplices," thundered Laubardemont. "You should consider the salvation of your soul and not your worldly reputation, which will be of little use to you after your death."

The condemned man retorted, "I wish I would be allowed to spend whatever time I have left in preparation for God's grace and mercy rather than continue to be tormented."

Laubardemont ordered him to be put on "the interrogation rack." At that moment, the Queen, Tréville, and his companions were in danger. But Cinq-Mars overcame his fears. According to Father Griffet, "He declared that he had already said as much as he knew, and that all the tortures in Christendom and beyond would not persuade him to divulge any more." Laubardemont had him unstrapped and returned him to the courtroom, where they exchanged a few words which were never reported. When Laubardemont left him, he had tears in his eyes. Cinq-Mars rejoined François de Thou and embraced him.

"Friend, how much I regret your death," wept Henri.

"We are lucky to be dying the same death," comforted de Thou.

De Thou then went to his confessor, Father Mambrun. Cinq-Mars objected to confessing under the eyes of so many guards and was allowed the privacy of a separate room for his confession to Father Malavalette, who had just obtained special permission for Cinq-Mars to mount the scaffold with his hands untied.

Henri confessed for over an hour, and then fainted from hunger. He had not eaten anything all day long. Father Malavalette called for some eggs and wine, but Henri "merely rinsed his mouth and swallowed nothing." He told Father Malavalette "that what he found hardest to bear was the painful realization that he had been abandoned by all his friends, which he would never have believed."

"Such has always been the way of the world," explained his confessor.

According to Vittorio Siri, Henri wrote the King a letter which was intercepted. However, there is no substantial evidence of any such letter of farewell. We do know that Cinq-Mars wrote to his mother, who had certainly played a part in his tragic misadventure. Richelieu allowed Madame d'Effiat to receive the long letter, "as His Majesty was indifferent as to whether she did or did not receive it."

> Madame, my dear and most honored mother, as I am unable to pay my respects to you in person, I am writing to ask you to favor me by granting me two last marks of your goodness: to pray as much as you can for my soul and my salvation. Then I would ask you to obtain from the King the price and value of my post as Master of the Horse, which I would have received had I lived to sell it. Should you be refused the sum, I entreat you to settle with my creditors. I know that this request may be distasteful to you, Madame [Cinq-Mars fully appreciated his mother's avarice], because being so near to death I am acutely aware of the value of worldly considerations. Farewell, Madame, and forgive me if I did not respect you enough while I lived, and be assured that I shall die your very humble and obedient son and servant,
>
> *Henri d'Effiat.*

De Thou prepared to meet his death in a state of religious excitement. He felt so close to the Lord that he was terrified of harboring the least trace of vanity because of it. He did all he could to humble himself. "When I die I want everyone to say that I was a vile coward and an ill-mannered hothead who did not know how to manage his affairs. I want them to have this opinion, to despise and blame me. I desire this for the love of God."

De Thou wrote to Monsieur Dupuy, his cousin, and to the Princesse de Guéméné, who had caused him so much suffering: "Madame, never in my life have I felt so obliged to you as I am now that I am about to lose my life. I am losing it with less grief because you have made it so unhappy. . . . I beg you to forgive me, Madame, for everything I may have done to displease you, and

I make the same prayer to all those I came to hate because of you, assuring you, Madame, that inasmuch as my faith which I owe to God permits me, I die only too assuredly your most absolutely humble and obedient servant." Richelieu did not allow the Princesse to read this bitter message.

"There's the last thought I want to have for this world," de Thou said when he had finished writing. "Let us talk about Paradise." He started intoning the *Miserere* "with such incredible ardor and violent tremblings of his body that one felt that he was levitating and about to leave his body."

The Place des Terreaux, about sixty to eighty yards square, began to fill with the thousand soldiers who took up their positions in readiness for the execution. A scaffold seven feet high and of about nine square feet was erected in the middle of the square, and a small stepladder of eight rungs was placed against the platform. An enormous crowd "of all conditions, ages, and sexes" converged on the square and pressed in behind the deep formation of the guards. Hundreds of others clambered on to the surrounding rooftops and hung out of every window to watch.

Twenty-One

"My God, What a World!"

꿹 FOR HIS LAST parade, the former leader of fashion revived his dandy's habits. His suit was brown, trimmed with yards of golden lace, his shoes were of green silk tied with a white ribbon; from his shoulders swung a great scarlet cloak with large silver buttons, and he wore a black hat cocked in the latest Catalan style.

At about five in the evening he was with his confessor when the officers arrived to escort him to the scaffold. He was suddenly in a hurry. "They are come for us. . . ." he said. "Let's go. It will soon be done." In the courtroom, he met François de Thou, dressed in a black mourning suit of Spanish cloth with a short coat. "Let's go, Monsieur, let's go," he said. "It's time."

They descended the marble staircase. Monsieur le Grand went first, holding Father Malavalette's hand. Cinq-Mars bowed low and graciously to the crowd that lined the steps, and many were moved to tears. At the foot of the stairs he faced his judges and thanked them—perhaps ironically—"for the kindness they had shown."

An enormous throng had gathered outside. "Messieurs," he cried out, "how very good of you to let two criminals ride to their death in a carriage when we deserve to be carted off and dragged through the mire. The Son of God was so reviled before He died for all of us!" The two young men "bowed long and low" as if they were at the Louvre, and drove off in the waiting carriage.

The proximity of death seemed to have shaken de Thou's reason somewhat. Throughout the interminable journey, he chattered compulsively, recited prayers, psalms, and "other pious invocations." He invoked the martyrs, begged Cinq-Mars' pardon. Cinq-Mars forgave him, and de Thou embraced him and thanked Heaven for allowing them "to eradicate all their crimes with a little infamy and to conquer Heaven with a little shame." He urged his friend not to regret his life and cried, "I regard our death as an infallible sign of our predestination for which we are more obliged to God than if He had given us all the good fortune on earth!"

The unfortunate Henri found it hard to preserve his equanimity and withhold his tears under this prolix torrent. He stuck his head out of the carriage window and asked the people for their prayers, for which he received sobs and moans. A cluster of young girls gave out with a wail that moved Father Malavalette to tears.

"Father, are you more sensitive to my misfortune than I am myself?" Cinq-Mars said. "I beg you not to make us sad. We need your strength to maintain our own."

The carriage inched slowly through the jostling crowds. Behind it, on foot, followed an aging porter who tortured condemned prisoners. Because no executioner was available, he had been chosen to do a job he had never done before.

Henri said he wanted to go first, because he had been tried first and was the guiltier of the two. "I would only die twice if I went last."

Monsieur de Thou objected on the grounds that he was older than Cinq-Mars. "You are indeed older," Father Malavalette intervened, "but you are also the more generous."

"Yes! Yes!" cried Henri.

"Ah, well, Monsieur, you will open the path of glory for me," François answered.

Father Malavalette settled the question by deciding that Monsieur le Grand would have his way.

When they caught sight of the scaffold, de Thou became very excited. "Monsieur, here it is! It's from here that we must enter into

Paradise! Is it possible that as miserable a creature as myself should take possession today of a blessed eternity?"

The carriage finally came to a halt. Henri embraced his frantic friend who proceeded to give him a lengthy oration: "Here comes the separation of our bodies and the union of our souls. . . . Go on, Monsieur. . . . We shall be apart for a few minutes, but then we shall be together again in the presence of God for all eternity. . . . You have achieved greatness on earth, but you will be infinitely greater in Heaven and your greatness shall never perish. . . . Show that you know how to die."

Cinq-Mars leaped out of the carriage. "He appeared with his head high and a smiling countenance." The trumpets sounded three blasts, and Pallerue on horseback read the sentence again. Henri flourished a courtly bow, donned his hat, and started up the stepladder. He was stopped on the second rung by Lenfray, the guard, who picked off Henri's hat and said, "You must show some modesty, Monsieur!"

Henri wheeled round and treated the insolent fellow with a taste of his old haughtiness. "Give me my hat!" he cried.

Malavalette put Lenfray in his place and returned the hat to the prisoner who continued up the stairs "with as much courage as if he were going into battle." When he reached the platform, he seemed to have regained his seductive powers. He raised his left hand to his side and bowed low in the manner of a court dandy. He repeated this gracious gesture three times as he walked round the scaffold. He answered the crowd's desolate cries as he had Father Malavalette, "What's the matter, Messieurs? You are more sensible to my misfortune than I am myself." He then threw himself into his confessor's arms and whispered urgently in his ear for a long time.

Richelieu later claimed that Henri was telling Malavalette that he wanted to rebel against his silence and make a public pronouncement about the King and that Malavalette dissuaded him. In any case, Malavalette persuaded him to kneel and receive absolution.

Henri was surprised to find that there was no proper executioner's block and that he was expected to lay his head down on a tree stump. He bent forward to test it and was then asked to remove his doublet. Before he did so he handed Father Malavalette a diamond-studded box. "Inside is the portrait of the lady I loved. Burn it and give the box to charity." He snatched the scissors from his executioner's hands and trimmed off a couple of his brown curls and begged Malavalette to burn them with the portrait. He may have hoped that the priest would give these relics to Princesse Marie. We do not know if he ever did.

Finally, Henri requested that Father Malavalette's assistant, and not the executioner, should cut his hair off. As his hair fell about his shoulders, Cinq-Mars sighed, "My God, what a world."

After praying for a few minutes he turned to his executioner and snapped, "What are you doing? What are you waiting for?" From a sack the man removed an ax "that looked like a meat cleaver, only larger and squarer."

"Let's go," Cinq-Mars whispered. "It's time to die. My God, have pity on me!"

He was not blindfolded. Monsieur le Grand "with incredible self-control . . . placed his neck squarely on the stump and faced the front of the scaffold. He hugged the stump tightly, shut his eyes, clenched his teeth, and waited for the blow.

"The executioner stood on his victim's left, clasped the ax in both hands, raised it into the air, and let it fall slowly and heavily. Receiving the blow, Henri gave a loud cry like an 'Ah!' that was drowned in blood. His knees jerked up as if he were about to stand, then knelt back again. The blow had not severed the head completely. The executioner stepped around Cinq-Mars from behind, grabbed his hair in his right hand, and sawed at the part of the tracheal artery and the piece of skin which had not been severed."

The charming head which had troubled so many hearts rolled across the length of the scaffold to drop into the crowd below. "The cries of horror and the groans made a sound so horrible that one forgot where one was." Henri's body was removed with great difficulty, for his arms remained locked around the stump. The executioner covered the head and body with a cloth.

It was then François de Thou's turn. Perhaps trying to allay his terror by grandiloquence, he jumped from the carriage and "bounded up the scaffold, cheerfully discarded his coat, threw open his arms and kissed his executioner, saying, 'Ah, my brother, my dear friend, how I love you. I must embrace you because you are going to bestow eternal happiness on me today. You are going to put me in Paradise.' "

He bowed to the crowd and gave himself over to transports of piety, humility, and resignation. But as soon as he saw his friend's blood and covered body, he stopped playacting and said soberly, "Gentlemen, I confess that I am a coward. I am afraid to die. . . ." He turned to the executioner and said, "You will have to bind my eyes."

"Monsieur," answered the brute, "I have no blindfold."

De Thou turned to the crowd. "I am only a man. I am afraid to die. This object [Cinq-Mars' body] frightens me. I ask you to take pity on me and bind my eyes." Two handkerchiefs were thrown up at him. He caught one and said, "May God give it back to you in Heaven."

The hideous preparations lasted a long time. De Thou finally put his head on the stump and said his last words: *Maria, mater gratiae, mater misericordiae . . . In manus tuas . . . .*" Then "His arms began to shake as he waited for the blow, which fell too near his head to cut more than halfway through his neck. The blow threw his body sideways to the left, turning his face to the sky. . . . His legs twitched, and he weakly tried to raise his hands. The executioner wanted to turn him to his original position to finish what he had started, but frightened by the angry shouts of the crowd, he frantically swung down on de Thou's throat and severed the head at the third or fourth blow. The head remained on the scaffold."

Horrified, the Lyon crowd all but lynched the clumsy executioner. The bodies were quickly bundled into the carriage, and the executioner followed with the heads. Both had their eyes still open and seemed to be still alive.

The city of Lyon was similarly moved, as was the rest of the kingdom. The two young men won their greatest political victory by dying as they did. The French nation felt no gratitude whatever to the Minister who had that one year given them Roussillon and Catalonia in spite of his ill health and near ruin. His success in no way mitigated the public indignation at the sacrifice of two gallant young men on the altar of that insatiable Minotaur. Madame de Pontac, François de Thou's sister, had his body exhumed and reburied in the family graveyard at Saint-André-des-Arts. No one went to such lengths for the former favorite, whose friends and relatives were terrified of incurring the Cardinal's persecution. But Monsieur de Guay, Treasurer of the Lyon region, was so moved by Cinq-Mars' untimely end that he had the body interred before the high altar of the Church of the Feuillants.

To facilitate the handling of the litter that was slowly carrying the Cardinal back to Paris, it was necessary to tear down walls and disembowel private houses. Resentful, fearful eyes watched the progress of the enormous scarlet machine with its twenty-four porters and its army of guards. But Richelieu was too satisfied with his recent achievements to give a thought to popular opinion, as his letter to Chavigny on September 15 shows. The humiliations the favorite imposed on him must have been very grave indeed.

"Monsieur le Grand," he wrote to Chavigny, "was his haughty self to the end. . . . It is said he often bragged that he would die more resolutely than Monsieur de Montmorency and Monsieur de Saint-Preuil, but I am sure that they died a more Christian death. I think the Abbé d'Effiat deserves to be demoted. His is a bad little spirit which cannot see the ways of God. The King should remove him from the Mont-Saint-Michel Abbey [which Louis XIII had given to Cinq-Mars' brother despite the Cardinal's objections]. . . . Madame d'Effiat should be allowed three or four weeks more at Chilly where she is staying to settle her son's debts, which I very

much doubt she wants to, and then she should be sent to Touraine.
. . . Such people do no good too close to Paris."

Richelieu's thirst for revenge seemed to have no bounds. He
did not feel guilty in the least in persecuting the innocent family of
his faithful friend Maréchal d'Effiat. Needless to say, Richelieu
vehemently opposed surrendering the hundred thousand écus from
the sale of the Master of the Horse's office to settle the debts of his
dead rival. Louis XIII personally paid the thirty or forty thousand
écus owed by his "dear friend." The towers of Cinq-Mars' castle
were torn down and the forests felled "to the level of his infamy."
Truly obsessed by the affair, the Cardinal wrote a long memorandum in which he again enumerated and wildly exaggerated the
crimes of "that miserable, damned, hellish devil."[1] He asked Séguier for the names of the two judges who had resisted sentencing
de Thou to death.

Richelieu was also obsessed by those whom he had not succeeded in condemning. After the execution of his accomplices, Bouillon took to his heels and abandoned Sedan, which Mazarin occupied
in the name of the King. He had been promised a pardon, but the
Cardinal was only biding his time before he pounced again. Monsieur
had taken refuge at Blois. He spent his time "trying to dispel the
gloom that had settled over him in Savoie." He felt safe enough
until Richelieu presented him with a terrible surprise: the abroga-
tion of his rights to succession.

The Cardinal was eaten away by the realization that the whole
affair would have been impossible without Louis XIII's acquiescence.
The Cardinal had a short memory; he could dismiss Maréchal
d'Effiat's loyalty as conveniently as he could dismiss his own
sizable share of the blame. It was he, after all, who had forced
Cinq-Mars on his reluctant master. Nonetheless he decided to make
the King, too, pay dearly for the whole tragic episode.

His Majesty had arrived at Fontainebleau on July 23, where the
Queen joined him the following day. Louis suspected her complicity

---

[1] Archives des Affaires Étrangères.

and thus "was quite animated against her." Marie de Médicis'
death depressed him as much as the sinister trial. The court went
into mourning for the Queen Mother, which at least kept the
sovereign from having to conceal his grief.

The mournful King hunted out his sorrow from Fontainebleau
to Saint-Germain, from Versailles to Chantilly, from Nanteuil to
Monceaux. At the beautiful chateau at Monceaux which had once
belonged to Belle Gabrielle, he heard about the sentence and execution.

Louis still talked about Cinq-Mars. He mentioned him in anger,
as if to justify Cinq-Mars' horrible death with memories of his
friend's desire to hasten his own. He was reticent with his courtiers
and refused to confide his sorrows. There is a tale which claims
that on the day of the execution, he looked at his watch and said,
"An hour from now, Monsieur le Grand will have a bad time of it."
In another version of the story, he worked himself into a state of
false hatred, just as de Thou had become overexcited and overpious,
and interrupted a game of chess with a vicious "I should like to
see Monsieur le Grand's expression now." These stories are not
very convincing, as it is almost certain that he learned of the deaths
and the fall of Perpignan from Richelieu's letter which arrived
several days after the fact.

He returned to Paris on September 17 to attend a *Te Deum* in
honor of his victories. Louis XIII offered thanks for the glories
that God had bestowed on his reign, and he may have felt a twinge
of regret for the price he had been made to pay for them.

Twenty-Two

The Dead Bury the Dead

AFTER VAINLY TRYING to recuperate at Bourbon-Lancy, Richelieu reached Fontainebleau on October 13, and moved into the Albret palace. He did not go to see the King, who had taken to working at his Minister's offices to lessen the risk of assassination. Now that he had reconstructed the Lyon attempt on his life, Richelieu was terrified that he would meet the same end as his former patron Concini. He even knew the names of his near-assassins—Tréville, des Essarts, Tilladet, and La Salle, still in their posts in Louis' royal guard.

Louis reversed etiquette and called on Richelieu at the Albret palace. Chavigny and de Noyers helped the Cardinal to his feet and the two men embraced theatrically, but with an absence of enthusiasm. Those who witnessed the scene were surprised by the coldness of their encounter and by the stony silence that followed. The King finally dismissed everyone from their presence.

It was the second time they had met since the discovery of the conspiracy, but the atmosphere differed greatly from the previous one four months earlier. Richelieu had then feared Cinq-Mars and the King's attachment to him, and he had not known that the King had almost consented to a plot on his life. He had been anxious to win over his equivocal King and to restore their old confidence. Now Henri d'Effiat was safely underground, however, and Richelieu's awful knowledge poisoned his relationship with Louis. The

King, embittered and lonely, could never forgive the Scarlet Courtier for sacrificing his friend. They had nothing left with which to mend their disputes. Their fellow feeling had been severed on the scaffold at Lyon.

The ghost of the decapitated favorite haunted the three-hour conference. We have some idea of what occurred between them because Richelieu always put down their important conversations on paper and then submitted a summary to the King. His account of the Fontainebleau interview is full of daring reproaches, refuted accusations, and thinly veiled sarcasms.

"Knowing the King's jealous nature, Monsieur le Grand persuaded him that my renown dimmed his glory and that the authority he had given me detracted from his own; even though everyone knows that I have always considered it a great honor to walk in my master's shadow. . . . Monsieur le Grand played on the King's suspicious nature to cast doubt on all my actions. . . . Your Majesty has won many great victories, not the least of which are those he had won over himself. For two years Your Majesty had to contend with the ploys of a young man who maliciously tried to alter your government and reverse your policies. Your decision to conquer this inclination was one of your finest victories. It was no easy matter to convince you of the evil consequences of these designs and of his evil influence on you and on your affairs, but God took compassion on us all and revealed the truth and helped you overcome your old inclination and revive your good opinion of your old and faithful servants." [1]

The King and his Minister were far less happy and satisfied by the outcome of this encounter than by their last one. The old magic, the absolute trust that had weathered so many trials, had finally disappeared.

Nor did the two men's proximity to death help reconciliation. Both anxiously prepared for the other's disappearance and replacement. The Cardinal, on the one hand, had no intention of leaving

[1] Avenel, *Letters of Cardinal Richelieu.*

the state to the Queen and Monsieur. He aspired to the position of Regent himself and set about accelerating the Duc d'Orléans' dispossession.

He was also concerned by the immediate future. The memory alone of his dead rival was a serious menace. The King had not recovered from the affair, and Tréville and others made it their business to keep Henri's memory alive. Their constant defense of their hero made Louis bitterly resent his Minister and regret the loss of his friend. The Cardinal had not yet routed Cinq-Mars completely.

Richelieu went on to Paris on October 17, determined to have done with the constant danger once and for all, even if it meant forcing Louis' hand as he had never dared before. Richelieu had always been respectful, even if it meant swallowing his own pride. Now, however, when the Queen did him the extraordinary honor of coming to see him at his Palace; he did not rise to greet her. "I dare to hope that Your Majesty will forgive my remaining seated in her presence, as I know she is well acquainted with the privileges of Cardinals in Spain."

Anne of Austria retorted quickly, "I must have forgotten them in becoming a Frenchwoman."

They sized each other up while exchanging formal pleasantries. Young and healthy, Anne had enabled the dying Minister to score a great victory, and he now intended to use his regained supremacy to dispossess her. But Richelieu's frailties were Anne's strengths. Anne's betrayal of the ill-conceived conspiracy had given her time to multiply her chances. De Thou would have died more readily had he known he was being of such service to his beloved Queen.

Richelieu behaved as if he had his whole life before him. On October 27, he threatened the King with his conditional resignation. "Monsieur le Grand used every possible argument and artifice to persuade a number of people whom he wanted to engage in his faction that the King was tired of his Cardinal and displeased with his services. Despite the worthlessness of an impostor's false judgments, the said Cardinal does not feel that he can satisfy his passion to serve Your Majesty . . . if such an impression as Monsieur le Grand insinuated to many souls within and outside the Kingdom has some foundation." Having proffered his resignation, he proceeded to enumerate his "five conditions." He would reconsider his decision if the King agreed to satisfy his impertinent demands: "First, His Majesty should never have another favorite and be content to occupy himself with the affairs of state." The King should trust in his ministers alone "and conceal nothing from them that is said to their detriment." "He should keep the proceedings of his Council to himself." "He should occasionally purge his Court of evil influences, and banish them rather than let them grow to be infamous and to choke others with their fatal influence (as happened in Monsieur le Grand's case)."

Richelieu had never before taken Louis to task like this, nor had he ever dared order the hero of the Pas de Suze to submit to his will. Shocked and surprised, the King might well have accepted his resignation if he had not been in such a state of confusion. His insolent "valet"—as Marie de Médicis used to call him—had timed his thrust perfectly. The Roussillon campaign planned for 1643 made him indispensable to the King. If Louis dropped his pilot now, he would have to admit that Cinq-Mars had died in vain.

Louis played for time. He acknowledged receipt of the memorandum "without bitterness," in Chavigny's words, but made no reply. Richelieu waited for nine anxious days, during which his health became more of a cause for concern. The King may have played on the Cardinal's nerves in the hope that the strain would accelerate his death and so save Louis the humiliation of submitting. But he had not allowed for Richelieu's immense reserves of energy. The Minister only launched another attack.

The Cardinal's memorandum to the King of November 5 is unadulterated blackmail. "God has not chosen to do the impossible, and the Cardinal finds it impossible to continue executing services and duties which are deemed inadequate." Since it is every man's duty to preserve his person when it is threatened, "it is my duty, therefore, to remove myself now that I am in danger. Your Majesty should know that a good deal has been learned from Monsieur le Grand, information which up till now has been withheld him. . . . Monsieur de Cinq-Mars was not submitted to a thorough interrogation for fear that he would reveal publicly what he had made known in private. His confessor had to restrain him from making such declarations from the scaffold as he had threatened to do, sparing no one if he were pressed beyond endurance."

Chavigny was entrusted with taking the menacing letter to Saint-Germain and with the task of repeating verbally all that Monsieur le Grand had told the Chancellor on the Lyon affair. Louis was infuriated by Richelieu's tactics and retorted that "he would have preferred the Chancellor to have allowed [Cinq-Mars] to say all he wanted, as that would have confirmed conclusively his wickedness and ingratitude in everyone's eyes."

Poor Louis! He had elevated his Minister to incredible heights and was rewarded by unparalleled insults and ultimatums. He had exalted and loved Cinq-Mars who turned on him, wished him dead, betrayed him, and remained loyal to his treacherous Queen. Louis had good cause to feel bitter and disillusioned.

On November 5 and 6, Chavigny pressed Louis for a reply, but the King still held out. Then on November 7 he brought Louis an incredible message. If the King refused to dismiss his suspect officers, "he would have to submit to the Cardinal's guards bearing arms in his presence in order to ensure His Eminence's safety against the insults of the King's men."

"Does the Cardinal have any more right to dictate the conduct of my men than I have of his?" demanded the King furiously.

"If His Eminence thought that His Majesty disapproved of anyone in his retinue, he would dismiss him instantly," Chavigny assured him.

"Then he'll never see you again, because I find you insufferable," the King snapped.

But Chavigny was undaunted. On November 8, he showed the King a letter which Richelieu had written him, dealing largely with state matters this time. "There are those who begin to suspect a rift between the King and myself. The suspicion is deleterious to my health and certainly detrimental to the King's interests." But Louis was unmoved, and Richelieu's health continued to deteriorate.

On November 13, the Cardinal made his final bid. He sent the King a third memorandum in which he summarily repeated his previous demands and hinted that the conclusion of the peace negotiations might amply compensate the King for his capitulation. "His Majesty is very humbly requested to state his intentions at the foot of this memorandum . . . and to add the conditions he wishes to put forward for the peace." His Eminence had thrust home. Cinq-Mars' handsome face could never have threatened French politics if Louis had not passionately desired to put an end to the war and conclude a lasting peace—and if he had not also doubted that his Minister had the same intentions.

The King pondered for twenty-four hours. The treaty would give him peace of mind and a clear conscience and would also put an end to his people's sufferings. But capitulation was still a bitter pill. Chavigny wrote to Richelieu on November 14. "The King clearly stated that he wished to comply with Monseigneur's wishes, on the condition that his honor was not made to suffer. I reassured him as best I could. I shall press him for an early reply."

Six more days were to elapse before Louis gave in. He wrote his reply at the foot of Richelieu's memorandum, again sullying the memory of the man he secretly mourned. "Having read the above, I have nothing to add except what my cousin Cardinal Richelieu already knows only too well: that Monsieur de Cinq-Mars was too malicious an imposter and a liar for . . . him to give credence to his slanderous imputations on the friendship and esteem I have for my cousin." He then copied down the Cardinal's conditions and surrendered unreservedly.

The terms of his capitulation would justify Madame de Motteville's trite opinion that "the greatest King in the world" was no more than a humble slave—if one failed to read the peace terms that followed. The son of Henri IV was not prepared to buy peace by total defeat. His conditions were those of a highly skilled statesman who intends to achieve a glorious peace without significant concessions: "I would become the laughingstock of Europe and let my enemies renew hostilities against me, if they were not made to pay for the war they have forced me to wage. There must be no question of conceding Lorraine, Arras, Hesdin, Bapaume, Perpignan, Roussillon, Brisach, or the Alsatian territories that border on Lorraine. I acquired Pignerol by too legitimate a title ever to think of giving it up. My nephew the Duc de Savoie should be restored to his lands, or I will not consider any peace settlement. If these conditions are accepted, I shall be agreeable to whatever schemes are deemed necessary to facilitate a general peace which will bind me to my allies."

This document conclusively demonstrates that Richelieu's policies were really those of Louis XIII. These postscripts are dated November 20. The two old colleagues were reconciled just in time to acquit themselves before history. But the Cardinal's last energies had been spent on their battle. While the King instructed Monsieur de Guitaut to banish his four compromised guards officers, and dispatched the letters patent of dispossession to Monsieur, Richelieu began to complain of an acute pain in his side which the doctors diagnosed as "false pleurisy."

On December 2, Louis learned that the Cardinal was spitting blood and that his physicians were admitting their concern. He left Saint-Germain, went to the Cardinal's palace, and saw Richelieu at two o'clock. The sick man turned to him and said, "Sire, this is our last farewell. In taking leave of Your Majesty, I have the consolation of leaving your kingdom greater than it has ever been before. . . ." And he could not refrain from adding, "and all your enemies struck down and humiliated."

Richelieu was not boasting. In 1624 France had been a chaotic state. Now the French Bourbon line was the strongest in Europe, checkmating the Habsburg dream of European domination. France had acquired an army and a navy. She had conquered Artois, Alsace, Roussillon; occupied Lorraine and Savoie; colonized Canada, the

Antilles, Madagascar, and Senegal. The Protestants had not been persecuted but absorbed into the national community. The provinces of France had been united under the single authority of the Crown.

Nonetheless, Richelieu died much too soon. His immense external achievements paved the way for further expansion, his foreign policies were absolutely irreversible, but he would have needed a good hundred years more to achieve the royal revolution of the country's internal policies. The Crown was not to find a man capable of changing and reorganizing the mildewed foundations of the old order (the fiscal system, the venality of parlementary procedure) and breaching the dangerous rifts that continued to widen until 1789, when they finally submerged the country in total revolution. Richelieu could not possibly have achieved all this in one lifetime, though he might have lived a few years longer had he not been worn down by the terrible fears and anxieties that dogged him throughout 1642. But he could blame no one but himself for this calamity. He was originally responsible for throwing two equally reluctant men together, and he must have regretted his self-destructive plan to his dying hour.

The Cardinal recommended his three Ministerial aides, de Noyers, Chavigny, and Mazarin, to the King's service. He asked Louis to execute his will and testament and to favor his relatives and heirs, to whom he left his infinite fortune. But he was wise or grateful enough to bequeath his palace and a large share of his furniture and jewelry to the King. Louis might have been delighted at Richelieu's impending death, but he gave no evidence of such pleasure. At the Cardinal's bedside, he at least affected "tenderness" and solicitude: Richelieu was brought two egg yolks and Louis insisted on giving them to him himself.

Leaving Richelieu's chamber, he strolled a while along the galleries of the Cardinal's magnificent palace that was soon to be his. His own Louvre next door seemed old-fashioned and comfortless by comparison. He laughed "while looking at some paintings," and many ascribed this gaiety to avarice. But it seems unlikely that Louis, who seldom laughed, should have been tickled by the thought of gaining so much for so little. It would be more in character if Louis was laughing at one of his morbid private jokes: to see Cinq-Mars' executioner expiring less than three months after his victim.

Louis stayed at the Louvre, for he was reluctant to leave Paris before knowing "the outcome of the malady." That night the Cardinal received extreme unction before a large audience. When Monsieur Le Tonnelier, the curate of Saint-Eustache, asked him whether he had forgiven his enemies, he proudly delivered the famous statement: "I have had none other than those of the state." Many a pious witness was shocked by his lie. Cinq-Mars was just one example of such a nonpolitical enemy. He began to hate Henri when he had refused to become his spy, which refusal predated the conspiracy by a long time.

The King returned to the Cardinal's palace on December 3. He looked sad and stayed with the dying but lucid man for an hour. As that ice-cold night fell, the King's household left Paris. The separation that had so often been expected, desired, and feared throughout their eighteen years together finally took place. Richelieu died near noon on December 4. As soon as the King heard the news he assured Chavigny, de Noyers, Mazarin, and Richelieu's family of his goodwill and favor. Before returning to Saint-Germain, he made a public declaration that "there were those who might think the day was lost or won, but in fact nothing had changed. His policies would be maintained even more rigorously, if that were possible, than they had been in Monsieur le Cardinal's lifetime." [2]

Louis did not attend the Cardinal's impressive commemorative service the following month. The sadness which had assailed him during the last few months seemed to vanish. He seemed almost relieved. He must have welcomed the dissipation of the guilt his Minister had imposed on him since the discovery of the conspiracy. According to Montglat, "He was delighted at the bereavement and did not deny it to his close friends."

---

[2] Letter from Le Duchat to his brother, quoted by Gabriel Hanotaux and the Duc de la Force.

The young poet Paul Scarron gives us an idea of how the public took the Cardinal's departure:

My plans, compared with my services,
Made it doubtful whether I was a king or a vassal.
Whether I worked for good or ill,
I always found faithful accomplices.
Either heaven and hell was so propitious to me
That no one knows which made me Cardinal.
I made the son reign, killed the mother,
And had I lived, I'd have ruined the brother.
Those who wanted to ruin me felt my power.
To trick Spain, I ruined France,
You judge if I was an angel or a demon.

The day after Richelieu's death, Parlement registered Monsieur's dispossession, and Cardinal Mazarin entered the Council as its president.

In fact, nothing had changed. Richelieu's political machine continued to function normally. The royal "slave" was a freer man and could follow his own bent, if that had ever differed from Richelieu's. But Louis was determined never to allow another man to take such liberties with him again. Many historians have closed Louis XIII's political career with Richelieu's death, but they have not given him credit for making one of the most important decisions since he had elected Richelieu as Minister in 1621—he now chose Mazarin to follow in his master's footsteps. The Italian grandson of a humble fisherman of possibly Jewish origin was to be the guardian of the future Louis XIV.

The King had always been suspicious of foreigners, especially of his mother's countrymen, but he had come to admire and respect the one-time double agent who had evolved into a suave Cardinal. But above all, Louis welcomed the fact that Mazarin had not been involved in the Cinq-Mars affair, as had his two colleagues. His Cardinal's purple was not stained with blood nor with unhappy memories. Louis was also persuaded to favor Mazarin because of his growing concern for his salvation, and Mazarin proved an excellent savior. He counseled the King to be clement as Corneille had vainly done before him in writing his *Cinna*. In January, Monsieur was returned to Court and restored to his rights and privileges. He was "so gay that one would have thought nothing had befallen Monsieur le Grand and Monsieur de Thou," as his daughter, the Grande Mademoiselle, was to write. He was quickly followed by all the other exiles, except for Châteauneuf, Madame de Chevreuse, and Madame de Hautefort. Louis could not bring himself to forgive the first two, and Madame de Hautefort would have revived too many sad memories. But even Fontrailles was soon back at Court. Had Richelieu died a little sooner, Cinq-Mars would undoubtedly have won back Louis' favor, and the King might well have lived a little longer.

But Cinq-Mars' fate hastened Louis' death, just as his life had Richelieu's. The King was haunted by the thought of his friend's handsome head rolling across the scaffold. His grief exacerbated his already chronic condition. He had had pneumo-intestinal tuberculosis for twenty years, but he no longer had the strength or the desire to keep it in check. The tragedy's three protagonists were to succumb almost simultaneously, in the true classical manner.

From February 21, the King was bedridden at Saint-Germain. On March 27, he ordered Bouvard to reveal the extent of his illness. The physician dared not answer, whereupon Louis sighed, "I see by your silence that I must die." He then added, "God knows life never pleased me, and I shall be delighted to go to Him."

Unexpectedly, Anne of Austria was a model of conjugal solicitude. She did not leave her husband's bedside, where she wept copiously. She asked his confessor to persuade him to renounce his conviction that she had been a party in the Chalais attempt on his life.

"In my present state," Louis answered, "I must forgive the lady, but I am not obliged to believe her." He may have forgiven her that complicity, but not her role in the conspiracy, and he intended to deprive her of all power. But it was then that Mazarin showed his talents. He convinced the King that the dispossession of the future King's mother would not only be ineffectual but dangerous. He suggested a clever alternative—the creation of a Regency Council of able and responsible men who would run the state and deal with all crucial decisions. Anne could then bask in the glory of her useless presidency, but she would not have effective powers.

Louis was persuaded. Mazarin then convinced the Queen of his loyal services and obedience. He assured her that she would be sole Regent and that she would reign supreme as Marie de Médicis had done before her. Anne believed him, admired his skill, and even felt grateful and tender toward her failing husband.

On April 20, Monsieur de La Vrillère read "His Majesty's declaration on the government of His Estates," which proclaimed one of history's only constant laws: "France has shown that united she stands invincible and that her greatness depends upon her continued unity, just as her downfall depends on her internal division."

The Dauphin was baptized the next day. Once the King settled his worldly affairs, he turned his thoughts to heaven and to those whom he had loved. Louis, whose whole life had been a secret, died on May 14, 1643, with a finger pressed to his closed lips.

In eight short months, the grandiose or pitiful characters in Cinq-Mars' story had disappeared from the scene. But the author of the drama, who had artfully manipulated the scenes to their final conclusion, survived them all to wrest grandeur from baseness. The Spanish Queen, who had been involved in so many plots and conspiracies and who had even negotiated with the enemy in wartime, suddenly became the personification of a united France.

One day, as she was passing before a portrait of Richelieu, she looked up and mused, "If that man were alive today, he would never have been so powerful." Poor de Thou must have turned over in his grave.

Epilogue

CINQ-MARS' CONSPIRACY differs from the usual favorite-inspired conspiracies that influenced the destiny of nations during the seventeenth century. Unlike his counterparts, he had no influence on the policies and the destiny of his own nation. Historians have always despised Henri d'Effiat, while poets and novelists have romanticized his memory; the historians have been too unfair and the poets too generous. He was a typical adolescent of his class who shared the aspirations of his kind to excel in battle and to conquer beautiful women. He was endowed with too excellent good looks and with too illustrious a patron. Henri was made a bait and lured into a trap which also caught the King and the Cardinal and endangered the lives of millions.

Henri was Richelieu's greatest tactical error and Louis XIII's greatest temptation. The King had resisted such temptations before, but he died for having almost yielded to Cinq-Mars' lure and for having made himself pull back.

In order to judge Cinq-Mars, we must assess whether Richelieu's policies—which Louis rigorously enforced on all, including himself—warranted the cruel sacrifices they demanded. They have been criticized, and they have been highly praised; but the twentieth century has found them some notable detractors, particularly outside France.[1] They have been held responsible for creating the

---

[1] Among others, Aldous Huxley's *Eminence Grise.*

economic and social conditions which produced the Revolution and for favoring the rise of Prussia by ridding Germany of the Austrian preponderance in Europe—which is supposed to have prepared the way for our twentieth-century catastrophes.

But Richelieu had no particular theories of absolute monarchy. He created an absolute monarchy because he had no other tool with which to unify France and remove the constant threat of civil war, which would have brought the Bourbons to a Merovingian end. The Revolution of 1789 became inevitable precisely when the monarchy proved incapable of accomplishing a royal revolution over its privileged classes—that is, when it could not bring the Cardinal's work to its natural conclusion.

The Treaty of Westphalia may have sowed the seeds of the Prussian climb to power. But Richelieu could not have been expected to make France a Habsburg satellite simply in order to forestall possible German expansionism. In any case, such a policy would not have provided against an ultimate confrontation between the European block and Russia and the Anglo-Saxon nations. If we consider the governments of Vienna and that of Madrid still controlled by the Inquisition, we might have some idea of the disastrous effects such an arrangement would have had on Western civilization.

Louis XIV and Napoleon certainly borrowed some of Richelieu's principles, but they distorted them and thus smeared his reputation. No statesman can be held responsible for his successors' abuses. Whatever his political genius, he was only a man, and he was fallible. History, unfortunately, only elects to register the progression of evils and lesser evils, of imperfect systems and less imperfect ones.

Every century of French history has its share of invasions, and it is to the Cardinal's credit that he created a political structure which escaped them from 1659 to 1792. It was also during that time that France gave the world a number of brilliant men who managed to alter the complexion of the world. This is enough reason to justify the Cardinal's reputation. Louis XIII had no reason to repent preparing his country's Golden Age, even if it meant breaking his most cherished affection.

INDEX